THE COMING PENAL CRISIS

THE COMING PENAL CRISIS

A criminological and theological exploration

edited by

A. E. BOTTOMS

Centre for Criminological Studies
University of Sheffield

and

R. H. PRESTON

Department of Social and Pastoral Theology
University of Manchester

1980

SCOTTISH ACADEMIC PRESS

Published by
Scottish Academic Press Ltd.
33 Montgomery Street, Edinburgh EH7 5JX

ISBN 0 7073 0265 X

Printed in Great Britain by
R. & R. Clark Ltd., Edinburgh

Contents

Preface

The chapters of this unusual book were presented to, or arose out of, a Consultation held in 1978 under the auspices of the Department of Social and Pastoral Theology in the University of Manchester.

The decision to mix criminological and theological concerns in the Consultation was a deliberate one, and the terms of reference for the occasion were formulated as follows:

(i) To examine, in the light of the best available criminological knowledge, the present and future policy options in the general field of the punishment of offenders. This would attempt to make a contribution in its own right to British penology, and would be one of the first specifically British symposia to consider in depth the situation faced by penal policy in the light of the extensive collapse of the 'rehabilitative ideal' which has informed much of post-war penal thought.

(ii) To consider whether the social theologian has any meaningful contribution to make to this debate.

The Consultation came about due to a happy conjunction of interests of the Editors. One of us is a criminologist who is a Christian believer, and who had been driven by various academic developments within his subject to consider more carefully the relationship of his faith to the presuppositions of various intellectual positions taken up by criminologists. Through a mutual friend he was put in touch with the other Editor, whose relatively new University Department had begun a series of inter-disciplinary Consultations, the purpose of which was stated as being to take 'some issue of public concern which involves making moral judgements, but on which public opinion is divided and confused' (Preston 1975, p. 1), and to reflect upon that issue, using the tools of various academic disciplines, including theology. The first such Consultation was held in 1974, on the subject of strikes, and was subsequently published (Preston 1975); the second, on the Future of Leisure, was held in 1976 but not published. Our penal policy Consultation was thus the third of a series, and followed a methodology which had been carefully worked out on the earlier occasions. In the remainder of this Preface we give a brief account of the criminological background, explain the methodology of the Consultation more fully, and try to state why, and how, theology should become involved in social issues of this kind.

The Criminological Background

Until about the late 1960s, criminology in Britain was dominated by a particular intellectual tradition. This tradition, which can be broadly designated as 'positivist', had the following features:

(i) It assumed that a natural science methodology could be unproblematically applied to the study of criminology.

(ii) It assumed the existence of theory-neutral facts.

(iii) It assumed a deterministic model of man.

(iv) It (usually) assumed that the sources of crime were ultimately found in the individual, not in society.

(v) It assumed that the definition by society of acts as criminal was unproblematic, usually by ignoring the issue or, if pressed, by adopting a position that it was 'natural' for societies to prohibit killing, theft, etc.

(vi) It assumed that a primary task of criminology was a 'correctionalist' one, that is for criminologists to act as technicians helping policy-makers and penal agents to reduce the amount of crime in society and 'correct' criminal tendencies in individual delinquents.

(vii) As a consequence of (especially) (v) and (vi) above, a close working relationship developed between criminologists and government agencies, a relationship which the criminologists mostly perceived as unproblematic.

This tradition was subjected to devastating attack in what became widely recognised as a major intellectual reorganisation which took place in the late 1960s and early 1970s (for accounts of these developments, see Cohen 1974; P. Wiles 1976, ch. 1). Out of these upheavals has come a rich variety of differing positions taken up by criminologists, including several versions of Marxism, phenomenology, symbolic interactionism, and transcendental rationalism (see Taylor, Walton and Young 1975; Downes and Rock 1979). These competing positions necessarily involve raising fundamental issues as to the nature of knowledge ('epistemology') and the nature of being ('ontology'). Since the Christian tradition has much to say especially about ontology, it was natural that a criminologist who is a Christian should begin to ask fundamental questions of his colleagues, wondering if their ontological presuppositions were correct.

But this book is not about such purely intellectual issues; it is about the more mundane question of penal policy. Why is this, given that the original impetus driving a criminologist to seek theological co-operation was straightforwardly intellectual? There are three reasons: *first*, the Consultation series was designed to be about issues where theory and practice are related rather than simply theoretical issues; *second*, the theologians concerned (none of whom had any prior specialist knowledge of criminological matters) thought it necessary that they should be compelled to approach the intellectual questions through reflection upon the practical outworkings of criminological thought and policy; and *third*, we wished to address, so far as possible, a lay as well as a specialist audience in promoting criminological–theological collaboration, and for such an audience policy questions are much more appropriate.

And let there be no doubt that there are major penal policy issues worth addressing in a forum of this kind. In particular, as chapter one explains more fully, present penal policy is much preoccupied with the 'collapse of the rehabilitative ideal', that is to say the radical undermining, on both empirical and theoretical grounds, of those methods of 'treatment' of offenders which gained a dominant hold over many sections of the penal field in the post-war period. The 'collapse' looks likely to be as decisively important for penal practitioners as was the collapse of scientific positivism for academic criminology (and the two issues are, of course, closely related). Yet there has been surprisingly little British comment on the 'collapse', and for this reason we hope that this volume will be carefully read by those with an interest in penal affairs, even if they regard its theological concerns as hokum.

The Methodology of the Consultation

The methodology of the Consultation arose out of three key considerations. These were, *first*, that it is difficult to get people as busy as those invited to the Consultation together for much more than a short time; and it is essential that they should all be there all the time. *Second*, it is potentially creative for representatives of different intellectual disciplines or different areas of the same disciplines, to meet together with practitioners 'in the field' of the disciplines studied by the academics; but this has to be carefully prepared for, otherwise the participants are very likely to misunderstand one another, get at cross purposes and fail to communicate. *Third*, only a limited number of people can be invited if there is to be a serious meeting of minds in the time available; we limited the number to 30.

A basic position paper was written by Anthony Bottoms (chapter one) to illuminate the background to the main areas of discussion which in preliminary consultations we had thought would be the most significant. This was circulated to those who were invited to prepare papers, and all their papers were written in the knowledge of it. All the papers (except one) were available to the participants about a month before the Consultation. At the Consultation a session was given to each paper, and each writer briefly introduced his paper; discussion followed. Rapporteurs kept a note of the main points raised, and at the last session they were able to provide an analysis of the trends of the discussion, which itself was then discussed. Each contributor subsequently revised his paper in the light of the proceedings at the Consultation and, after a limited amount of editorial work, they now appear in this volume. One additional theological paper, that by David Jenkins, was also added at this stage. The different contributions are therefore much more closely related to one another than is usually the case in a published symposium.

The fact that this was an inter-disciplinary Consultation meant that neither criminologists nor theologians could write merely for fellow-professionals. They were asked to write for a general public, of the kind that reads the 'quality' papers and journals. This means that they were asked to eschew the technical terms and 'shorthand' method of writing which assumes a range of expert knowledge in the reader. A plainer style is no barrier to their fellow experts and at the same time makes their writing accessible to a wider public, which is important for the formation of public opinion. How far we have been successful in this only the reader can judge. He can be assured, however, that behind the chapters lie the experiences not only of theologians and of academic criminologists (not all of them Christians), but also of practitioners in the various aspects of the judicial and penal processes, and of prison chaplains, who were all represented at the Consultation.

The Contribution of Theology

It is perhaps necessary to add a few introductory comments on the nature of theology, if only because the position has changed so much since theology was generally accepted as 'the queen of the sciences'. We feel sure that a number of professional criminologists and penal practitioners will be astonished to find theologians involved in a discussion with criminologists on criminological issues. This may be partly because they think of theological studies as concerned with establishing the best texts of sacred books, or with the exegesis of them, or with the historical study of their embodiment in systems of doctrine and ecclesiastical institutions down the centuries. Theology is indeed concerned with these and other specialist matters. But it is also concerned with a whole understanding of the nature and significance of human life and human well-being in society, including structures of the State and the legal and penal systems which go with it. Behind these are value judgements about man-in-society with which theology must be concerned. Those who regard the whole discussion with which theology deals as outmoded, and its persistence as an irrelevant intellectual survival which is being eroded and on the way to disappearance, will not be impressed by this. However the proof of the pudding must be in the eating. The theologians in this volume are not claiming access to any esoteric knowledge, but are trying to point to considerations derived from their faith and tradition which they think may illuminate current criminological issues. The reader can judge for himself whether this is so. That hoped-for illumination comes from the Judaeo-Christian understanding of life, which is the religious tradition which has deeply influenced our civilisation and culture, and still does even in the days of a plural society. Moreover if cogent insights into human life and institutions spring from that religious tradition it may well be the case that they can be seen independently of the faith which underlies them in the writings of the theologians themselves. The implications of this, and how far it can persist, are not questions which can be pursued here.

This kind of theological contribution cannot be made in any 'take it or leave it', *de haut en bas*, manner, as if a voice from Sinai is uttering. It can only be made if theologians bring their insights alongside those engaged in the areas under consideration. Moral and social theology cannot operate on its own, from outside, or from afar. It requires inter-disciplinary involvement. That is why a Consultation such as this is so valuable. One of us has given in chapter six some account of the problems facing a Christian theologian in making a contribution, because of difficulties in the history of his own tradition and misunderstandings of it in our plural society. A further difficulty lies in becoming sufficiently competent, amid many other preoccupations, in the area of discussion under review, to make an intelligent contribution to it. The theologians involved in this Consultation have done their best in this respect, but are aware that their best is inadequate.

A Note on Timing

Inevitably there is delay in getting a volume of this kind to the public. This has dated some of the references — for example, in chapter one there is mention of the possibility of a Conservative Government, which since May 1979 has been a reality. We have not usually sought to alter such references, since we do not believe that these slight anachronisms alter the essential message of this volume. Readers should be aware that the author's final revision of most contributions was made in December 1978. Chapter one is a rather special case, since it is the basic 'position paper' from which other contributors worked (see above on the methodology of the Consultation); accordingly its text has not been fundamentally altered, but some updating to the end of 1978 has been carried out in the footnotes.

Acknowledgements

We gratefully acknowledge our indebtedness to the Principal and Staff of the Northern Baptist College, Manchester, which provided a congenial setting and atmosphere for the Consultation; to the Ferguson Trustees for a small grant to defray essential expenses; to Michael Taylor and Richard Jones, who acted as *rapporteurs*; to Jack Keiser the Consultation Secretary; and to Brenda McWilliams for much painstaking work in preparing this volume for the press.

August 1979   A. E. BOTTOMS
                                               R. H. PRESTON

List of Participants at the Consultation

Department of Social and Pastoral Theology

The Rev. Dr. J. Atherton
The Rev. Canon David Jenkins
The Rev. R. G. Jones
Mr. J. Keiser
Professor the Rev. Canon R. H. Preston
The Rev. Michael H. Taylor

Other Participants

Miss Elizabeth Barnard, University of Sheffield
Mr. J. Bolger, Greater Manchester Probation Service
Dr. A. K. Bottomley, University of Hull
Professor A. E. Bottoms, University of Sheffield
Mr. Dean Clarke, University of Sheffield
Mr. Nicholas Coote, Catholic Social Welfare Commission
Dr. David Downes, London School of Economics
Mr. Dermot Grubb, H.M. Prison Service
Mr. W. A. Heath, H.M. Prison Service
Mr. K. L. Hollingsworth, Essex Probation Service
Dr. Marjorie Jones, Penal Affairs Committee, Society of Friends
Mrs. Joanna Kelley, formerly of H.M. Prison Service
Mr. John McClenahan, Northern Ireland Office
Professor F. H. McClintock, University of Edinburgh
Mr. William McWilliams, South Yorkshire Probation Service
Mr. M. J. Moriarty, Home Office
Professor T. Morris, London School of Economics
Dr. K. Pease, University of Manchester
Dr. Raymond Plant, University of Manchester
The Rev. M. Riddell, formerly one of H.M. Prison Chaplains
Professor Eric Sainsbury, University of Sheffield
The Rev. Austin Smith, H.M. Prison Chaplain
Mr. Colin Thomas, South Yorkshire Probation Service
Mr. Martin Wright, Howard League for Penal Reform

1

An introduction to 'The Coming Crisis'

by A. E. BOTTOMS

What is this talk of 'crisis'? Isn't it rather melodramatic?

The difficulties (which might or might not amount to 'crisis') are at two levels: theoretical and practical. At the theoretical level, there is a serious likelihood of a vacuum in penal thought following the coming certain collapse of what I shall call the 'rehabilitative ideal'. At the practical level, there is serious overcrowding in the local prisons; a tense — perhaps increasingly tense — atmosphere in the high-security 'dispersal' prisons; and considerable uncertainty of role in the probation service.

But let us take it stage by stage, and begin by trying to understand more fully our present situation. Two very recent English policy documents neatly encapsulate most of the crucial elements of the present penal situation[1] — the 'Serota Report', i.e. the Advisory Council on the Penal System's Interim Report on *The Length of Prison Sentences* (A.C.P.S. 1977); and the consultative Home Office Working Paper, *A Review of Criminal Justice Policy* (Home Office 1977a). I shall pick out four themes which can be found in both reports, and which seem to me to be of special importance.

Four Themes in Contemporary British Penal Policy

First, and the dominant factor in much current penal consideration, comes *the collapse of the rehabilitative ideal.* Reformation as a principle in the handling of offenders has a long history (at least as far back as John Howard), and was increasingly important in the penal system of the inter-war period, when a series of liberal reforms of prisons were made, and the probation service grew steadily in strength. The Criminal Justice Bill of 1938–9 (lost through the commencement of war) was heavily based on liberal-reformist principles. In the post-war period, 'reform' became 'rehabilitation' — that is, religious and moral

1

impulses in reformation became secularised, psychologised, scientised. By about 1960, there was a strong liberal consensus of informed penal thought in Britain, which believed that rapid strides would soon be made scientifically towards the identification of specific types of effective treatment for specific types of offender. The nascent science of criminology would actively assist in this process (the Institute of Criminology at Cambridge was set up at this time); courts would get better social information (to enable better 'diagnoses' to be made); prisons began practising group counselling; the probation service had moved away from its Evangelical missionary roots and had become strongly attached to Freudian-based casework theory. There was pressure for an increase in the use of indeterminate custodial sentences, so that offenders could be let out when, and not before, they had been successfully 'treated'. Judges and magistrates were advised to avoid passing very short prison sentences, because these would not allow sufficient time for rehabilitative techniques to be brought to bear on the offender; and so on. (For perhaps the key official document of this period, see Home Office 1959.)

Of course, this view was not an unopposed one. At about the same time, Conservative women were pressing strongly for a reintroduction of corporal punishment, a campaign which the then Conservative Home Secretary, R. A. Butler, resisted only with difficulty; there was a serious disturbance at an approved school which led to a tightening of legislative control; many sentencers continued to believe strongly in tough, retributive penalties. But the intellectuals, the probation officers, the prison governors and assistant governors, and the Home Office officials — they were much more likely to be committed to the 'rehabilitative ideal'.

And this ideal is now in the process of evaporating. A succession of negative research reports has — with a few exceptions which do not seriously disturb the conclusion — suggested that different types of treatment make little or no difference to the subsequent reconviction rates of offenders (Lipton *et al.* 1975; Brody 1976; Greenberg 1977). As the Serota Report (A.C.P.S. 1977) succinctly put it:

> A steadily accumulating volume of research has shown
> that, if reconviction rates are used to measure the success or
> failure of sentencing policy, there is virtually nothing to
> choose between different lengths of custodial sentence,
> different types of institutional regime, and even between
> custodial and non-custodial treatment. (para. 8)[2]

Very recently, the Home Office's *Review* has endorsed this view (Home Office 1977a, para. 14 and Annex C), and has commented seriously and pertinently that 'the broad policy implications of that (research) now have to be considered'.

But the objections to the treatment (or rehabilitation) ethic have not been solely based on empirical demonstrations of lack of efficacy. Strong theoretical objections have also been raised, perhaps most influentially in the American Friends Service Committee's (1971) *Struggle for Justice*, which argued that there was:

> compelling evidence that the individualised-treatment
> model, the ideal towards which reformers have been urging
> us for at least a century, is theoretically faulty,
> systematically discriminatory in application, and
> inconsistent with some of our most basic concepts of
> justice. (p. 12)

What lies behind these claims? I will leave it to Keith Bottomley to provide the full context of the Friends' document; but some general points can be made here, to illustrate (in my words, not theirs) the burden of the three main complaints:

(i) *'Theoretically Faulty'* — because, it can be claimed, the treatment model implies that criminal behaviour has its roots in the deficiencies of the individual and his upbringing, and that if these are remedied, the crime rate will be cut; but this medical analogy is inappropriate, and crime is far more a result of the overall organisation of society than of the deficiencies of the individual.

(ii) *'Systematically Discriminatory'* — because the treatment model typically takes more severe coercive action in cases of 'unsatisfactory' home circumstances or 'dubious' moral background; but these judgements are made by middle-class workers who unwittingly but systematically discriminate against the poor and the disadvantaged, and in favour of the 'good' homes of the privileged.

(iii) *'Inconsistent with Justice'* — because judgements involving the liberty of the individual are made (in the name of 'casework' or whatever) on the basis of extremely impressionistic evidence which is usually not revealed to the offender, and which he cannot therefore challenge; and the result may be, for example, that some will serve long sentences for trivial crimes because their 'attitudes have not improved', while others convicted of serious crime but who have allegedly 'responded' are let out.

Underneath criticisms like these, it will be noted, lies a fundamental conviction by the critics as to the essentially *coercive* nature of the rehabilitative ideal — a matter to which we shall return later. Many adherents of the ideal blinded themselves as to this coerciveness, in the false belief that benevolent intentions preclude a coercive result: thus a social work lecturer could write that legal limits on official powers over juveniles were actually irrelevant, since 'the whole purpose . . . is to concentrate on treatment needs, *and therefore what is done for a child is done in the interests of his welfare*' (Boss 1967, p. 91, italics added). That way, say the critics, lies potential tyranny — or, as C. S. Lewis (1953) had put it some time before, 'the "humanity" which (this theory) claims is a dangerous illusion, and disguises the possibility of cruelty and injustice without end'.

The second element of current British penology which can be adduced from the Serota Report and the Home Office *Review* is the contemporary air of *penological pragmatism*, with no clear or coherent philosophical or other theoretical basis. In the heyday of the rehabilitative ideal it was all very different: those at the forefront of penal policy-making formulated with pride Prison Rule No. 1, the ideal against which everyday practice in prisons was to be measured:

> The purpose of the training and treatment of convicted
> prisoners shall be to encourage and assist them to lead a
> good and useful life.[3]

But now? Rule No. 1 is still on the books, but it is increasingly regarded as unrealistic by prison officials: the Chief Inspector of the Prison Service wrote recently:

> Traditionally, the Prison Service has attracted to its ranks
> staff at all levels who have been encouraged to identify
> closely with the treatment aspects of custody. . . . Of recent
> years, however, . . . the prison community . . . has rejected
> paternalism in favour of a more pragmatic approach in
> which management, control and more realistic objectives
> have been the keynotes. (Fowler 1977, paras. 352–3)

Notice, in this passage, the explicit reference to pragmatism, its curious identification with 'realism', and the complete absence of long-term or overarching goals. It is the same when one turns away from prisons to a wider consideration of the penal system: thus the three final 'main conclusions' of the Home Office *Review* are essentially pragmatic in tone[4], while the Serota Report, having implicitly accepted the demise of the rehabilitative ideal, has nothing much to offer in its place:

> in our view, a sound penal philosophy must place a greater
> reliance on data about the effectiveness of our penal system
> and move away from tradition and emotional reactions.
> (para. 20)

But however important data on effectiveness are (and they *are* very important for many purposes), they can of course in no sense provide or constitute a penal philosophy. So where is this new philosophy to come from, now that the rehabilitative ideal is collapsing? There is no answer in the official documents — just a heavy preoccupation with the urgent practical problems of the moment, the overcrowding of the prison system, to be met (it is hoped) by shorter sentences and more diversion to non-custodial sentences. This pragmatic preoccupation with current difficulties is by no means ignoble — but it is also no adequate basis on which to rethink the shape of the penal system of the future.

These comments lead naturally to the third element discernible in the Serota Report and the Home Office *Review, the crisis of penological resources.* This crisis takes two forms: the size of the prison population, and the demands on the probation and after-care service.

The prison population in England and Wales currently stands at a record figure of 42,000, as against 11,000 just before the Second World War. On the face of it this sounds like a considerable extension in the use of coercive social control by the State; but one must be cautious before offering any such interpretation, since there has in fact been a considerable *decrease* over the same period in the proportionate use of imprisonment for persons convicted of indictable offences. The major fact which underlies these two different statistics is the vast rise in the annual rate of convictions: very many more are convicted, proportionately fewer are sent to prison, but the total prison population nevertheless has increased very considerably.[5]

In the present economic circumstances, the country simply cannot afford a much larger prison population, even if this were regarded as desirable. So various attempts have recently been made (with increasing urgency) to halt the steady increase in prison numbers — the provision of alternatives to imprisonment, an increase in the scope of the parole scheme, more generous bail laws, and so on. The Home Office *Review,* which stresses that achieving an actual *reduction* in the prison population must now be a 'particular preoccupation' for policy-makers, declares that the best hope of achieving this lies in 'shorter sentences, either as a result of changes in remission or parole or through a change in the sentencing practice of the courts' (para. 10); and the main message of the Serota Report is also an urgent call to sentencers to shorten the prison terms they impose. Both reports hope also for a further switch of sentences from imprisonment to non-custodial alternatives, but in neither report is this stressed as much as is the need to shorten the prison sentences which are passed.

The main reason for this is spelt out clearly in the Home Office *Review*: it arises from demands on the probation service, which itself has risen from 1,000 full-time officers in 1950 to 5,000 now, but which cannot for economic reasons be further substantially increased at present. Thus:

> the possibility of financing an increase in probation-based facilities through a major shift in resources from the prison service is unrealistic . . . it will not be possible as it has been previously to make the central feature of policies for the reduction of the prison population the development of

facilities for the offender to be dealt with in the community, *where fresh resources are required.* (para. 8, italics added)

This does, however, leave open one possibility which is not fully discussed by either the Home Office *Review* or the Serota Report, namely a switch into non-custodial sentences not involving the use of probation manpower. And in fact, there has during the whole post-war period been a tendency for more and more convicted offenders to receive sentences which do not place them under surveillance by either the prison or the probation services — our two sources of what the Americans call 'correctional manpower'. (This trend is shown clearly in *Table 1*.) A further switch in this direction can

TABLE 1

Adult Indictable Offenders: Types of Sentence
(includes all persons finally sentenced in years shown)

		1938 (per cent)		1975 (per cent)	
(a) *Prison Service*	Imprisonment	32.8		13.4	
(b) *Probation Service*	Probation	15.1		7.0	
	Community Service	—	15.1	0.5	8.6
	Suspended Sentence with supervision	—		1.1	
(c) *Other Sentences*	Fine	26.9		55.3	
	Discharge	23.3		12.0	
	Suspended Sentence without supervision	—	52.1	10.1	78.0
	Other	1.9		0.6	
Total		100.0		100.0	
N		38,896		209,709	

perhaps be predicted is a result of the severe resource problems currently facing the prison and probation services.

The fourth and final element of current British penology discernible from the two reports under review is what I have called in a previous paper a tendency towards a policy of *bifurcation* (see Bottoms 1977). In presenting its clarion call for shorter prison sentences, the Serota Report draws a sharp distinction between, on the one hand, 'dangerous' crimes and offenders, and, on the other, what it variously calls 'ordinary' or 'run-of-the-mill offenders'. The shorter sentence policy, it makes clear, is to be restricted to the latter category; as the Chairman puts it, 'our comments do not apply to the question of dangerous crime, where long sentences will, we believe, continue to be appropriate' (p. v; and see para. 5). Similarly, the Home Office *Review*, for all the urgency of its wish to reduce the prison population, clearly exempts from such considerations the 'dangerous offence and offender' from whom society is to be protected by appropriate terms of imprisonment (paras. 3(ii)(a), 9).

Official policy-makers now seem increasingly to be making explicit this dichotomy between the 'dangerous' and the 'rest';[6] but, as I tried to show in my earlier article, it is a dichotomy with an emerging history which can be traced back some years, notably in sentencing practice, where on the one hand there has been a considerable decrease in the proportionate use of imprisonment (see above), and on the other hand there has actually been a proportionate increase in the use of very long sentences of imprisonment.

Yet, if we are to draw this sharp distinction between the 'dangerous' and the 'run-of-the-mill', it only raises the more starkly the question as to what and who are to be considered 'dangerous'. The issue of 'dangerousness' has suddenly in the last few years leapt into an unprecedented prominence in British penology, not least as a result of proposals in the Butler Report (1975, ch. 4), and by the Scottish Council on Crime (1975, ch. 4, sec. 2). My own views on this 'renaissance of dangerousness' are on record elsewhere (Bottoms 1977); *inter alia*, I believe (i) that the proposals are not soundly based, since they would (on present evidence) involve locking up three people for indefinite terms in order to prevent one violent crime; (ii) that the Butler Committee and the Scottish Council were at fault in operating with implicitly class-loaded conceptions of dangerousness — lower-class assaultists were included, but drunken drivers and the keepers of persistently unsafe factories were not. Thomas Mathiesen (1974), the Norwegian criminologist, was in my view exaggerating a little but nevertheless pointing to an important truth when he said:

> In our society, acts dangerous to human beings are
> increasingly being committed. Largely, however, these
> acts are committed by individuals and classes with
> considerable power in society. . . . Punishment, in our age
> imprisonment, is largely used against petty thieves and
> other relatively harmless individuals. (pp. 77–8)

If, then, 'dangerousness' is to be the key concept in a bifurcated penal policy which separates clearly the 'serious' from the 'ordinary' offender, it is essential that the issues as to the identity of the dangerous, and the justification for separating them off for particularly major penal intervention, be squarely faced.

Responses to the Collapse of the Rehabilitative Ideal

If we pause to take stock at this point, we have identified (using the two recent reports as convenient vehicles) four current facets of

English penology: the collapse of the rehabilitative ideal; penological pragmatism; the crisis in penal resources; and the bifurcation tendency. Of these, penological pragmatism may be regarded as an inadequate response to present difficulties, and which must therefore be transcended; and the crisis in penal resources is simply a most important material limitation in any penal policy which is to be enunciated. This leaves us with, as the two central conceptual features of contemporary English penology, the collapse of the rehabilitative ideal and the bifurcation tendency.

I ought to say at once that the relationship between these two features, at the level of historical and sociological explanation, raises very major issues about recent developments in the State and in punishment. It would not be appropriate to tackle these problems here, though I intend to do so elsewhere. Here, I shall first spell out in some detail the main responses which have been made in various quarters to the collapse of the rehabilitative ideal; and then I shall give a slightly fuller consideration to the implications for penal thought and policy if (as seems likely) the bifurcation tendency is indeed pursued as a major strand in future official strategies.

Responses to the collapse of the rehabilitative ideal have, naturally, been various. I shall identify five main alternative approaches.

(i) *Rehabilitation Revisited.* There are some who wish to keep alive the treatment ethic, in various guises. They correctly point out, for example, that not all the research results have been wholly lacking in support for treatment effects; and they often suggest, much more doubtfully, that more encouraging results might well be achieved *either* by more sophisticated classification of types of offender in relation to different types of treatment, *or* if more financial resources were allocated to treatment programmes, *or* if research workers were allowed (as they usually are not, for ethical reasons) to carry out fully controlled random experimentation with offenders. Better versions of this 'defence of treatment' thesis usually take account also of the criticisms of the previous excesses of the rehabilitative model: thus for example the dust cover of Norval Morris' (1974) *Future of Imprisonment* declares that the author 'retains what is valuable in the "rehabilitative ideal" while eliminating the corruptive effects of our current prison programs'.

Perhaps the most sophisticated contemporary British defender of 'treatment' in penology is Nigel Walker, the Wolfson Professor of Criminology at Cambridge (see, for example, his discussion of the parole concept: Walker 1975). Walker devoted his recent Sandoz Lecture to a general philosophical defence of treatment, a choice which he made specifically because 'what is happening to the notion (of treatment) in America and Scandinavia seems likely to happen here' (Walker 1976, p. 5); a prospect which he views with disquiet, since he believes that, provided a healthy scepticism about treatment is maintained, 'we should not abandon all efforts to devise effective forms of treatment' (p. 20). But sophisticated as is Walker's argument at many points, at the end of the day one is left wondering quite what this defence amounts to; for he gives away so much of the game to his opponents that the remainder seems of rather marginal significance (a danger familiar to theologians, one imagines!). Thus, for example, as regards the sentencing of sane adult offenders, Walker suggests that a 'treatment' disposition may justifiably be imposed only if the offender consents; if the resources for treatment already exist; if the extent of restriction on the offender's liberty is no greater than would be the case if he were sentenced without treatment considerations influencing the decision; *and* if 'the prospects of success really are substantial'. These criteria are in fact so stringent — far more stringent than most courts today habitually apply — that they would in my view virtually eliminate the use of probation orders (as currently understood) if courts were to take them seriously.[7]

In fact Walker's arguments, important enough in one context, miss the real point of the contemporary debate. Penal decision-makers are still operating in a way that takes major account of treatment considerations, and they used to do so to an even greater extent. Thus, people have been sent to borstals in large numbers in the belief that the training offered in borstal will help to 'cut off the supply of adult recidivists'; many others have been placed on probation because guidance from a probation officer was thought essential to help them keep away from crime; others have been and are still regularly released on parole under supervision because 'he will stand a much better chance of survival with supervision than without it', and so on. If, for both empirical and theoretical reasons, the justification for such claims seems increasingly doubtful,[8] it follows that the *primary* question should be — what should be the general aims and shape of the penal system if we can no longer make the widespread assumptions about treatment which we used to make? An important *secondary* question certainly then is 'and what scope is there left for treatment?'; and it is this question which Walker essentially tries to answer.[9] But it is only a secondary question, and the central defect of treating it as if it were a primary question is that the answer to it might very well vary according to the answer given to the primary question.

At the level of the primary question, no one now seriously pretends (as once they used to) that 'rehabilitation' has any major utilitarian value in the general reduction of crime rates, or in the prevention of the recruitment of recidivists. Important ethical and other questions remain about the residual role of 'treatment'; but for the purposes of the general planning of the penal system (and hence for this paper), it would seem that the rehabilitative ideal cannot be effectively revivified.

(ii) *The Justice Model.* By far the most important and influential alternative to the rehabilitative ideal, particularly in the U.S.A. and Scandinavia but increasingly in Britain also, has been the so-called 'justice model'. 'If we cannot ensure rehabilitation, and if rehabilitation in any case often produces injustice, then let us at least have justice' has been the cry. Justice, in this context, has meant primarily the *elimination of arbitrary discretion* by decision-makers: so the main practical effect of the justice model has been in attacks on disparities in sentencing and in parole decision-making, and in pressure for fixed penalties for specified offences. In some radical prisoners' movements, this has become translated into the slogan of 'the right to punishment': the right, that is, to be let out as soon as you have served a just sentence, and to serve your time without interference from psychiatrists and social workers if you want to. There have been some important practical consequences of the justice model approach, such as the State of Maine's abolition of parole and reversion to a fixed-sentence system, and the U.S. Federal Parole Board's adoption of standard 'guidelines' to reduce discretion; a similar attack on the parole concept in Britain has been launched by Hood (1974a, 1974b) and supported by N.A.C.R.O. (1977b).

As Dean Clarke (1978) has usefully pointed out, different advocates of the justice model have operated with rather different theoretical assumptions — in particular, there is a divergence between those (such as Hood) who are seeking only for a new formalism in the application of criminal justice, and those such as the American Friends Service Committee (1971) who are concerned with much wider issues of injustice in society. Interestingly, however, even amongst the latter group there has been little attempt to link the 'justice model' debate with the very large literature on Justice in the field of social and political philosophy. Indeed, even the extremely influential contemporary *magnum opus* of Rawls (1972) is not systematically discussed in any penological 'justice model' text known to me.

This failure to connect with wider debates on justice perhaps explains some of the theoretical confusions of the 'justice model' texts. Consider, for example, the most recent complete statement of the model, the Committee for the Study of Incarceration's *Doing Justice* (Von Hirsch 1976), a document which deliberately seeks to reinstate the concept of 'desert' at the centre of modern penal thought. Two of the Committee's members, in their introduction, specifically endorse the Kantian imperative that 'certain things are simply wrong and ought to be punished' (p. xxxix); that is, that moral desert is both a necessary *and sufficient* ground for punishment. Yet the report itself says on the contrary (see pp. 54, 160) that desert in itself is a necessary but *not a sufficient* ground. (For a stringent review of other confusions in the book, see Walker 1978). Indeed, the Committee seem to be very half-hearted retributivists — in the introduction it is stated that their solution 'is one of despair, not hope'; and one of the signatories of the report, the British criminologist Leslie Wilkins, says that he endorses the report only 'without enthusiasm . . . it seems that we have rediscovered "sin" in the absence of a better alternative' (pp. 177–8). In short, the Committee's desert-based philosophy lacks both clarity and conviction; and, significantly perhaps, the other main text of the 'justice model', the American Friends' report, was specifically utilitarian in its general justifying aim (pp. 149–50), though few have noticed this difference between the two volumes. The only things that really unite all adherents of the justice model are suspicion of the individual treatment model, and the reduction or elimination of discretion by decision-makers: beyond that, there are real difficulties and confusions. Arguably, this explains the paradox that, although the justice model has been formulated by liberal and Left groups, it is in fact easily capable of appropriation by the Right, who have no difficulty with concepts of desert and of equal sentencing, but would insist on *long* fixed sentences rather than the short fixed sentences proposed by justice model adherents.[10]

Because of the central importance of the justice model in the emerging contemporary debate, we have devoted two chapters to it in this volume. Keith Bottomley concentrates on exegesis and criminological comment, while Raymond Plant considers the issues from the wider standpoint of moral and political philosophy.

(iii) *Radical Approaches.* The American Friends' document devotes a chapter to the 'repressive functions of the criminal justice system'. After examining evidence for *systematic* discrimination in the system according to economic status; ethnic group; age; sex; membership of unconventional life-style; and political affiliation, it concludes:

> In a free society (the repressive functions of the criminal
> justice system) should be minimised or eliminated. We
> hope that an awareness of the pervasiveness of these
> functions in the American system can lead to change. We
> will not be able to do away with these repressive functions
> until social prejudice and inequality are uprooted and
> eradicated from society as a whole. (p. 123)

Similarly, the Committee for the Study of Incarceration includes a final chapter on 'just deserts in an unjust society' which concludes that while its proposals for punishment are less unfair than the existing system, 'as long as a substantial segment of the population is denied adequate opportunities for a livelihood, any scheme for punishing must be morally flawed' (Von Hirsch 1976, p. 149).

As we have already seen, however, neither Committee really grounds its report in the wider context of social philosophy. From the point of view of a Marxist analysis, therefore, aspirations such as the above can be regarded as merely misguided idealism, with no real understanding of the nature of the capitalist system or of how it is to be changed; whilst more 'formalist' approaches to the justice model, such as Hood's, can from the same viewpoint be considered as legitimations of the criminal justice systems of advanced-capitalist societies (Clarke 1978).

If the demonstration of systematic (and not just accidental) discrimination in criminal justice is accepted, it follows that any true 'justice model' of criminal policy must face the wider issues of the nature of Social Justice, and indeed the age-old question of the Good Society. I shall not debate this here, though it is to be hoped that this question will be centrally faced in the Consultation. In the meantime, and before the Good Society is achieved, two questions arise.

The first of these is as to how our existing penal system handles the so-called 'crimes of the powerful' (see Pearce 1976), whether improvements in this respect are required in the name of justice, and whether such improvements are attainable without a radical transformation of society. These difficult issues are to be confronted in this volume by Terence Morris.

The second question concerns the tactics of reform. Traditional penal reform organisations have worked quite close to Government, and indeed the Howard League at one point in its post-war history had a Secretary (H. J. Klare) who, according to his own statement, believed that reform could 'best be achieved through discussions with enlightened decision-makers like Sir Lionel Fox (Chairman of the Prison Commissioners) and R. A. Butler (Home Secretary)' (quoted in Wright 1975, p. 92). A much more radical stance is taken by Thomas Mathiesen (1974), undoubtedly the most influential radical writer in the strictly penal field in the recent past. His concept of 'abolition', fully explored by David Downes in this volume, is concerned with the abolition of prisons and other penal apparatus in western liberal-democracies, and is essentially aimed at a process of chipping away at the power face of the State through a series of 'negative' reforms. ('Negative' reforms remove some State power; 'positive' reforms do not, though they may make inmates' lives more comfortable — they are to be avoided, in Mathiesen's view, as leading to a greater entrenchment of State power.) Mathiesen's strategy, based on this concept, was not followed by the British prisoners' union, PROP, in the celebrated 1972 prison confrontations; but

PROP has subsequently come round to a Mathiesen-based strategy (Fitzgerald 1977). It remains a most important question for any penal reformer how far Mathiesen's analysis and strategy is to be followed (see also Cohen 1975).

(iv) *Incapacitation and General Deterrence.* A completely different approach to the present conjuncture has been offered by the so-called 'incapacitation' strategists in the United States. Perhaps the most celebrated adherent of this view is James Q. Wilson (1975, ch. 10) of Harvard, though his influential book, *Thinking about Crime,* is concerned with much wider issues than simply incapacitation. (For another influential text, see van den Haag 1975, esp. ch. 21).

The main premises of Wilson's approach to incapacitation are, as he himself states, two-fold. The first is a pessimistic theory of human nature, and the consequent need for firm social control. The second is the assertion that 'most serious crime is committed by repeaters'. Such assumptions are, he believes, much more acceptable than the existing ones: as he put it in an article in the *New York Times Magazine* (9 March 1975) under the bold title 'Lock 'Em Up':

> Our futile efforts to curb or even understand the dramatic and continuing rise in crime have been frustrated by our optimistic and unrealistic assumptions about human nature. . . . It is strange that we should persist in the view that we can find and alleviate the 'causes' of crime, that serious criminals can be rehabilitated. . . . Wicked people exist. Nothing avails except to set them apart from innocent people.

Wilson is very optimistic about the effects of his strategy. He believes that a 20% reduction in street robberies could be achieved by the simple device of locking people up for longer — 'the reduction . . . would be solely the result of incapacitation, making no allowance for such additional reductions as might result from enhanced deterrence or rehabilitation'. This is, of course, based on the (doubtful) premise that there is a finite number of violent repeat offenders and that, by locking up some of them for longer, they would be prevented from reoffending, and others would not be recruited to take their place. Wilson's assertions have led to detailed statistical work on the possible effects of incapacitation strategies, at least some of which concludes that the impact on crime rates would be much less dramatic than he supposes (Van Dine *et al.* 1977, and subsequent controversy in the same journal).

An intellectual movement of this kind has not yet been influential in this country. Indeed, as we have seen, the official pressure here has been almost wholly in terms of *reducing,* not increasing, the lengths of prison sentences. Nevertheless it is by no means impossible that a movement along Wilsonian lines will develop. As we have seen, the message of the justice model can in fact be easily appropriated by those such as Wilson who want *long* fixed sentences. And there is evidence that the Conservative Party is planning to make 'law and order' a populist issue at the next General Election:[11] an incapacitation strategy would fit in well with such an approach.

In England, incapacitative sentences have, in the recent past,[12] been used only for a very small group of people who have committed serious offences — usually either 'professional criminals' or the psychiatrically disturbed. It is significant that such offenders are largely excluded from the recent relaxations of the parole system; they are in a real sense the top end of the dichotomy being created by the bifurcation tendency. Recently, the Butler Committee (1975) and the Scottish Council on Crime (1975) have wanted to add to this group by creating more indeterminate sentences for so-called 'dangerous offenders'; but the strategy of these reports is very different from that of J. Q. Wilson. The British proposals are based on scientifically selecting *individuals* who are alleged to be dangerous (as indicated earlier in this chapter, a very difficult exercise, and one which invariably results in a high proportion of 'false positives', or those predicted to be violent who will in fact not be so). Wilson's proposal is by contrast, based on a *class* incapacitation strategy which would lock up all those convicted of specified crimes, and which therefore does not require the specific prognosis of the allegedly dangerous individual. Yet both the American and the British initiatives in this field are clearly connected with the decline of the rehabilitative ideal.

So too is another related but separate intellectual movement, which might be described as the 'renaissance of general deterrence'. In the heyday of the rehabilitative ideal, it was fashionable to ignore general deterrence, or to suppose that the capital punishment debate had disposed of the issue. These naïve positions could not be long maintained once the rehabilitative ideal began to crack, and there has been a veritable spate of renewed academic interest in general deterrence in recent years (e.g. Zimring and Hawkins 1973; Ehrlich 1973; Andenaes 1974; Gibbs 1975; Beyleveld 1978). In intellectual terms, this has been wholly healthy, having brought to light many important and neglected research issues. The policy implications for penal sanctions are less straightforward. One short but important Home Office study showed, for example, that a wholly exceptional 20-year detention sentence on a teenage 'mugger' in Birmingham had had little or no discernible impact on the robbery rates in Birmingham or other large cities in England (Baxter and Nuttall 1975); and Gibbs (1975, p. 238) concludes his sophisticated book on deterrence by explicitly stating that 'there is no immediate prospect of deterrence research having an impact on penal policy: all social scientists can do at present is to emphasise the difficulties in assessing evidence for or against the deterrence doctrine'. Nevertheless, there is plainly a temptation in the present penal situation for some to want to argue a rather simple 'law and order' case based on the deterrence doctrine, following the collapse of rehabilitation; and in certain contexts this can be easily married with an espousal of incapacitative strategies — as it is, to an extent, by J. Q. Wilson.

No paper specifically on incapacitation or general deterrence has been included in this volume, but these potential strategies should be carefully borne in mind in reading the various contributions.

(v) *Reparation.* In a recent discussion pamphlet, the Howard League for Penal Reform (1977a) has produced ideas for a new policy, based on the concept of reparation. Summarising this thesis in its Annual Report, the League (1977b) argues the case in this way:

> If a policy based on rehabilitation is unlikely to do offenders much good, and punishment is likely to harm them, what is left? The answer is surely not to do things to them, still less to put them somewhere out of the way and then not to know what to do with them, but to require them to do something constructive to make up for the harm they have caused. In some cases, personal restitution is possible. Otherwise the offender should make reparation to the community (as in Community Service Orders) . . . only in the most serious cases, or when a person was totally uncooperative, would this work have to be done in prison. (pp. 5–6)

The League claims substantial advantages for the approach. Punishment proportionate to the offence, as advocated by the justice model, is retained — 'but as a by-product, not an end in itself, and in a way which is constructive, not damaging'. Rehabilitation and attitude-change is not sought: if it occurs, 'so much the better, but even if (it) doesn't at least he has been required to do something useful'. Perhaps most interestingly of all, it is argued that efforts at checking the crime rate are no longer concentrated on the 'blind alley' of changing individual offenders, 'and can instead concentrate on a realistic policy combining security precautions and social reform'.

This victim-oriented reparation policy is not a sudden new phenomenon. The post-war years in England have seen a succession of moves towards a more victim-oriented approach: the initial pioneering work of Margery Fry which led eventually to a State compensation scheme for victims of violent crime (1964); the extension of compensation in the criminal courts following the report of the Advisory Council on the Penal System (1970b); the advent of voluntary victim support schemes, to provide victims with emotional support, and practical help and advice, at a time of difficulty; and the enactment in 1972 of community service orders, which are seen by many as having a strongly reparative element in them.

Nor is the rise of a victim-oriented approach restricted to this country. The Norwegian Nils Christie (1976) has recently advocated a thorough-going return to a less centralised, neighbourhood-based, lay court system. After a finding of guilt, the next task of the court would be a detailed discussion of satisfaction to the victim — and only after that would any question of punishment arise. Again, the Dutch criminologist Louk Hulsman (1976) has, in similar fashion, called for the blurring of the distinction between crime and civil wrong, with a consequent increase in victim-oriented solutions to harmful actions. And in the U.S.A. Robert P. Rhodes (1977) has said — as only an American could — that:

> A victim perspective can provide a comprehensive,
> quantifiable indicator to measure the success of a policy for
> social defence against crime. It shifts the balkanised focus
> of interested groups from subsystem objectives (e.g.
> recidivism and treatment) back to the fundamental purpose
> . . . of protecting the citizen. (p. 194)

I do not believe that this relatively sudden recent upsurge of interest in the victim, and in reparation, is in any sense accidental; and for this very reason I would expect it to grow in strength in the coming years. Some help in understanding why the trend is occurring comes from the work of the French sociologist Émile Durkheim (1901), who formulated a general proposition that 'the intensity of punishment is greater the more societies approximate to a less developed type'.[13] This is due, Durkheim asserts, to the different kind of *conscience collective* — collective consciousness or conscience — in those societies. We can distinguish two kinds of crime — crimes against collective things, such as religion and public customs and authorities, and crimes against individuals, such as theft and violence. Less developed societies tend to include within their penal laws only the first type; such crimes are seen as deeply odious, and elicit very strong sanctions. As societies developed, the contents of their criminal codes became more individualistic and less collective or religious; and punishment became less severe because the harm to the victim, and the subsequently meted out harm to the criminal, were seen to be of the same type — so respect for the human dignity of the offender could therefore attenuate the penalty in a way not possible for the collective or religious crimes. In such a movement, one can well expect that the logical end result would be a tendency to redress the imbalance between the offender and the victim, rather than simply to mete out sanctions against the offender.[14] In a period such as the present when there has been a progressive lessening of the penalties awarded to 'ordinary' offenders (for reasons not unconnected, I would suggest, to the twentieth-century secularisation process), it is therefore predictable that one should in the end, for such offenders, turn to an abandonment of penal sanction and a return to civil redress between parties.

Two questions arise from this discussion. The first seems to be a difficult problem in ethics: once we understand a little more fully how we come to be where we are in terms of penal thought, how far is it justifiable that this should constrain our ethical choices — and if we do allow this, does this make our work simply a legitimating ideology? Secondly and more practically, an alternative emergent response to the present situation would seem to be, not to stress *reparation* but *regulation* — that is, to work out a purely regulatory scale of penalties, of which the fine is the most obvious example, but local detention, and adult attendance centres, are other possibilities. (Interestingly, the fine has recently been the fastest growing penal sanction in England, even at the time of the ascendency of the rehabilitative ideal.) In cases where no personal restitution is appropriate, it is perhaps for the Howard League to justify why the 'compulsory reparation to the community' (such as a community service order) is more appropriate than a regulative penalty such as the fine.

Bifurcation and its Consequences

Having considered these five approaches to the collapse of the rehabilitative ideal, we must return to a consideration of the bifurcation tendency. If I were asked to guess at the likeliest actual shape of future penal policy (regardless of the question of desirability), then I would guess that bifurcation will play a key role. At the serious end of the dichotomy, there will be isolated the 'dangerous', who will be on the one hand those regarded as very disturbed, and on the other, those regarded as straightforwardly wicked (i.e. respectively the 'mad' and the 'bad'). For the remainder of offenders, there will be an attenuation of penalties, a progressive abandonment of rehabilitation, a reduction of discretion in sentencing and parole, and a move towards either regulatory or compensating penalties. Many things might make this prediction go wrong — such as the return of a Government heavily committed to an incapacitation strategy. But I hope it is permissible for me to treat this prediction at any rate as a working hypothesis, and to ask some questions about it.

The first question concerns *models of human action*. A dichotomy such as the one suggested would isolate at one end of the spectrum both the 'involuntary actor' and the 'evil'; whilst for the less serious offenders there would be talk of 'situational pressures to offend', related to the overall structure of society. Whether, and if so how, it is possible to hold with philosophical coherence these three different views of offending within a single theory of human nature, remains unclear (see further, Bottoms 1977).

Secondly, there is the question of *social policy in crime prevention.* What is interesting about the possible shape of penal policy as sketched above — and indeed about many contemporary approaches in penology — is that they are virtually abandoning any hope of having significant effects on the crime rate through action with individual offenders. In theoretical terms, I am sure that this is correct. To illustrate the point — I recently attended a seminar at which six local practitioners were asked to speak on the question whether juvenile delinquency had increased since the war, if so why, and what could be done about it. (They were given ten minutes each!) They all agreed that delinquency had increased considerably, and suggested various social causes for this, in terms of general developments in British society since the war: but when they came to speak of remedies, the talk was all of action on and for the individual offender. The incongruity between the 'social' nature of their diagnosis, and the 'individual' nature of their remedies, was very striking, and underlined the fact that only social changes and social policy of a broad kind are really likely to have much impact on crime rates.[15] This has recently been grasped in the Home Office *Review*:

in view of the limitation in the capacity of the agencies of the criminal justice system to reduce the incidence of crime, the scope for reducing crime through *policy that goes beyond the boundaries of the criminal justice system* merits particular attention. (para. 15, italics added)

Quite what these policies should be is, of course, an extremely difficult and complex question, which is addressed in this volume by Elizabeth Barnard. One possible approach, much in vogue in the U.S.A. at present (Newman 1973; Jeffrey 1977) is that of 'environmental prevention', involving such things as redesigning housing estates, and fitting steering locks to cars (Mayhew *et al.* 1976). All this certainly has some marginal promise, but in my view does not really tackle the central social policy issues involved. Briefly and provocatively for the sake of discussion, I might suggest that one possible hope for crime reduction lies in the revivification of neighbourhood and of community within an urban society, along the lines argued by Christie (1976) but without following him all the way into his rural romanticism. Such a policy, if taken seriously, might well involve a major restructuring and rethinking of the nature of social services departments, probation, and community work (see, on aspects of this theme, Sainsbury 1977).[16]

I have deliberately inserted the previous paragraph because if taken seriously, it would certainly affect my third question, the *future role of the prison and probation services,* which are considered in the chapters by Frederick McClintock and Ken Pease respectively. The probation service is currently undergoing a process of internal self-appraisal (cf. Weston 1978; Thomas 1978; Haxby 1978), and this is by no means unconnected with the collapse of the rehabilitative ethic, so central to its previous ideology. Indeed the *Probation Journal* has recently reported rumours from high places that the probation service has had its day (vol. 24, p. 1: and see Croft 1978, p. 4). However this may be, it is surely the case that the erosion of claims of particular professional skills in the handling of offenders, coupled with hints that any possible hope of crime-rate reduction must lie in the working with communities in a very broad sense, should surely reopen (in a very new context) the old debate about the possible merging of probation and social services departments.

As to the prison service, they will be involved in different ways as the bifurcation policy develops. On the one hand they will have a relatively small, but probably increasing, group of 'dangerous' high-security prisoners; as the Hull riot of 1976 amply showed, not all the problems of handling this group have by any means yet been solved (see Thomas 1977). On the other hand, if the policy of the Serota Report and the Home Office *Review* is followed, 'ordinary' prisoners will be held for shorter periods, and, if the attack on parole develops as one would expect, then prison staff will not need to trouble themselves with parole reviews for the majority of prisoners.

Let us look in a little more detail at the first group, the 'dangerous offenders'. One half of these, the 'psychiatrically disturbed', will no doubt continue to be the subject of keen clinical attention, — if not for treatment, then at least to assess continuing 'dangerousness' and therefore whether or not to release them. The other half, the 'professional criminals', will be viewed with the greatest possible suspicion because of potential escapes. Therefore, clinically, or physically, or both, this 'dangerous' group will be under extensive *surveillance* (see Cohen and Taylor 1972). In a wider context, there is evidence in Britain of the increasing power of the State, manifested most obviously in the criminal context in the growing centralisation of the police, and the increasing tendency to set up within the police forces special units who might develop (and, some say, already have developed) into a 'Third Force'. All the evidence suggests also that the prison service is not reluctant to see an increase in its centralised powers over the group perceived as 'dangerous', and is likely to resist any attempt to bring in outside lawyers or other watch-dogs who might want to question the use of this power. That such a situation has its potential dangers needs little emphasis here. Perhaps the most eloquent testimony to the dangers came — surprisingly — in an article in the *Prison Service Journal* in which a borstal governor who is also a Church of Scotland minister seriously and explicitly warned his fellow-members of the prison service against what he saw as a potential slide towards attitudes which would be compatible with Fascism in prison management (Fyffe 1977). As he pointed out also, the 'real action' in the prison system is increasingly to be found in the seven high-security 'dispersal' prisons where the 'dangerous' are all held.

It is said that Malraux saw as a key problem of our time whether it is 'possible to pursue an active but pessimist philosophy that is not, in fact, a form of Fascism' (*New Statesman*, 4 April 1975). This seems to encapsulate the problem for the Prison Service. The abandonment of the rehabilitative ethic has led to a widespread abandonment of hope. The somewhat chilling phrase, 'secure and humane containment' (Home Office 1977b, p. 17) seems to command growing support as policy. The rehabilitative ethic, and perhaps still more the liberal-reformism which preceded it, was an ethic of coercive caring; but at least there was caring. Will there be real care in the era of humane containment?

Envoi

I should like to end with some discussion of ideas prompted by Michel Foucault's (1975) recent essay in prison history. Foucault argues that the end of the eighteenth and the beginning of the nineteenth century saw a great transformation both in the nature of punishment, and also (and of course closely related) in the way in which the central power of the State is manifested at the local and individual level. Briefly, the mode of punishment was transformed from the 'corporal' (the infliction of physical pain or shame on the body, a public demonstration of Royal power), to the 'carceral' (the prison, invisible to the public, conducted on a strict time-table, under close surveillance and discipline, with a regime of work, education and religious exercises). What has happened, says Foucault, is that, in a word, the *soul* has replaced the *body* as the object of punitive power: the modern prison was from the outset concerned with reformation, but it was very much *coercive reformation*, the soul in the body to be coerced into the dominant morality. It can be argued that this has remained essentially the same (despite the obvious differences) ever since — from the chaplain in the first reformed prison system in England;[17] through Bentham's secular 'Panopticon'; to the late-nineteenth-century treadwheel; Paterson's liberal paternalism (Ruck 1951); and on to the group-counselling techniques of the 1960s.

Foucault points out, though, that there was a third model of punishment available — but not taken up — at the end of the eighteenth century. This was the model of the social-contract reformists such as Beccaria (1764); and Foucault describes the three models as follows:

> In monarchical law, punishment is a ceremonial of
> sovereignty . . . it deploys before the eyes of the spectators
> an effect of terror as intense as it is discontinuous. . . . The
> reforming jurists, on the other hand, saw punishment as a
> way of *requalifying individuals as subjects, as juridical*
> *subjects.* . . . Lastly, in the project for a prison institution that
> was then developing, punishment was seen as a technique
> for the coercion of individuals (pp. 130–1, italics added)

In an interview about his book Foucault (1977) was asked whether it was not a 'striking phenomenon' that today people are 'returning from the schema of delinquence (i.e. prison-type coercion) to that of infraction (i.e. that recommended by the eighteenth-century jurists)'. He did not really answer the question, but it remains a highly pertinent one. It is always difficult to see clearly what is happening in one's own time, but it is certainly of considerable interest that not only are we increasingly using punishments not involving penal agents (see *Table 1*); but also that, even in cases where we do send law-breakers to prison or place them on probation, we seem now at last to be on the point of abandoning coercive soul-transformation. In short, we may even be at the beginning of another decisive moment in penal history, in which we leave behind the coercive reformatory technique, and seek for most offenders (through fines, compensation, or short non–treatment prison terms) the classical project of 'requalifying individuals as subjects, as juridical subjects'.[18] But even classicism allowed banishment for those who completely fail to uphold the social contract (Beccaria 1764, section XVII); and perhaps also we are developing our own form of banishment, to the high-security prisons. In those prisons there is still as much surveillance as in Bentham's Panopticon: but the purpose is now different. In Hulsman's (1976) memorable metaphor, this is increasingly a 'prisoner-of-war' type of detention.

These schematic ideas based on Foucault are tentative, and perhaps in need of revision: but they seem at least worth airing as an aid to understanding our present situation, and hence to assist in reflection on desirable options for future policy.

I have said nothing about theology — and there is an obviously good reason for this. But I have spoken of theories of man; of the State; of Hope, and of Caring; of Coercion, and of Justice. In such themes, there is surely adequate scope for the theologian's reflection, to help forward our joint endeavour.

NOTES

1. Two limitations of scope are made in this chapter. First, juvenile offenders (under 17) are excluded because, while much of what is said here is also relevant to them, there are additional legislative considerations which greatly complicate the picture. Secondly, the chapter covers only England and Wales, and omits the separate Scottish jurisdiction — though the Scottish system is by no means without its problems, and perhaps even its crisis (Moore 1978). Aspects of the Scottish prison situation are dealt with in the chapters by McClintock and Downes.

2. The Report goes on to say that 'for some types of offence fines do appear to be more effective in discouraging recidivism than prison sentences', but the evidence for this is in my view unconvincing (Bottoms 1973).

3. Prison Rules, 1964, Rule 1: re-enacting with a slight change of wording Prison Rules 1952, Rule 6.

4. They are: (i) that reduction of the prison population must remain a particular preoccupation; (ii) that in view of the pressures on the penal agencies, a particular focus in policy development must be to reduce the input into the criminal justice system; (iii) the assumptions upon which the system rests should continue to be kept under review (para. 17). The third conclusion, if imaginatively conceived, could transcend the pragmatic, but there is little real evidence of this kind of approach in the rest of the document.

5. A further variable which is relevant is length of sentence; there are technical complexities about analysing this, but it can safely be said that its influence has not been anything like as great as the rise in conviction rates.

6. After this chapter was written, the Advisory Council on the Penal System (1978) published its final report following a major review of maximum sentences. The report explicitly advocates a two-tier sentencing structure in which maximum sentences for most crimes would be reduced to 'the level below which 90% of sentences of immediate imprisonment passed by the Crown Court for the particular offence have fallen in recent years'; while for some 'dangerous' offenders, preventive determinate sentences without maximum limit may be passed. So the infant Bifurcation has leaped, like Athena, fully armed from Zeus' head: but without Athena's quota of wisdom. For criticisms of the Council's report, see Radzinowicz and Hood (1978a, 1978b), and Hall Williams (1978).

7. Particularly if the condition that 'the prospects of success really are substantial' is interpreted strictly to mean that 'the prospects of success really are substantially greater than if no treatment were attempted'.

8. After this chapter was written, the Home Office produced some empirical evidence showing that males sentenced to terms of imprisonment of over

four years were less often reconvicted (in a two-year follow up) if released on parole rather than held in prison until the normal release date (Home Office 1978, ch. 8). However it is not certain that this is a true result, since, as the report notes, 'the lower reconviction rate of those on parole could have resulted from the use by the Parole Board of relevant selection criteria not taken into account in the classification of risk' in the research design.

9. See especially pp. 16–20 of his paper, where he essays a series of *reductio ad absurdum* arguments as to what a penal system would look like if the treatment were to be 'outlawed' altogether. *Inter alia*, he argues that the elimination of treatment 'must overcome great difficulties, not least of which would be the hopes both of staff and offenders'; but this comes close to making the false assumption that only a treatment ideology can produce hope. For a paradigm for future probation practice which explicitly abandons treatment but attempts to retain hope, see Bottoms and McWilliams (1979).

10. The Howard League (1977b, p. 5) has indeed recently assumed that the justice model is all about 'going back to punishment', and has argued against this that it would 'mislead the public, because it would give the impression that punishment 'works' as an individual or general deterrent, whereas there is no evidence that it is any more 'successful' than treatment'. In fact, I know of no justice model theorist who upholds the model on these grounds, though it is easy to see how such assumptions can be made from their work — even by some who should know better, such as the President-elect of the American Society of Criminology (Jeffrey 1977, ch. 1).

11. See Mrs. Margaret Thatcher's speech to the Conservative conference, October 1977: 'the people of Britain would make crime an issue at the next election. . . . I do not intend to sit on the sidelines, wringing my hands, while London, Glasgow, Manchester, Birmingham and the rest of our cities go the way of New York' (*The Guardian*, 15 October 1977).

12. A previous incapacitative sentence ('preventive detention') was abolished in 1967. Intended for the professional criminal, it caught, largely, rather tragic habitual petty offenders.

13. The proposition continues: 'and the more the central power assumes an absolute character'. Although very important for many purposes — not least in the context of Durkheim's own thought — this need not be fully considered in the present context.

14. Actually, Durkheim in an earlier work had suggested a general historical move from repressive to restitutive sanctions (Durkheim 1893); but there is no doubt he was ignorant of the great extent of the role of restitution in primitive societies. There has been no adequate exploration of the way in which the State took over these restitutive sanctions and turned them into repressive ones — which it now seems to be about to reconvert.

15. Even then, these changes may easily be regarded as undesirable on other grounds. A criminologist attached to the United Nations used to be asked by the trainee rulers of developing countries how they might prevent their crime rate from increasing. They were told, with heavy irony, that 'on no account should they develop substantial industries', that 'village societies are entirely capable of maintaining any discordance . . . within their own social frameworks', and that the people should remain 'ignorant, bigoted, and ill-educated'. (Morris and Hawkins 1970, p. 49). In strictly criminological terms, the advice was undoubtedly correct.

16. This 'brief and provocative' suggestion, originally written in November 1977,

led to sustained discussions with the South Yorkshire Probation Service and the eventual appointment of a Special Projects Team to work in a local neighbourhood with the aims specified. In the light of these discussions, and my own subsequent reading, my views on the way in which the aims might be achieved have been considerably modified and refined: see now Bottoms and McWilliams (1979, Aim 4).

17. Namely Gloucestershire: see Whiting (1975, pp. 33–7). The Chaplain believed in 'Solitude, Labour, and Religious Exercises'; he pressed for and obtained a 'solitary system'; 'he was not a neutral figure ... he was part of the establishment'. Christians should note with shame that among his routine activities was the visiting of condemned men for the express purpose of questioning them about their (undetected) accomplices, and that, in order the better to achieve this, news of reprieves from execution were sometimes deliberately withheld from the men concerned.

18. Several months after this was written, I encountered Cohen's (1977, p. 227) alternative suggestion, namely: 'Foucault described one historical take-off in terms of the move from 'simple' punishment to the concentrated surveillance of the asylum. We are living through another change: from the *concentration* to the *dispersal* of social control' (italics in original). Both suggestions have some plausibility, but I remain of the view that the apparent abandonment of coercive soul-transformation is ultimately the more fundamental development.

2

The 'Justice Model' in America and Britain: development and analysis

by A. KEITH BOTTOMLEY

Attempting to identify particular historical trends within criminology and penology is a notoriously hazardous task. Nevertheless, I wish to suggest that a consideration of post-war penological thought and practical developments in America and several Western European countries could lead to the plausible claim that the 1970s be seen as the decade during which the dominant 'rehabilitative ideal' of the '50s and '60s gave way to the 'justice model', as a basis for critical thinking, if not always for dramatic policy changes.

In this chapter I propose to outline the development and origins of this concept in the United States, with an indication of some of the major themes shared by the various proponents of the 'justice model' as well as some of the differences in emphasis that are also to be found. The second part of my discussion will concentrate on the various 'ripples' of the model that are to be found in critiques of criminal justice and penal policy in Britain. Finally, I shall conclude by drawing attention to what I see as some of the unresolved issues in the formulation of the justice model, which nevertheless in my view provides the most valid framework for a critical penology of the future.

The Justice Model for Corrections in the United States of America

It appears that the phrase 'justice model', as applied to corrections in America, originated with David Fogel, an energetically reformist Commissioner of Corrections in Minnesota from 1971 to 1973 (see Kwartler 1977; Fogel 1975, 1976). Fogel not only spelled out his ideas in a number of academic publications, but applied them in the day-to-day running of prisons in Minnesota, which ensured that notice was taken — both positive and negative — and opinions quickly crystallised around the core concepts. Despite the location of the literal origins of the 'justice model' in the work and writings of

Fogel, he was by no means a lone pioneer. Coincidentally, perhaps, 1971 can be seen as a particularly significant year in the development of the justice model: not only did it mark the appointment of David Fogel as Commissioner in Minnesota, but it saw the publication of the highly influential report *Struggle for Justice*, drawn up by the American Friends Service Committee (1971), and the setting up of the Committee for the Study of Incarceration, which published its report, *Doing Justice: the Choice of Punishments*, in 1976 (Von Hirsch 1976).

Thus the five-year period from 1971 to 1976 can be viewed as the 'coming of age' of the justice model in American corrections. I shall analyse in some detail the main arguments and conclusions of those two reports, together with the individual contributions of David Fogel (1975) and Norval Morris (1974). However, before proceeding to this central task, it is important to consider the background.

The Seed-Bed of the Justice Model

Three related elements appear to have contributed to the emergence of the justice model: (i) a growing *loss of faith in the 'rehabilitative ideal'*; (ii) *the extension of due process procedures*, and (iii) widespread *criticism of discretionary decision-making* in criminal justice and the penal processes.

Loss of faith in the 'rehabilitative ideal'. It is possible to trace the theoretical roots of the 'rehabilitative ideal' at least as far back as the second half of the nineteenth century, when a positivist-determinist criminology flourished in Italy, with a strong emphasis upon the need to study the individual offender in order to find ways of correcting him and thus preventing crime. At the turn of the century, the ideas of this school of criminology were eagerly embraced in the United States by the established legal and medical professions involved in criminal justice and penal management. Consequently this correctional and individually oriented version of criminology shaped the direction of American penal thought for most of the first half of the twentieth century, and directed it towards the goal of the *individualised treatment of offenders*. It was particularly influential in the development of a separate system of criminal justice for juvenile offenders, and the widespread use of parole and indeterminate sentencing for offenders of all ages.

In *Struggle for Justice* the American Friends Service Committee (1971) commented on the way in which the rehabilitative ideal had been uncritically accepted over the years:

> The individualised treatment model, the outcome of this
> historical process, has for nearly a century been the
> ideological spring from which almost all actual and
> proposed reform in criminal justice has been derived. . . .

> Like other conceptions that become so entrenched that they
> slip imperceptibly into dogma, the treatment model has
> been assumed rather than analysed, preached rather than
> evaluated. (pp. 36–7)

An early academic critic of this dominant paradigm within American corrections was Francis A. Allen (1959, 1964). It is indeed to him that we owe the phrase 'rehabilitative ideal'. Writing in 1959 he pointed out that the previous fifty years had seen major penological developments in the establishment of juvenile courts, probation, and systems of parole; in addition, big strides had been made in the study of crime, both by criminologists and by psychiatrists. He was able to detect one common element running through the period under review, and that was 'the rise of the rehabilitative ideal'. The complex of ideas that characterised this common element included a belief that human (including, therefore, criminal) behaviour was the product of antecedent causes, which could be identified and thereby manipulated for 'the scientific control of human behaviour'. Most importantly, it was held that 'measures employed to treat the convicted offender should serve a therapeutic function', to effect changes in his behaviour in the interests of his own happiness (?) and the interest of social defence (Allen 1959, p. 226).

Allen's brief critique indicated several undesirable, and often unintended, consequences that had accompanied the rise of the rehabilitative ideal. Like the positivist criminology, which I have suggested was one of its theoretical mainsprings, it concentrated all attention upon the *criminal,* thereby neglecting crucial legal and sociological aspects of the *nature of crime.* Allen further suggested that the rehabilitative ideal in *practice* was a debased version:

> Under the dominance of the rehabilitative ideal, the
> language of therapy is frequently employed, wittingly or
> unwittingly, to disguise the true state of affairs that prevails
> in our custodial institutions and at other points in the
> correctional process. (Allen 1959, p. 229)

He had in mind disturbing trends in the psychiatric treatment of delinquent children, and legislation such as the sexual psychopath laws. Further debasement of the application of the ideal was seen in the frequency with which it led to increased length of penal measures.

Allen's final proposition related to the fundamental way in which the application of the rehabilitative ideal conflicted with the values of individual liberty and legal rights, raising questions about the appropriate limits for the exercise of power by the state over the individual. More specifically, it resulted in frequent laxity and irregularity in the procedures for ascertaining legal 'guilt' and in failures to incorporate safeguards for limiting 'treatment'.

The pervasiveness of what Allen had called the 'rehabilitative ideal' in the way society responded to the threat posed by different forms of deviant behaviour, in the second half of the twentieth century, was confirmed by Nicholas N. Kittrie's comprehensive and often disturbing survey of the power of the 'therapeutic state' to enforce therapy upon deviants of all sorts, whether juvenile delinquents, psychopaths, mental patients or alcoholics (Kittrie 1971). Whatever its official pretensions towards a primary concern for the welfare of the individual, Kittrie identified as an equally dominant aim of the 'therapeutic state' that of the isolation and control of 'socially dangerous persons':

> The new therapeutic state has from the beginning contained
> mixed strains of both social defense and individual welfare,
> carrying out programs of confinement and compulsory
> therapy which could not be justified by considerations
> other than those of social defense, yet relying upon its
> manifest dedication to welfare in order to combat criticisms
> of its disregard for the traditional safeguards of the criminal
> process. (Kittrie 1971, p. 360)

In the criminal justice context the loss of faith in the rehabilitative ideal and a growing awareness of the outreach of the powers of the therapeutic state raised serious doubts in some quarters about the system of indeterminate sentencing and parole. The traditional justifications for imposing indeterminate terms of imprisonment included a belief in the *legitimacy* of rehabilitation as a primary penal objective and a belief in the *possibility* of rehabilitation occurring in penal custody. In view of the negative aspects of indeterminacy, both in terms of the ethical justification of extended custody for treatment purposes, and the humanitarian concern for the effects of constant uncertainty for the individual prisoners, it was perhaps surprising only that challenges had not come earlier. However, when empirical evidence began to accumulate that questioned the rehabilitative efficacy of penal measures (e.g. Bailey 1966; Logan 1972; Clarke and Sinclair 1974; Martinson 1974; Lipton *et al.* 1975; Brody 1976), this acted as a catalyst for more positive action, and resulted in swingeing critiques of indeterminacy such as that by Judge Marvin Frankel (1973).

As far as the 1960s were concerned, the main practical challenge to the rehabilitative ideal in America occurred in the context of the juvenile court system. Reform of juvenile justice was a major concern of Francis Allen, and he insisted upon greater honesty in acknowledging the latent social defence functions underlying a manifest commitment to the rehabilitation of juvenile offenders:

> It is, in my judgement, both inaccurate and deceptive to

describe the operation of the juvenile court in this area as the exercise of a rehabilitative or therapeutic function. . . . The primary function being served in these cases . . . is the temporary incapacitation of children found to constitute a threat to the community's interest. (Allen 1964, p. 53)

This rehabilitative 'double-think' encouraged, in Allen's view, a 'laxness and unfairness in the procedures employed by the juvenile court in executing its charging, adjudicatory and dispositional functions' (Allen 1964, p. 54). In its turn this led directly to increasing demands for *due process* in juvenile justice, which I have identified as a second contributory element to the emergence of the justice model.

Extension of due process. The history of 'due process' in the American legal system is long and complex, with roots leading from the Magna Carta to the Bill of Rights and beyond (see Miller 1977). No attempt will be made here to survey the whole of this development; instead, attention will be drawn to just two examples that illustrate the sort of practical and theoretical issues which provide relevant background for the present discussion.

The first relates to the reform of juvenile justice in the United States during the 1960s. Changes that took place within the American juvenile court system during this time foreshadowed future thinking and development of the justice model for adult corrections in more ways than one. They were a result of the questioning of the rehabilitative ideal and an accompanying demand for greater protection of the legal rights of juvenile offenders. Edwin Lemert has provided a classic account of the processes which led to a 'revolution' within the Californian juvenile courts system in 1961, and which was followed by increasing insistence upon due process for juveniles throughout the United States (Lemert 1970). In his discussion of the various anomalies and issues which gave general cause for concern about juvenile justice in California, including *excessive detention* on 'treatment' grounds and the widespread persistence of *'informal justice'* for juveniles, Lemert showed how the *legal rights* of juveniles came to dominate the pressure for reform. After the Governor's Special Study Commission on Juvenile Justice had been set up at the end of 1957, a number of personal, professional and political factors guided its thinking along the lines of primacy of the legal rights issue. Among the main explicit principles that shaped the final report in 1959 was that of 'the rights of minors to fair treatment under formal guarantees of procedural law' (Lemert 1970, p. 119), and this was a dominant theme in the subsequent legislation of 1961. Lemert identified a number of radical postulates that underlay the Commission's thinking and which were to have an impact outside the boundaries of California. The first postulate was that 'courts for children are places where justice is a prime issue', and another was that 'the interests of minors and parents are best served by a balance of interaction in the court, secured by narrowing of its jurisdiction, instituting special procedural rules, and structuring of roles' (Lemert 1970, p. 211). Five years after the Californian legislation a number of Supreme Court decisions were to provide the juvenile defendant throughout America with increased legal safeguards at various stages of the court process, so that between 1966 and 1975 the gap between juvenile and adult criminal court procedure narrowed quite considerably (Rutherford 1977). The most important of these Supreme Court cases was that of *Gault*, which ensured that juveniles should have a right to notification of the charge, a right to counsel, and a right to full review on appeal. Additional interest is attached to the case of *Gault* for our present purposes, in the judicial views that were expressed about 'due process' and 'justice'. According to the majority opinion a distinction should be drawn between 'due process' of law as a *means* and 'fairness', 'efficient procedures', as an *end in themselves*. Lemert's assessment of this majority view indicated its significance for consideration of the justice model:

> The Supreme Court judges were agreed that formal or legal rules are only a part of juvenile justice. . . . Study and comparisons of juvenile justice must move beyond formal procedure to scrutinise the consequences of administrative practices and legal subculture. Juvenile justice at this level requires evaluation by criteria of 'background fairness', in contrast to those of formal procedural fairness. (Lemert 1970, p. 225)

The second illustration of the role of due process in penological thinking comes from Herbert Packer's well known elaboration of two 'models' of the criminal process, described as the Due Process and Crime Control models. He did not present these models either as literally accurate descriptions or as purely abstract conceptions, rather he saw the exercise as an attempt to identify two separate value systems that compete for priority in the operation of the criminal process. Packer compared the Due Process Model to an obstacle course, in which a succession of impediments is presented to the passage of the accused person along the road to the status of convicted criminal. An emphasis upon due process leads to a rejection of *informal* fact-finding processes in the investigation of crime or determining of guilt, and demands formal adjudicative processes with the case against the accused heard by an impartial tribunal. In the constant tension between bureaucratic efficiency in the fight against crime and reliable decision-making, the ideology of the Due Process Model is firmly behind the latter:

> If efficiency demands short-cuts around reliability, then
> absolute efficiency must be rejected. The aim of the process
> is at least as much to protect the factually innocent as it is to
> convict the factually guilty. (Packer 1969, p. 165)

Many of the central values of due process can be summed up, in Packer's view, under the complementary concepts of the *primacy of the individual* and the *limitation on official power*; the legal 'presumption of innocence' also links many practical applications of due process in the stages of law enforcement and criminal justice administration up to and including the formal conviction. At the end of his review of the two models in operation, Packer concluded that although in practice the criminal process operated fairly closely to the dictates of the Crime Control Model, yet the increasing trend was for the formulation of official norms and standard procedures that were much closer to what he had described in the Due Process Model. He summarised the main aspects of the trend:

> Its principal thrusts have been to 'judicialize' each stage of
> the criminal process, to enhance the capacity of the accused
> to challenge the operation of the process . . . and to equalize
> the capacity of all persons accused of crime to take
> advantage of the opportunities thus created. (Packer 1969,
> p. 239)

Although Packer felt able to identify with some confidence a trend towards due process, he was also aware of the essential precariousness of its foundation, based largely on the judicial decisions of the Supreme Court. Nevertheless, the essential characteristics of the Due Process Model gave Packer great hopes of its survival and extension. It thrived on visibility. The more cases of denial of rights and other breaches of due process that came to light, the harder it became to maintain that the process should remain primarily administrative and managerial in orientation:

> At root, the Due Process Model depends on the functioning
> of what has been called the sense of injustice. . . . It is self-
> sustaining because its own operations uncover the raw
> material that fuel its continued growth. (Packer 1969,
> p. 243)

Discretionary decision-making. The final element that can be identified as an important precursor of the justice model is a growing awareness of the role of discretionary decision-making in the criminal justice process. The empirical underpinning for this awareness was provided by the increasing amount of research being carried out by sociologists and criminologists interested in how the exercise of discretion at various stages of the process vitally influenced the practical realities of criminal justice, as opposed to any theoretical expectations that may be derived from regarding 'the law' in isolation from its application. The most comprehensive research of this kind during the early period was the work of the American Bar Foundation, whose team of researchers systematically surveyed the decision-making practice of police, prosecutors, judges and parole administrators in several states, and published a series of impressive reports which left no doubts about the extent and importance of discretion (LaFave 1965; Newman 1966; Tiffany *et al.* 1967; Miller 1969; Dawson 1969).

Apart from the essential contribution made by empirical studies such as these, there was a need for a more integrative analysis of the characteristics and problems posed by the extensive exercise of discretion in criminal justice, to provide an overall framework for understanding and, if necessary, changing the situation. This was provided in timely fashion by K. C. Davis (1969), in his book *Discretionary Justice: A Preliminary Inquiry*, in which he drew parallels and comparisons across a wide field of decision-making. It is difficult to form an accurate estimate of the impact of this book, with its careful analysis and eloquent call for the need to *confine, structure* and *check* the use of discretion. However, it was impossible for any subsequent consideration of discretionary justice to ignore the convincing case made out by Davis, and although it is rare to find any overt acknowledgement in the literature on the justice model, we shall presently see the extent to which the new model is indebted to Davis' ideas and framework for structuring discretion (Davis 1969, pp. 97–141).

The Justice Model: Variations on a Common Theme

Arguably the single most important issue responsible for the emergence of the justice model, and one which has not yet been directly mentioned, was the perceived *'crisis' situation in American prisons.* However far beyond the confines of the prison walls some of the features of the developed model may extend, the fact is that all the major studies were firmly grounded in an overwhelming concern to ameliorate the situation of contemporary imprisonment. Without wishing to credit the American Friends with the prescience of Cassandra, it is highly significant that the year (1971) of the publication of *Struggle for Justice*, was also the year of the uprising at New York's Attica prison, in which more than 40 prisoners and guards lost their lives. It is not fanciful to see in the Attica tragedy a symbolic reflection of the everworsening prison situation which finally communicated the message (in some quarters) that the only hope of avoiding such tragedies in the future lay in a radical reappraisal of the principles and practice of imprisonment and criminal justice.

We have already seen how the authors of *Struggle for Justice* placed substantial blame upon the 'individualised treatment model', which they roundly attacked as 'theoretically faulty, systematically discriminatory in administration, and inconsistent with some of our most basic concepts of justice' (American Friends Service Committee 1971, p. 12). Despite their strength of feeling on that issue, they were unequivocal in denouncing the *lack of social justice* in the wider society as the root cause:

> The quest for justice will necessarily be frustrated so long as
> we fail to recognize that criminal justice is dependent upon
> and largely derives from social justice. The only solution
> for the problem of class and race bias in the courtroom or by
> the police or correctional systems is the eradication of bias
> from American life. (American Friends Service Committee
> 1971, p. 13)

> To the extent, then, that equal justice is correlated with
> equality of status, influence, and economic power, the
> construction of a just system of criminal justice in an unjust
> society is a contradiction in terms. Criminal justice is
> inextricably interwoven with, and largely derivative from,
> a broader social justice. (American Friends Service
> Committee 1971, p. 16)

This focus upon the link between criminal justice and social justice is, at one and the same time, the single most important and yet frustratingly not fully expounded contribution of *Struggle for Justice* to the entire debate. The other major proposals in the report laid the foundations for much of the common ground shared by later proponents, and centred on the following issues:

  (i) rejection of the individualised treatment model;
 (ii) the need to control the exercise of discretion;
(iii) restriction of the role of the criminal justice system;
(iv) openness and accountability of decision-making.

In the view of the Committee the unchallenged hegemony of the concept of 'individualisation' in criminal justice resulted from the traditional focus of 'scientific' study upon the criminal rather than the act of law violation, and the acceptance of the primacy of rehabilitative aims in the treatment of offenders. Once individualisation had become an accepted principle it was used at every stage, from police arrest and prosecution to release on parole, to justify the exercise of discretionary power, extensive use of secret procedures, and lack of accountability in decision-making.

The main thrust of the report's recommendations related more to matters of procedure than principle. Police discretion should be controlled by public guidelines from the community or police departments; discretion should be eliminated from the sentencing process, with all sentences fixed by law; and parole should be abolished. The outreach of the criminal justice system should be reviewed, and the traditional reliance upon the penal system as the main instrument in the solution of the crime problem should be abandoned. Finally, the entire system should be made more publicly visible and accountable both to the community and to the convicted prisoners.

David Fogel published his book *'We are the Living Proof': the Justice Model for Corrections* in 1975, some years after he had begun to introduce his ideas in a very practical way into the prisons of Minnesota. There can be no doubt in his case, therefore, of the centrality of a concern with the contemporary prison situation in his formulation of what he was the first to call 'the justice model'. Furthermore, his analytical sketch of correctional history as a series of attempts to change the officially ascribed status of inmates from that of *pariah* and *penitent*, through *prisoner* to *patient*, and now *plaintiff* (Fogel 1975, pp. 62–3), clearly showed an appreciation of the legal rights of prinsoners comparable to that which informed the reform of American juvenile justice in the 1960s. Fogel's emphasis upon prisoners' rights distinguishes him somewhat from other advocates of the justice model, but apart from the value of this *per se* many interesting parallels can be drawn between the attempt to establish a model of justice within the 'micro-world' of the prison community and the need for similar justice to operate for the 'macro-world' of the community outside prison. Particularly obvious parallels are the need for legal safeguards and due process in internal prison disciplinary hearings and a greater openness and accountability in classification, transfer and indeterminate release decisions.

It is to Fogel's credit and our advantage that he did not stop short at considering the implications for prison organisation and objectives alone, but widened his discussion into the whole field of criminal justice, introducing into his scheme Rawls' concept of 'justice-as-fairness':

> Justice-as-fairness is not a *program*; it is a *process* that insists
> that prisons (and all agencies of the criminal law) perform
> their assigned tasks with non–law–abiders lawfully. (Fogel
> 1975, p. 184, italics in original)

Justice-as-fairness, in Fogel's terms, can be seen as incorporating the main procedural recommendations of *Struggle for Justice*, with which he was in basic agreement: namely, the narrowing and control of discretionary decisions, and wider accountability to the 'consumer' of criminal justice. He encapsulated the desired consequences in another apt turn of phrase:

> Properly understood, therefore, the justice perspective is not so much concerned with administration of justice as it is with the justice of administration. (Fogel 1975, p. 192)

More specifically, he wished to abolish indeterminate sentences and parole, thus returning more power over the limits of imprisonment from the executive to the judiciary, who should sentence within statutory guidelines (pp. 245–6). Finally, he reiterated that one of the main themes underlying justice-as-fairness in the prison was the maintenance of individual responsibility, so that every opportunity should be created in prison for the inmate to make choices and influence his day-to-day life in preparation for the time of his release.

The other individual contribution to the debate is Norval Morris' (1974) study of *The Future of Imprisonment*, which was also centred very much on future strategies for prisons, although it made no explicit claims to represent a justice model scheme. Morris' starting point was the conventional recognition that rehabilitation as a penal objective was no longer tenable, but that it should be seen as the 'noble lie' which in truth it was. He did not take the implications of this recognition as far as many of the proponents of the justice model, but felt there was still a role for a newly-liberated concept of rehabilitation in prisons (which he envisaged as being, like the poor, always with us). In particular, he advocated that the rehabilitative aspects of prison regimes should move from the role of 'coerced cure' to that of 'facilitated change', whereby any inmate could voluntarily choose to take advantage of educational and vocational programmes being offered in the prison. Morris' middle-of-the-road position was also illustrated by his unwillingness to abolish all parole as a matter of principle; nevertheless he favoured a major swing towards greater judicial determinacy in sentencing, with special provision for those given indeterminate sentences to agree on a 'parole contract' release date during the first few weeks of the sentence.

It is in Morris' discussion of the principles which he feels ought to guide the decision to imprison that we find his main contribution to the development of a fully-fledged justice model. He emphasised the principle of 'parsimony' by which he meant that 'the least restrictive (punitive) sanction necessary to achieve defined social purposes should be imposed' (Morris 1974, p. 59), and decisively rejected the increasingly popular view that at least for certain kinds of offender it was possible and valid to base the decision to imprison them on a predictive assessment of their potential *dangerousness* to the community. His final principle was that of *desert*: 'no sanction greater than that "deserved" by the last crime or series of crimes for which the offender is being sentenced should be imposed' (Morris 1974, p. 73). Apart from the almost passing reference in *Struggle for Justice* to the need for the punishment to fit the crime, neither the American Friends Service Committee (1971) nor Fogel (1975) spent much time on thinking through alternative principles to replace the rehabilitative ideal. Morris rectified this, and placed the concept of desert at the heart of critical penology, thereby linking it to an issue of long-standing concern in philosophical and theological circles.

He spelled out his interpretation of the principle of desert as one that accepted retributive purposes as a limitation on punishment and affirmed that 'as a matter of justice, the maximum of punishment should never exceed the punishment "deserved", either to cure the criminal or protect the citizenry'. He claimed to view 'desert' not in relation to 'salvation' or ethics, but rather as related to mundane social organisation, and the question of admission or readmission to the company of citizens in the here and now. It was in this context that he raised the question of the distinction between deserved punishment as *rejection* or *expiation,* concluding that:

> Imprisonment is not now seen as a permanent social
> rejection; it is at the most a temporary banishment; the
> prison gates open for all but a very few. Imprisonment is
> thus, in terms of this distinction, expiative and not
> rejective. . . . *The concept of desert in this chapter is thus limited*
> *to its use as defining the maximum of punishment that the*
> *community exacts from the criminal to express the severity of the*
> *injury his crime inflicted on the community as a condition of*
> *readmitting him to society.* (Morris 1974, p. 74, italics added)

Morris emphasised that to say that a punishment was deserved, in this sense, did not imply that it ought to be imposed; rather the concept being advanced was one of a retributive maximum — 'a licence to punish the criminal up to that point but by no means an obligation to do so' (p. 75). Parsimony, humanity, mercy and other principles could all properly influence the choice of punishment below the maximum. Despite this emphasis upon the concept of desert Morris' broad view encompassed the legitimacy of other penal objectives, so that among the preconditions of imprisonment he set down were that 'either (i) any lesser punishment would depreciate the seriousness of the crime(s) committed or (ii) imprisonment of some who have done what this criminal did is necessary to achieve socially justified deterrent purposes' (p. xii). He summarised the relationship between these objectives and 'deserved punishment' as follows:

> The criminal law has general preventive purposes in
> relation to crime, cohesive functions in relation to society,
> educative and deterrent functions in relation to potential

criminals, all of which bear upon the determination of the
proper punishment. The punishment equation relates these
social purposes to the sentence on the convicted criminal up
to the deserved punishment. (Morris 1974, p. 75)

This integrative approach to penal objectives has a certain
superficial attraction, but on reflection it is little more than a
restatement of and reversion to the existing ambiguity of aims, which
many advocates of the justice model believed the centrality of 'deserts'
would avoid. The concept of desert can have no major impact on
criminal justice policy unless it is seen in a bolder light than simply that
of traditional 'limiting retribution'. In this context, it is helpful to
recall the comments of C. S. Lewis about the relationship between
justice and deserts, and humanitarian or utilitarian theories of
punishment:

> The Humanitarian theory removes from Punishment the
> concept of Desert. But the concept of Desert is the only
> connecting link between punishment and justice. It is only
> as deserved or undeserved that a sentence can be just or
> unjust. . . . We may very properly ask whether it is likely to
> deter others and to reform the criminal. But neither of these
> two last questions is a question about justice. . . . Thus
> when we cease to consider what the criminal deserves and
> consider only what will cure him or deter others, we have
> tacitly removed him from the sphere of justice altogether.
> (Lewis 1953, p. 225)

The final major statement to be considered is the report of the
Committee for the Study of Incarceration, *Doing Justice: the Choice of
Punishments* (Von Hirsch 1976). This report firmly placed justice and
'just-deserts' at the centre of its proposed scheme for reform of
sentencing and imprisonment, with an emphasis upon *justice as an
objective* rather than merely *procedural justice.* Although there are some
questionable arguments and loose ends in the course of the report, it
nevertheless stands as a document which raised most of the issues
which have to be faced in the formulation of a justice model.

The moral premises upon which the Committee's analysis was
based were that (i) the liberty of each individual is to be protected so
long as it is consistent with the liberty of others; (ii) there should be
strict parsimony in state intervention, and (iii) the requirements of
justice ought to constrain the pursuit of crime prevention, so that no
policy can be justified solely on the grounds of its usefulness in
controlling crime, without first considering whether the policy is a
just one. The main burden of the report lay in its elaboration of the
nature and implications of a justice model based on 'commensurate
deserts'. Qualified scepticism was expressed concerning the tradi-

tional assumptions of rehabilitation, predictive restraint, and individualised sentencing. Justice put a limitation upon the rehabilitative disposition, even if a particular penal 'treatment' was known to be effective (Von Hirsch 1976, p. 18). Predictive restraint posed special ethical problems, not only with regard to the moral acceptability of mistakes of overprediction but in terms of the justification for punishment *in advance*, on grounds of what someone is merely expected to do. Widespread discretion in sentencing on an individualised basis created unacceptable disparities, which could only be eliminated by the creation of sentencing standards derived from a coherent conception of purposes (Von Hirsch 1976, p. 32).

The concept of 'desert' at the centre of the Committee's analysis derived from a revival of certain aspects of the notions of punishment found in the writings of Kant and Beccaria. From Kant was taken the explanation of deserved punishment based on the idea of fair dealing among free individuals, whereby the imposition of punishment restored the equilibrium that had been upset by the infringement of another's rights, and deprived the offender of any temporary advantage over others that may have been gained:

> The penalty is thus not just a means of crime prevention but
> a merited response to the actor's deed, 'rectifying the
> balance' in the Kantian sense and expressing moral
> reprobation of the actor for the wrong. (Von Hirsch 1976,
> p. 51)

From the ideas of Beccaria about proportion between crimes and justice, the Committee elaborated the principle of 'commensurate deserts'. For Beccaria, however, the principle of proportion in punishment was mainly based on strict utilitarian arguments about deterrence, whereas in *Doing Justice* it was supported on rather different moral grounds as an essential requirement of justice.

The principle of 'commensurate deserts' was rooted in common-sense notions of equity and fairness, and unlike the principles of deterrence and social defence it ensured that the rights of persons who are punished are not unduly sacrificed for the supposed good of others in the cause of crime prevention. In the allocation of punishment it looked retrospectively to the *seriousness* of the offender's crime, which involved the twin elements of actual *harm* done and the extent of the offender's *culpability*.

Unlike Norval Morris' use of the concept of desert as merely setting an *upper limit* to what was permitted, the Committee was careful to make it clear that its principle debarred disproportionate leniency as well as severity; furthermore, it had priority over other objectives:

> We think that the commensurate deserts principle should

have priority over other objectives in decisions about how
much to punish. The disposition of convicted offenders
should be commensurate with the seriousness of their
offences, even if greater or less severity would promote
other goals. For the principle, we have argued, is a
requirement of justice, whereas deterrence, incapacitation,
and rehabilitation are essentially strategies for controlling
crime. (Von Hirsch 1976, pp. 74–5)

This stands as an impressive statement of faith to be reckoned with and
argued about, even though in other places of the report it seemed to be
qualified in a number of directions, with regard to the roles of
deterrence and rehabilitation.

Having worked out a comprehensive (if at times inconsistent)
blueprint for a justice model, the Committee was rather less
impressive in its secondary task of describing the precise details of the
machinery needed to operate the model. There was a rather naive
confidence in the ability of communities to reach agreement on the
'seriousness' of crimes, and when tricky questions were raised about
the assessment of individual culpability, refuge was taken in stating
that in any case 'harm' takes precedence. Once the traditional
assumptions of rehabilitation and predictive restraint have been
abandoned, in favour of the principle of commensurate deserts, the
basis for the exercise of discretion in sentencing was undermined. The
Committee saw the need for *sentencing standards* to be articulated to
ensure equity in application, with each crime category assigned a
'presumptive sentence' from which courts should depart only if there
were clearly defined aggravating or mitigating circumstances. As
indeterminate sentences would also disappear, there would be a need,
in the Committee's view, for the average length of sentences to be
substantially scaled down.

In the last analysis, the logic of this argument resulted in a reluctant
(and conditional) acceptance of the continued need for imprisonment
as the currently most acceptable 'severest' punishment for the few
most serious crimes — and in spite of the hazardous relativity of all
these terms. Not only this, but they introduced *incapacitation* as a
secondary justification (or 'not unacceptable consequence') of imprisonment, and one which did not rely upon predictions of
dangerousness:

Incarceration can be prescribed as the only authorised
severe punishment — so that all offenders convicted of
sufficiently serious crimes would be confined, irrespective
of their likelihood of their returning to crime. As long as
this group contains *any* potential recidivists, confining the
whole group will prevent some crimes from occurring.

And no offender — dangerous or not — would be punished
more severely than deserved by his past offence. (Von
Hirsch 1976, p. 113)

With a certain poetic justice, at the end of this survey of the
American 'coming of age' of the justice model, the final lingering
question raised in the last chapter of the Committee's report was the
one to which the authors of *Struggle for Justice* gave an unequivocal
answer in their very first chapter, five years before — namely, that of
'just deserts in an unjust society'. This question was not given an
adequate answer, beyond the rather apologetic protestation that 'our
earlier defense of the existence of punishment necessarily presupposes
at least a partial acceptance of this society's laws', whereas the more
radical social critics condemned not only society but its entire system
of punishment and social control. It may well be that just as there are
very different questions to be raised and solutions proposed for justice
as an *objective* and justice as a *procedure*, so there may be for justice in
penal policy and the wider issue of *social justice* (see especially Clarke
1978).

Emergent signs of Justice Model thinking in Britain

There have been certain trends in British penological thinking during
the last few years similar to those we have identified as leading to the
emergence of the justice model in America in the 1970s, but there has
been little explicit reference to a 'justice model' as such (exceptions
include Parsloe (1976), the Howard League (1975, 1977b) and most
recently Clarke (1978)). Instead, criticism has for the most part been
directed piecemeal fashion at selected aspects of criminal justice and
penal policy, with few attempts to link specific critiques under any
broader perspective. The value of the development of the justice
model in the United States lies in the way it enables us to see possible
connections that we might otherwise have overlooked, and to assess
how valid and useful such an approach may be.

The most obvious parallels with America are the ongoing (if rather
sporadic) criticisms in Britain during the last three or four years of
central aspects of our own parole system (introduced in 1968), and the
related debates about certain proposals of the committee on the Young
Adult Offender (Advisory Council on the Penal System 1974). There
have also been important changes in the organisation of juvenile
justice in England and Wales, and Scotland (see Bottoms 1974; A.
Morris 1974, 1976), which provide striking contrasts with the changes
taking place in America. Important lessons might have been learned
by those responsible for penal legislation in the reform of juvenile

justice if there had been a greater awareness of justice model thinking, and many of the subsequent problems might have been avoided or at least foreseen. However, for reasons of space, we must concentrate our attention on the adult offender and the experience of imprisonment which in Britain as elsewhere has been at the centre of the movement for change.

Undoubtedly the most important contribution so far to critical thinking along these lines in Britain has come from Dr. Roger Hood. In his important lecture *Tolerance and the Tariff*, presented to a N.A.C.R.O. meeting at the House of Lords in July 1974, Hood (1974b) welded together criminological theory, practical penology and moral observations in a way that is all too rare in discussions of penal policy. The main attacks of Hood (see also Hood 1974a, 1974c), have been levelled at the rehabilitative assumptions and consequent *indeterminacy* of the parole system and the Younger Committee's proposals for offenders aged 17–20 years old, incorporating discretionary release into the community for the second part of a sentence (Advisory Council on the Penal System 1974). He based his argument on (i) the lack of any evidence that rehabilitation 'works' in any clearly identifiable way that can be utilised in sentencing or penal management; (ii) the unacceptable nature of indeterminacy in imprisonment, in terms of the status and integrity of the individual prisoner and its effect upon his family, and (iii) the potential abuse of the discretionary power of the executive over release dates, afforded by any system which is in effect indeterminate and non-judicial. Hood drew the following conclusions:

> Any decisions to reduce the lengths of deprivation of liberty
> should be made not in terms of their effectiveness but by a
> clear decision to re-draw the 'crime-punishment equation':
> in other words to examine the kinds of behaviour which are
> regarded as sufficiently serious to justify incarceration, to
> re-consider the concept of dangerousness, to reassess the
> degree of tolerance which we should show towards
> offenders. . . . Put this way, the nature of the discussion
> changes drastically. We move back from what has been
> called 'Correctionalism', based on a deterministic
> conception of criminal behaviour, towards the Classical
> Enlightenment. (Hood 1974b, p. 5)

The ideal was seen to be a 'twentieth-century enlightenment', based on rather different views of human behaviour and response to punishment than were commonly held by scholars of the eighteenth-century enlightenment. In particular, general deterrence would not have the major emphasis it enjoyed then and still does today in some circles. Account could still be taken of the individual circumstances of the offender, but this would be neither for purposes of assessing primitive retribution nor modern rehabilitation but for the moral assessment of the seriousness of the crime and the harm done:

> Thus I believe a system which arrives at the length of
> sentences based more on moral evaluation than on appeals
> to utilitarian philosophy of deterrence and reductivism,
> would be fairer, not necessarily less effective, possibly less,
> not more, punitive and appeal to that sense of social justice
> on which any system of acceptable social control must be
> founded. (Hood 1974b, p. 7)

We can no look in more detail at how a new perspective of this sort can be applied to the two aspects of penal policy which have been the focus of attention from Hood and other critics: namely, parole and the proposed custody and control orders for young adult offenders in England and Wales.

Early critics of the English parole system concentrated upon procedural aspects that appeared to militate against concepts of fairness and 'natural justice'. Particular targets were the failure to give reasons to prisoners refused parole, and the lack of opportunity for personal hearings before the parole boards. Keith Hawkins elaborated upon these procedural criticisms in his proposals for an alternative approach, and showed how close his ideas were to those underlying the justice model in American corrections. He believed that if the parole system were to continue in its existing form then a 'fair procedure' should be incorporated:

> A fair procedure is taken to mean . . . one which helps to
> give the individual prisoner a sense of protection against
> oppression and injustice, and of confidence in his dealings
> with the authorities, one which will at the same time serve
> to check any possible abuse of power. (Hawkins 1973, p. 6)

One of the basic premises of Hawkins' arguments was that 'fairness' was a good in itself, and that 'notions of fairness and justice transcend the aims of the parole system' (Hawkins 1973, p. 8). He insisted that the issue could not be avoided by claims that prisoners have no right to complain about the way the State grants privileges, or that fair procedures do not matter when the authorities have the rehabilitative interests of the offender at heart. Furthermore, fairness in parole decisions could have profound implications upon the integrity and morale of prisoners, individually and collectively, and could be abused in the interests of prison management. Finally, Hawkins emphasised that arguments about fair procedures were strictly separate from the issue of parole 'effectiveness':

> It is often assumed that 'fairer' decisions are somehow
> 'better' decisions according to the usual criteria of parole

success, and the debate about the appropriateness of fair procedural standards is usually based on this assumption. It is quite possible that some parole decisions may be 'better' as a result of fairer procedure since more rational and more informed decisions may follow. But arguments about fairness do not rest primarily on this ground, and those who criticise fairness in these terms miss the point. (Hawkins 1973, p. 9)

In concrete terms, he advocated the right to a parole hearing for those prisoners who wished, the disclosure of reasons for parole refusals, and the introduction of a system of appeal. To accommodate these proposals, considerable modification in the structure of the existing system would need to take place, perhaps involving the creation of regional parole boards staffed on a more full-time basis. The only proposal that seems to have been seriously considered by the Parole Board is that of disclosure of reasons, but on each occasion so far it has been rejected on grounds of the difficulty of formulating the reasons for a complicated panel decision of this kind, and because many reasons are outside the control of the prisoner himself (and thus, it is assumed, not worth communicating!).

In response to procedural criticisms of this sort, J. E. Hall Williams considered the extent to which elements of natural justice could be incorporated into the parole system. He saw that the issue of disclosure of reasons was closely linked to other proposals for personal hearings, representation and the right of appeal. It would be difficult, in his view, to allow a right of appeal where no reasons had been given for the initial decision; conversely, giving reasons for parole refusal would naturally suggest the need for some method whereby the reasons could be challenged or the decision appealed against (Hall Williams 1975, p. 91). Hall Williams accurately diagnosed the main source of the problem in the nature of our conception of parole:

It needs to be recognised that what we have in this country is *an arrangement for the discretionary award of a privilege by the executive*, acting on the advice of an independent advisory board. The choice which has to be squarely faced is whether this should continue to be the basis for the parole recommendation, or *whether a model based more closely on judicial lines is preferable, looking at parole more in terms of a right than a privilege.* Only on the assumption that this latter course is correct are some of the criticisms valid, and substantial modifications are required. (Hall Williams 1975, p. 223, italics added)

Roger Hood's approach to parole went beyond the purely procedural aspects of fairness, to some of its more fundamental issues.

The official intention in introducing parole (beyond a practical concern with the increasing prison population) was to release prisoners at the time most suitable for their re-entry into the community, especially as indicated by 'response to training'. The fact that there exists very little empirical evidence to support this official 'model' of parole at all its most crucial points meant that its introduction was more an act of faith than anything else. In addition, it brought with it all the problems of indeterminacy grafted onto a determinate sentencing structure based largely on tariff principles (see Hood 1974a; Thomas 1974). Hood's solution was to eliminate the indeterminate element in sentences of imprisonment (affected by parole), except when it could be justified by reason of public policy, and to provide a system for the automatic release of most prisoners at an earlier point than the current two-thirds remission-earned stage. The courts would have the power to indicate those offenders whose release should be subject to review by the Parole Board, giving reasons for their decision which would be subject to appeal. Hood envisaged that a relatively small number of prisoners would come into this category and the court's decision would be based on 'the extremely serious nature of his offence and his potential dangerousness in terms of possible repetition of serious crimes against the person' (Hood 1974a, p. 15). This reduction in numbers for consideration by the Parole Board would make it feasible to allow personal hearings and the giving of reasons for refusals to grant parole.

In the terminology recently suggested by Elizabeth Barnard (1976) the effects of proposals like those of Hawkins and Hood would push our system in the direction of a conceptual model of parole decision-making that was *judicial*, moving it away from the basic *administrative* model that it has resembled since its inception. Because of its relevance to the present discussion Barnard's description of this model is valuable:

> In the judicial model, parole is seen principally as a sentence, and the criteria that govern decisions are as those of sentencing. Primary among these are the importance of maintaining equity in the treatment of offenders in respect of the seriousness of the offence and the public interest in being protected from dangerous persons. . . . At the same time, justice demands the protection of the prisoner by due process . . . he should have legal representation; there should be provision for appeal. Parole and revocation both involve a new sentence, so both should be covered by due process provisions. Decisions should be made by a body wholly independent of prison management, and it should give reasons for its decisions. (Barnard 1976, p. 145)

She shared my doubts as to the likelihood of the judiciary accepting release for the majority of prisoners after considerably less than the current two-thirds, and felt that only incremental changes were likely to occur, in the direction of due process. In my view, the logic of many of the arguments of critics like Hood, particularly for those who doubt the ethics or viability of longer sentences for the 'dangerous' offender, leads to the more radical suggestion of *abolition* of parole. Politically, this seems unlikely to occur in Britain for many years, but justice model thinking presents a case which has to be met by those who wish to retain parole.

Criticisms of the Younger Committee's proposals understandably followed very similar lines to those related to parole, as certain features of the system recommended for young adult offenders were virtually an extension of parole principles to this younger age group. They recommended the introduction of a new custody and control order, whose outer limits would be decided by the courts ('in the light of the seriousness of the offence, the offender's record, and circumstances and the public interest generally' Advisory Council on the Penal System 1974, p. 8) with the crucial dividing line between custody and supervision in the community to be decided by a local licence advisory committee. The custody and control order (C.C.O.), with the additional possibility of a restricted release order, exhibited a similar compromise between the rehabilitative and social control objectives that characterised the ill-fated legislation for children and young persons introduced in 1969. Significantly, also, a strong minority group wrote a note of dissent, indicating their wish to move further towards a non-judicial rehabilitative model; they favoured an even more limited role for the courts, according to which the only decision in the hands of the judiciary would be the choice between any kind of supervision (whether custodial or non-custodial) and a fine/discharge alternative — and even this choice would be based exclusively on considerations of the welfare and reformation of the offender, with all attempts at adjusting sentence to degrees of criminal responsibility and seriousness of crime rejected.

In fact, the proposals for the C.C.O. seemed to be based on an inconsistent acceptance of a non-rehabilitative objective, as far as the selection of offenders for this order and the fixing of its length were concerned, combined with proposals for early release procedures based on traditional 'treatment' principles, with a confidence in the ability of institutional staff to recognise optimum release dates. In terms of the criteria for the selection of offenders for the C.C.O., it seems disingenuous to claim that non-custodial supervision (or control) is likely to achieve these objectives as adequately as custodial. The restricted release order seems to confirm this interpretation.

Thus, official thinking in British penal policy in the early 1970s has reflected a tenacious clinging to the once-progressive ideas of the rehabilitative ideal, particularly in defence of the newly established parole system and as the underpinning for a possible future structure for the treatment of the young adult offender. Among penologists, there have been a few 'voices crying in the wilderness' against these official assumptions, which seem anachronistic in comparison with developments on the other side of the Atlantic. What little progress there has been in getting any sort of message through to the authorities has been limited to an acceptance in principle of the desirability of certain due process measures, as in seeking ways to disclose reasons to prisoners refused parole or in experiments with providing forms of 'representation' in applications. Similarly, in the important related field of procedures for adjudications in penal institutions, the official response has been to accept the least radical of the proposals put forward (Jellicoe Committee 1975; Home Office 1975). Trying to learn a lesson from the American experience, it may well be that the situation in our prisons and courthouses has to become much worse before there is hope of a fundamental return to first principles. We may not have had our Attica uprising in 1971, but we did have the Hull riot in 1976 — which, in relative terms, might naïvely have been expected to have had a rather greater impact on official thinking and future strategy than has been apparent (Fowler 1977; Thomas 1977). Can the so-called 'justice model' provide us with any possibility of an agreed approach to penal policy in Britain for the 1980s, which has some chance of gaining widespread support and resulting in practical action?

Critical Penology and the Justice Model — some unresolved issues

The concept of the justice model has developed from a number of inter-related strands within criminal justice and penology, and its implications can properly be seen as extending into practically every sphere of activity involving the enforcement of law and the application of penal sanctions. Its value as a conceptual model can best be established, in my view, by concentrating initially on its relevance to the role of imprisonment in contemporary penal policy, and the decisions about the actual length of custodial sentences.

One of the important distinctions to have emerged from our survey of trends in America and Britain is that between *justice as procedure* and *justice as a policy objective*. Fogel talked about 'justice-as-fairness', which he described as being a *process* not a *program*. The judges in the *Gault* case emphasised the need to move beyond the establishment of 'due process' procedures to a more fundamental consideration of fairness as a directing principle. Any truly radical justice model must concentrate primarily on the issue of the principles of justice to be followed as an objective and as the foundations for an integrated policy programme. This strategy is bound to create tensions between the short-term amelioration of the system by procedural reforms (along due process lines) and more fundamental alterations in the basic principles, but unless the ultimate objectives are clearly spelled out and kept at the forefront of debate, there is a very real risk that a partial official response to pressure for procedural changes will ultimately serve only to delay the more radical reassessments that are required. Strategic choices will have to be made on the basis of shared values and political judgements about the continued existence of certain structural elements in our penal system.

At the centre of the justice model debate must be an elaboration of an appropriate *sentencing policy*, with a clear indication of the extent to which any *de facto* alteration of this policy should be in the hands of the executive. In my view such a policy should be formulated primarily in accordance with agreed principles of justice, with preconceived objectives in crime control terms relegated to a secondary level. One of the cautionary lessons to be learned from the recent penological debate is that apparently similar programmes can derive support from opposite ends of the ideological spectrum. This ideological dualism has been a feature of attitudes towards juvenile justice in both America and Britain. Historically, Tony Platt showed how both 'legal moralists' and 'constitutionalists' criticised the juvenile court system, the former for its ineffectiveness in social defence terms in controlling juvenile crime, the latter for its arbitrariness and violation of the rights of the individual offender (Platt 1969, pp. 152–3). Similarly, Sanford Fox showed how 'the child's right to punishment' was advocated by both liberals and conservatives:

> In spite of everything, the idea of treatment and
> rehabilitation still looks remarkably like being soft on crime
> and mollycoddling young criminals. What they need is
> some punishment for a change; let's think of the victim,
> treatment is too expensive, and so on. The demise of
> treatment in favor of a right to punishment will find few
> mourners in conservative ranks. (Fox 1974, p. 4)

When Roger Hood first spelled out his ideas to an English audience, he felt he had almost to apologise, as an academic criminologist, for arguing along lines that might appear to be directly opposed to what was traditionally regarded as 'progressive' penology, and more compatible with views held by 'reactionary' judges (Hood 1974b, p.

14). In America, major contributions to the justice model debate can be found across a very wide ideological spectrum, from the authors of *Struggle for Justice* (at the more radical end), through Norval Morris (in the middle), to criminologists such as James Q. Wilson (at the conservative end). Indeed, the vigorous thinking about crime and punishment over the years by Wilson is among the most difficult to categorise (Wilson 1975). He is firmly in favour of abandoning the idea of rehabilitation as the *primary* purpose of imprisonment, and would substitute for it a concept of punishment in sentencing 'to give appropriate expression to our moral concern over the nature of the offense and to conform to our standards of humane conduct' (Wilson 1975, p. 164). However, he goes further than this in supporting a policy of penal incapacitation, which in his version accepts the *possibility* of deterrence and has disturbing potential in preventive detention terms. Thus, it is important to be clear about the ideological basis and preconceived objectives of participants in the debate, and to decide how far these ought to dominate or be subordinate to the formulation of principles, that can be justified in their own right rather than in terms of their possible consequences. (See Clarke (1978) for an important elaboration of this whole issue.)

Sentencing policy should be firmly based on the moral concept of 'just-deserts', which should take precedence over the other (empirically descredited) utilitarian objectives such as deterrence, rehabilitation and incapacitation of the dangerous offender. The centrality of this concept entails the revival of the vocabulary of punishment and responsibility, and in practical terms raises difficult problems of the mechanics of arriving at an agreed 'deserved' sentence. Here we can look towards Roger Hood's proposals for a new approach in the articulation by judges of the moral judgements on which their sentences are based:

> The new approach addresses itself directly to the moral
> evaluations of these judges and the way they interpret the
> gravity or dangerousness of various offences in modern
> society. It does not take judicial opinions for granted and
> would aim to bring the judiciary into a critical debate over
> how our society should define its deviants and what system
> of punishments are justifiable in a social order still full of
> inequities and injustices. (Hood 1974b, p. 14)

From Scandinavia, Professor Nils Christie has provided even more challenging support for the idea of the criminal courts as institutions for 'the evaluation and creation of conflict' (Christie 1974, 1976):

> We need courts as clearly defined arenas for decisions on
> values uncontaminated by other aims. Nothing is thereby

implied about severity. The morality applied can be severe or mild; it can lead to the infliction of great pains, or minor ones. The point is that we should be made quite conscious of what is going on, so that we can thereby embark upon a rational discussion of what type of morality should form the foundation of the penalties imposed by the courts. (Christie 1974, p. 292)

The courts have for a long time been drifting in a stagnant lagoon protected by the belief that they are, through expertise, striving to reach attainable utilitarian goals. It is time that they were forced out of this and into the flowing waters of a clearly expressed and exposed morality. (Christie 1974, p. 296)

The moral evaluations necessary for sentencing of this kind should not be entirely unstructured and open-ended, but could usefully be based on several elements. In *Doing Justice*, the Committee for the Study of Incarceration distinguished the two elements of actual *harm done* by the criminal act and the *culpability* or *blameworthiness* of the individual offender. This provides a reasonable starting point, provided that the interpretation of *blameworthiness* is wide enough in scope to include several aspects of the 'individualisation' that has traditionally been closely tied to purely *rehabilitative* objectives. A crucial part of Hood's call for a new enlightenment approach was centred on just such a reassessment of individualisation in a non-rehabilitative context that would involve a moral evaluation of the harm caused by criminal acts 'in the context of our understanding of the motivation of the offender and the interactions in the situation surrounding his act' (Hood 1974b, p. 6). Similarly, Christie indicated the three types of evaluation he considered necessary: firstly, an evaluation of the perceived seriousness of the *criminal offence*; secondly, a more open discussion about the *choice of the type of suffering* that can be inflicted as a penal sanction; and thirdly, a moral debate about what *characteristics of the criminal and his situation* ought to count as extenuating or aggravating circumstances (Christie 1974, p. 293). It is this last point which is central to the justice model of the future, as it could incorporate at least partial recognition of the problems of justice in an unjust society. Innumerable conditions of socio-economic deprivation and political discrimination that may be deemed irrelevant in a penology based on individualistic treatment aims are factors that can and must be taken into account in assessing an offender's blameworthiness and the punishment that is deserved. Individualisation also enters into the punishment equation in assessing the *differential impact* of punishment on offenders — not just by way of financial equalisation, as in the Swedish day-fine system, but in paying closer attention to the personal and social impact of the full range of penal sanctions. Unfortunately, any kind of individualisation brings with it problems of discretion, so that sentencing under the just-deserts concept of individualisation will require standards for the structured control of discretion. There should, however, be no temptation to share the discretion with other executive bodies involved in penal management, as the sentence would be entirely 'backward looking', with no room for subsequent amendment in the light of 'response to treatment'.

What, then, of rehabilitation programmes in penal institutions? The rejection of rehabilitation as an objective of sentencing policy does not necessarily eliminate it completely from the penal system. Instead, following Norval Morris, we could accept the change from prison as 'coerced cure' to a new role as 'facilitated change', so that prisoners' participation in educational or other training programmes would be on an entirely voluntary basis, free from the existing constraints, that distort its possible value and impact both in individual and organisational terms.

Finally, the concept of incapacitation haunts discussions of the justice model and contemporary penal policy in a rather disturbing fashion (see the introductory chapter by Bottoms). As it does not seem disposed to go away of its own accord, it must be faced and challenged more openly than hitherto. The aspect of the concept that has received most attention has been its assumed foundation in the ability to predict dangerousness. Tony Bottoms has recently reflected at considerable length and to very good effect on the 'renaissance' of dangerousness in penal thinking, showing the weakness of its empirical foundations and suggesting an interesting concept of 'bifurcation' to explain the origins of its current popularity (Bottoms 1977). I would not wish seriously to question anything in that important review, which leaves little doubt about the insubstantiality of the claims to be able to identify the dangerous offender; but rather I want to think aloud for a few moments about the possibility of a modified 'neo-classical' version of incapacitation as a complementary justification for imprisonment.

Any version of incapacitation is open to criticism on the grounds that it is *really* based on positivist-correctional assumptions about predicting dangerousness or that it is a thinly disguised form of preventive detention, dominated by Packer's Crime Control values of the 'assumption of guilt'. Nevertheless, despite these very real risks of misunderstanding and possible distortion, it does seem worth considering whether the common-sense view that 'whatever they may do when they are released, they cannot harm the community while they are locked away' (see also Wilson 1975, p. 173) has any substance upon which to build a case.

I believe that a revival of emphasis upon certain elements of enlightenment thinking about crime may provide a possible solution to our search. If the Kantian notion of punishment as 'righting the balance' in social relationships that have been disturbed by an infraction is linked with 'social contract' ideas, it seems a logical step to accept that a doubly appropriate sanction would be exclusion (temporarily or permanently) of the offending member from the community whose norms have been contravened. Obviously, this can partly be supported in social defence terms, partly in conventional 'denunciation' theory — but there seems to be a further indefinable suitability of banishment or temporary 'social exclusion' as a sanction — which countless generations of parents have recognised in their dealings with deviant offspring in the home! A welcome respite from the offending behaviour is gained thereby, but the banning action is not usually based on any simple preventive objective (with predictive overtones), but on a complex web of factors including a communal feeling that the offender has relinquished his right to share in community life and association, *including* of course the opportunities for further deviance that this entails. It is much more closely tied to the just-deserts model than to any alternative, and satisfies a feeling that justice has been done not only by the *fact* of sanction but by the specific *type* of sanction (for a closely related discussion see N. Morris 1974, pp. 73–74; also Bottomley 1979, ch. 4).

This function of imprisonment as *temporary social exclusion* may also assist in the inevitably difficult task of evaluating the punitive appropriateness of a chosen sentence. In whatever way the 'crime-punishment equation' may be redrawn under the auspices of the justice model, a major qualitative leap occurs between non–custodial and custodial sanctions, so that one of the determining factors in the decision as to when to impose a custodial sanction may be the consideration of the social justifications for incapacitatory exclusion, as an expression of shared feelings within society about the nature of the offending behaviour.

To summarise: A justice model for future thinking and planning in penal policy can usefully start by focusing upon the role of imprisonment. It will involve a number of strategic choices between concentrating upon an extension of procedural aspects of 'justice-as-fairness' and the establishment of justice as a primary policy objective. Sentencing is at the heart of the matter, with the just-deserts of the offender taking precedence in the choice of sentence over other utilitarian objectives. The most difficult task will be that of organising appropriate structures to allow for the community's moral evaluations to be reflected in judicial decisions, and to be aware in certain circumstances of the special suitability of social exclusion as a function of imprisonment, but one which is not to be confused with ideas of incapacitation based on the prediction of dangerousness or preventive detention.

3

Justice, punishment and the State

by RAYMOND PLANT

Usually discussions of punishment raise the deepest questions in social and political philosophy because in the practice of punishment we come up against one of the most concrete expressions of the coercive power of the State. Both the institution of punishment and the kinds of arguments which are devised to justify it are going to reflect general philosophical views about the role of the State *vis-à-vis* the citizen, the nature of law and the relationship of its procedural rules to the wider society, and about the nature of persons and how they should be shown respect. For these reasons questions about punishment should always be debated. They concern every citizen and, because of the deep nature of the ethical issues involved, these questions cannot be entirely made over to experts — criminologists, penologists, social workers, etc. Although facts about different types of punishment and their effects on offenders are of course relevant, nevertheless such facts are always going to underdetermine values. To see punishment as a purely technical issue to be settled by expert opinion is an evasion of responsibility by the citizen. It is in the name of the political community that certain persons are deprived of their liberty, made to suffer pain and not infrequently death, and it is surely our responsibility as citizens that the institutions which have such a dramatic effect upon the lives of our fellow men should be kept under review and the values on which such institutions finally rest sould be subjected to the most rigorous analysis. However, the analytical basis of punishment cannot be divorced from the wider questions concerning the moral values and principles held within the political community, and must not ignore the degree of moral diversity which may be found in the community. As we shall see later on in the paper the importance of this connection between punishment and morally pluralistic society may have been ignored by retributivists. Because there are problems in determining the acceptability of retribution, there is always likely to be a call for utilitarianism in the philosophy of punishment just because utilitarianism, as has often been noted, is a very attractive basis for morality in a pluralistic society.

The Decline of the Rehabilitative Ideal

In the present context it is extremely interesting for a moral philosopher to observe the resurrection from within the penological world of views held by Kant, Hegel, Bosanquet and many others and moreover, views which modern philosophers have, on the whole, regarded as difficult to sustain. In this volume we are invited to assume that the rehabilitative ideal has collapsed, and both Professor Bottoms and Dr. Bottomley have traced the history of this collapse. I am not competent, nor is it necessary for me, to comment upon their reading of the history behind our present situation. What I want to do is to add a few of the doubts of a moral philosopher on the rehabilitative conception — not because I think that the philosopher needs to provide a further nail in the coffin of the rehabilitative ideal, but rather because I suspect that a philosopher's comments may be able to focus upon some of the moral values and principles lying behind the rehabilitative ideal and which will presumably collapse along with rehabilitative practice. This will enable us to be clearer in our minds about the moral issues at stake in the rehabilitative theory.

The rehabilitative ideal makes assumptions about the nature of persons, the nature of social science and what, in the light of a social scientific approach, an appropriate attitude of respect should be towards a person. I shall argue that it is precisely what is implied by the principle of respect for persons which marks the moral difference between rehabilitation and the 'justice' model. The rehabilitative ideal is clearly influenced by assumptions about the nature of human behaviour drawn from the social sciences, and these assumptions seem to be as follows:

(i) Human behaviour is explicable in causal terms, that is to say that behaviour is to be seen as an effect of a nexus of antecedent causal circumstances. These causal circumstances will be sought either in the physical and psychological make-up of the individual whose behaviour is to be explained, or in the environment within which the individual lives or, more plausibly, in some combination of both of these. In the case of criminal offenders their law-breaking behaviour is to be seen as the *effect* of causal factors of this sort.

(ii) This has the effect of shifting the emphasis away from such notions as responsibility and personal desert. If behaviour is the result of antecedent causes then it is at least plausible to suggest that the individual is not responsible for his actions and if this is so it is not at all clear in what sense he deserves anything — good or bad, punishment of reward — on the basis of his action. One can make claims for desert only on the basis of what one is responsible for; and precisely this factor is missing if we grant that human behaviour has a sufficient causal explanation. However, criminal behaviour will still need to be controlled or changed, but the justification of this is independent of otoise considerations about desert. Although B. F. Skinner is perhaps an extreme example, his book *Science and Human Behaviour* (Skinner 1953) brings out both this feature of responsibility and the previous feature about the nature of social scientific explanations:

> We do not hold people responsible for their reflexes, for example, for coughing in church. We hold them responsible for their operant behaviour — for example, for whispering in church or remaining in church while coughing. But there are variables which are responsible for whispering as well as coughing and these may be just as inexorable. When we recognise this we are likely to drop the notion of responsibility altogether and with it the doctrine of free will as an inner causal agent. (pp. 115–16)

(iii) In natural science prediction and control are closely related features and are central both to the aims of science and to the kinds of explanations of phenomena which natural science yields. A law-like generalisation such as $x\varphi(x)x\psi(x)$ allows us in a particular case to say $\varphi(x)$ therefore $\psi(x)$. We shall be able to predict the occurrence of $\psi(x)$ from the occurrence of $\varphi(x)$ and of course with prediction goes control. If we wish to produce that state of affairs $\psi(x)$ then we shall seek so far as possible to precipitate the antecedent conditions $\varphi(x)$. If on the other hand we wish to avoid the occurrence of $\psi(x)$ then we shall try to prevent $\varphi(x)$ from occurring. Similarly in social science if we believe that it is or will be possible to produce analogous generalisations about human behaviour such a view would lead us to think that it ought to be possible to intervene in the causal antecedents of such behaviour and either prevent its occurrence or to modify it to some degree. This kind of intervention is presumably the basis of rehabilitation. For example Karpman (1956) says:

> Basically criminality is but a symptom of insanity, using the term in its widest generic sense to express unacceptable social behaviour based on unconscious motivation flowing from a disturbed instinctive and emotional life. . . . If criminals are products of early environmental influences in the same sense that psychotics and neurotics are, then it should be possible to treat them psychotherapeutically. (p. 47)

In this passage the model cited above is clearly at work. Criminal behaviour has a sufficient causal explanation which makes notions like responsibility and guilt redundant, and such behaviour can be modified or controlled by intervening in the causal circumstances — childhood conditioning and the like — which has led to its development. In addition to this, the predictive element in the explanation of criminal behaviour is used as a basis for indeterminate sentences for those offenders whose prognosis is that they are likely to be of danger to society in the future. On such a basis individuals are 'punished' for what it is predicted they *would do* as much as for what it has been found out they *have done.*

(iv) The language of social science and the explanation of criminal behaviour in terms of social science generalisations has constituted the basis for the kind of 'clinical' terminology which is frequently used in the literature of rehabilitation. Notions such as responsibility, desert and punishment drop out in favour of notions such as cause, treatment, prognosis, etc. I have already cited examples of this but probably the very best piece of sustained writing in this particular genre is Karl Menninger's (1968) *The Crime of Punishment.*

(v) Finally there is the assumption that the rehabilitative approach is humanitarian. Treatment patterns are tailored to individual needs and problems. Investigations are made into the circumstances and psychological state of the offender — in short the whole process of treatment is individualised. Instead of being dealt with according to some kind of impersonal procedure the *particular* person is taken as a unique individual with his own needs, interests, desires and problems and this individualisation, so it is argued, is central to the principle of respecting persons — at least as it is understood by social workers and probation officers etc. Biestek (1961) for example argues as follows — that individualisation implies:

> The recognition and understanding of each client's unique
> qualities and the differential use of the principles and
> methods in assisting each towards a better adjustment.
> Individualisation is based upon the right of human beings to
> be individual, and to be treated not as *a* human but as *this*
> human being with his personal differences. (p. 46)

In the rehabilitative model we are presented with a tangled skein of beliefs and moral attitudes. Beliefs about the nature of human behaviour generally and about the explanation of criminal behaviour in particular, the possibility of the scientific modification and change of such behaviour and also the consequences of these beliefs for our overall moral outlook, particularly a shifting away of emphasis from notions like responsibility, guilt and desert, towards a more impersonal clinical view of human behaviour, a view which is well captured in the following section from Karl Menninger's (1959) 'Therapy not punishment' printed in *Harper's Magazine*:

> We, the agents of society, must move to end this game of tit
> for tat and blow for blow in which the offender has foolishly
> and futilely engaged himself and us. We are not driven as he

is to wild and impulsive actions. With knowledge comes power, and with power there is no need for the frightened vengeance of the old penology. In its place should go a quiet, dignified therapeutic programme for the rehabilitation of the disorganised one, if possible the protection of society during the treatment period and his guided return to useful citizenship as soon as this can be effected. (pp. 63–4)

However, as we have seen in Professor Bottoms's and Dr. Bottomley's chapters, many of the assumptions behind this approach have broken down — or at least there is no longer this simple faith which Menninger has in either the knowledge or the power which social science is supposed to bring into penology. But in addition to this there has been a moral crises over the replacement of punishment by rehabilitation. Is the latter in fact consistent with well-entrenched moral beliefs we have about respect for persons and similar practical attitudes towards persons?

Perhaps the first point to notice here is that the scientific background to the rehabilitative model is somewhat threadbare. In the first place of course, many would argue that such faith in the predictive and explanatory power of social science is quite misplaced (see, for example, Winch 1958; Taylor 1977); but leaving this argument on one side for the moment it is clear that the assumptions made by those who hold to the rehabilitative model are highly normative. Rehabilitation always has to be *to* something or other and in the present case presumably something like consensus expectations and social norms. Both rehabilitation and deviance have to be defined against the background of the norms of the society in question. The social scientific air of neutrality and objectivity has to be seen in the light of these assumptions and the support which social science gives to these values by defining in quasi-medical terminology the failure to meet them as pathological, and the subsequent ability to live in terms of them as rehabilitation. Of course, the critic will argue that the same is true of medicine — treatment and diagnosis take place against assumed standards of health and illness, and yet this does not seem to cast doubt on the role of medicine in our society. However, it is at least arguable that there is a much higher degree of consensus in society about the types of physical conditions which constitute health and disease, and there is a much higher degree of agreement that physical health and the absence of physical injury are valuable than is true of what might be called 'social health' and 'adequate social functioning'. In a pluralistic society there are bound to be disagreements about standards of behaviour and the extent to which we can define a norm of social health. These can range from the view that the norms of society do articulate as an adequate standard of social health to the anguished outburst of R. D. Laing (1967) when faced with theories of rehabilitation and adjustment: 'Adaptation to what? To society? To a world gone mad?'

Herbert Morris (1968) in an influential article has put the problem less dramatically but perhaps more rigorously when he argues that:

> The logic of cure will push us toward forms of therapy that inevitably involve changes in the person made against his will. The evil in this would be more apparent in those cases where the agent, whose action is determined to be a manifestation of some disease, does not regard his action in this way. He believes that what he has done is, in fact 'right' but his conception of normality is not the therapeutically accepted one. When we treat an illness we normally treat a condition that the person is not responsible for. He is suffering from some disease and we treat the condition, relieving the person of something preventing his normal functioning. When we begin treating persons for actions that have been chosen, we do not lift the person from something that is interfering with his normal functioning but we change the person so that he functions in a way regarded as normal by the current therapeutic community. We have to change him and his judgements of value.
> (p. 487)

Granted the possibility of a good deal of intractable disagreement about the norms of society, a conception of rehabilitation, defined in terms of *certain* norms rather than others, loses its veneer of scientific neutrality. Obviously there is the possibility in the context of rehabilitation for mental health and illness to be new words for describing moral values as Szasz (1968) has argued. It is not necessary for us to believe this to be the case — we may ourselves see the rules of society as embodying a healthy way of life, but the very fact that *some* may disagree with this and see these norms as repressive, or whatever, shows the necessity for the justification of these norms. And this justification which, as we have seen, defines the ends of rehabilitation, cannot be a scientific one — it has to be a *moral* justification.

This realisation of the normative assumptions behind the rehabilitative process and the questionability of those assumptions has been a major cause of the loss of confidence in it at a theoretical level. The other major moral problem with the rehabilitative ideal, and this perhaps takes us much closer to the heart of the matter, is that it appears manipulative and not to respect persons as persons. It appears manipulative in the sense that 'punishment' or 'treatment' is given not on the basis of what the crime deserved, but rather on the basis of how the person can be changed so that he/she will be able to meet more adequately society's expectations. It also seems to involve manipulation in that when the length of punishment is linked to rehabilitation, then release will only come when the offender has satisfied a group of experts that he is rehabilitated — rehabilitation which, as we have seen, is likely to be seen in terms of the moral consensus of society. An interesting and dramatic illustration of this is to be found in the tragic story of George Jackson:

> In 1960 Jackson at the age of 18 was convicted of second degree robbery for driving a getaway car while a friend robbed a petrol station of seventy dollars. Under the Californian state law, which claims to have the most reformist penal code, Jackson and his accomplice were sentenced to a period of between one year and life imprisonment. After serving the first year the parole board determines when the prisoner should be released on parole. Under that system, parole is granted when the board thinks a prisoner has been sufficiently reformed to be let out. Jackson's accomplice was released in 1963. Jackson remained until 1970 and subsequently died in prison. He claimed that his political beliefs prevented him from being granted parole — he was a black revolutionary — and as long as he expounded those beliefs he was not considered reformed. (Bean 1976, p. 10)

The critic of the rehabilitative ideal will argue that the reformist must shift the centre of attention away from the *crime* to the *character* of the criminal and that as a consequence the length of time to be spent in an institution becomes dependent on a board comprised of experts who claim to know when reform or rehabilitation has been achieved. This is thought to be manipulative — an offender has to act in a way consistent with the norms which define rehabilitation and these norms represent the interests of society at large, and may or may not reflect the offender's own values.

The claim that the rehabilitative process is manipulative is also justified with reference to punishment which is based upon a predictive estimate of the chances of the offender acting in a similar manner again in such a way as to be a danger to society. Here a person may be deprived of his liberty not because of what he has done, but of what he is thought likely to do. The fact that the deprivation of liberty is called therapy instead of punishment does nothing to disguise the substantive issues of personal liberty and due process of law which are being bypassed in this kind of procedure, a procedure which is clearly maintained as being in the interests of society. The moral principle of respect for persons involves the idea that a person should never be used solely for the purposes of others, but as an end in himself. Clearly to talk about therapy in these circumstances gives the impression that it is being done in the interests of the offender, but it seems clear with the introduction of the concept of 'dangerousness' that the interests of society are obviously at stake and the restraints on the offender are largely undertaken in response to a predicted danger to society.

The Rehabilitative Ideal and Respect for Persons

At the same time there does seem to be something odd about the claim that the rehabilitative ideal is inhumane. Surely it might be argued that it is this reformist rehabilitative ideal which has led penology out of the dark ages of brutal and savage treatment inflicted upon offenders in the name of retribution. Clearly, if being humanitarian means being concerned with *physical pain* inflicted upon human beings, then the rehabilitative model has some claim to be humane — it is clearly the case that punishment conceived in rehabilitative terms is likely to involve far less physical pain than would be the case with some other model — but nevertheless it is certainly plausible to suggest that the rehabilitative model is at the best insensitive to certain other aspects of humanitarianism, particularly in the crucial importance of notions of agency, moral capacity and responsibility in our conception of ourselves. Strawson (1974) in his important essay *Freedom and Resentment* has pointed out the extent to which our view of the humanity of another becomes attenuated when we see another person's behaviour as the result of antecedent causal factors. He points out that in normal human relations a whole range of attitudes, what he calls 'reactive' attitudes between one person and another, are central to their relationship, whereas in the case of a person whose behaviour is seen as pathological only 'objective' attitudes may be appropriate:

> To adopt the objective attitude to another human being is to see him perhaps as an object of social policy; as a subject for what in a wide range of sense might be called treatment; as something certainly taken account, perhaps precautionary account of; to be managed or handled, cured or trained. . . . The objective attitude may be emotionally toned in many ways but not in all ways . . . it cannot include the range of reactive feelings and attitudes which belong to involvement or participation with others in interpersonal relationships. (p. 9)

Reactive attitudes do seem to be bound up with our conception of a person and it is perhaps the main moral failure of the rehabilitative model to be insensitive to these aspects of humanity. It may well be the case that a good deal of criminal behaviour is due to bad social conditions and to psychological causes amenable to treatment, but if we assume that the offender has no moral capacity at all — is not capable of agency, of identifying himself with his actions and taking responsibility for them — it may well be argued that we are failing to show proper respect for the criminal's personality. Perhaps this comes out particularly clearly in the quotation from Menninger (1959) cited above where the very language which is used seems to place the criminal outside of normal human relationships and normal human responses.

Of course, the rehabilitation theorist still appears to have a very strong card to play in defence of his view that his position does embody a sense of respect for persons. The rehabilitative theorist will rightly claim that at least his model is *individualised* — he is responsive to the particular circumstances, the needs and desires of his particular client. Those who wish to replace rehabilitation with a system of discretion-free procedural justice punishing in the light of the crime rather than in terms of the needs of the criminal are, on the rehabilitative view, guilty of not respecting the unique individual personality of the offender. Individualisation is, on this view, the touchstone of respect for persons and the rehabilitative ideal is perhaps on its strongest moral ground at this point. However, the position is still open to the other charges in regard to its neglect of other central features of humanity, and the critic of rehabilitation may well say that the rehabilitationist's commitment to individualisation may not be all that it seems to be. Granted that the therapist is going to operate with *some* sociological or psychological model of human behaviour (if this is not so then the language of rehabilitation and therapy becomes redundant), this model is likely to determine in the end what are seen to be the needs, or better the 'real' needs or desires of the client or offender and perhaps even to be rather dismissive of the desires which the offender himself articulates. A good example of this which, because it operates with a strong although in my view unintelligible notion of the unconscious, is to be found in Clare Winnicott's (1967) article 'Casework and agency function' in which she talks about the role of the probation service in relation to crime:

> When a child or an adult commits an offence of a certain
> degree and kind he brings into action the machinery of the
> law. The probation officer who is then asked to do
> casework with the client feels that he ought to apply
> techniques implying the casework principle of self
> determination, but he loses everything if he forgets his
> relationship to his agency and to the court, since symptoms
> of this kind of illness are unconsciously designed to bring
> authority into the picture. (p. 108)

Here there is very little respect shown for the principle of individualisation. In the first place the probation officer is being advised not to treat his client as being responsible, and then the client's committing the crime is supposed to be seen as an illness which has been unconsciously designed to bring an authoritarian personality in to the life of the client. It is clear that whatever else we may mean by unconscious design it cannot mean something actually avowed as a desire by the client, but rather something ascribed to the client on the basis of some social scientific theory. In addition, of course, it is difficult perhaps to see how such basic moral principles as respect for persons, self-direction, individualisation etc, can in fact exist along-side a strong commitment to the view that human behaviour has sufficient causal explanation.

Rational Agents and Retribution

It is perhaps over this principle of respect for persons that the moral differences between the rehabilitative view and the critics of this position become most apparent. Indeed we should not be surprised by this because the present debate about the nature of punishment was mirrored in the late eighteenth and early nineteenth centuries in the debate between the Utilitarians on the one hand and Kant and Hegel on the other. The Utilitarians, following Bentham's lead, took the apparently humane view that punishment, as the intentional infliction of pain, is an evil and could only be justified in terms of the greater good which its infliction would yield. Punishment is an instrument of social control and should only be used in the terms necessary to achieve this. Kant and Hegel on the other hand, took the view, as do some modern critics of the rehabilitative ideal, that the humanitarian-ism of the Utilitarian view is in fact rather shallow and in fact, in inflicting pain, or therapy, as a form of social control infringes the right of the person to be treated as an end in himself and not merely as a means to the ends of others. As Kant argues in a famous passage:

> Judicial punishment can never be used merely as a means to
> promote some other good for the criminal himself or civil
> society, but instead it must in all cases be imposed on him
> only on the ground that he has committed a crime; for a
> human being can never be manipulated merely as a means
> to the purposes of someone else. . . . He must first of all be
> found to be deserving of punishment before any
> consideration is given of the utility of this punishment for
> himself or his fellow citizens. (Ladd 1965, p. 331)

Desert for Kant is therefore a central moral notion in thinking about punishment, and desert implies agency and responsibility. One can only make claims to deserve anything on the basis of things for which one can claim at least some degree of responsibility. Thus to entrench desert as a necessary condition of punishment, as Kant does in this passage, is to place at the very centre of his theory of punishment a very strong commitment to human responsibility. This is paralleled by Hegel (1821) who in *The Philosophy of Right* goes on to suggest that punishment is the right of the offender. It is an affirmation of the person's status as a human being and not just something to be controlled or, as Strawson (1974) says, to be taken precautionary account of. However, it is important when considering Kant's statement of his position as found in the above quotation that his use of the word 'merely' admits that there can be justifiable aspects of the dealing of society with the offender which do take into account the interests of society, but these are not to be seen as overriding. And the question of the infliction of punishment and the particular character which it has in each case should be decided independently of these other interests. On this sort of basis punishment would be justified on the basis of desert alone, and should be meted out in the light of the gravity of the offence, but equally during the sentence of an offender fixed by desert criteria there might well be offered the possibility of help, therapy, training, education etc., which might help him to be rehabilitated or reform; but equally these opportunities should be offered and taken up quite independently of considerations about the length of sentences, the possibility of parole etc. The length of a sentence should be based upon what the crime deserves and not on the basis of whether the offender has reformed or not.

If this was all that Kant and Hegel were arguing then it might appear to be entirely unexceptionable for all but the most thorough-going utilitarians, but it is not all that they were committed to in their arguments. Kant is arguing that desert is not just a necessary condition for punishment but also a sufficient one. If a person has been found guilty of a crime then not only does his guilt make it possible to punish him, it makes it necessary to do so.[1] There is no gap of justification between finding guilty as charged and therefore punishable, and actually punishing him. If he is guilty then he ought to be punished. Kant's reason for saying this is obvious — at least on first inspection — because if there was a gap between finding a person punishable and punishing him then the question, 'ought we to punish this guilty (punishable) person?', could only be answered by utilitarian arguments such as 'it is in the interest of society that we should do so', or 'it will deter him if we do'. But all answers of this sort for Kant can only be secondary if we take the principle of respect for persons seriously, because they all claim the right to inflict punishment in a manipulative way. However, while this accounts for why Kant wishes to resist any suggestion of a gap between guilt and punishment this does nothing to justify the principle 'the guilty ought to be punished', unless of course we take the view that it is the only consequence in terms of punishment which is allowable under an acceptance of the principle of respect for persons. Some commentators have suggested that Kant's argument is an illusion; either the principle 'the guilty ought to be punished' has to be taken as a fundamental moral intuition, or else the reasons we give for accepting it must be broadly speaking of a utilitarian type — the balance of social advantage lies in punishing the guilty. However, there is perhaps a third type of justification which we might call analytical[2] rather than either utilitarian or intuitive, although it is perhaps closer to the latter than the former. An analytical justification would be an attempt to see a particular theory of punishment, such as Kant's or Hegel's, as set within a broader framework of political and social analysis, and in particular an analysis of the nature of the State and social and political obligation. This is certainly the kind of argument which both Kant and Hegel sought to provide, and incidentally it is perhaps just what is lacking in the work of those who wish to resurrect, under the 'justice' model, some of the central features of Kant and Hegel's retributivism. Such an analysis would have to take us very deeply into each particular thinker's conception of the social and political order, the nature of the rules and laws which characterise that order and the obligations of individual citizens to that overall order. Perhaps only background theories of this sort are going to be able to provide the final basis for a desert-based theory of punishment which seeks to avoid either a utilitarian foundation which would be paradoxical, or lapse into an appeal to moral intuition which would be implausible to those who do not share the intuitions. However, the difficulties with such background theories is they are never finally capable of completely compelling the intellect. They are more like contestable visions of the actuality and the possibility of man's social life rather than scientifically testable hypotheses about the nature of social experience — although, as we shall see, empirical evidence is relevant in a crucial way to determine the applicability of the Kantian model to existing societies.

In this chapter it is obviously impossible to try and discuss in other than the most superficial terms the visions of society which inform both Kant and Hegel's views of punishment and I shall discuss here only Kant's view: partly because it is much more manageable, and also because I have discussed Hegel's theory, which is very different, elsewhere (Plant 1973). Kant's theory of political obligation is contractual, and he places a very great deal of weight on the notion of reciprocity. The laws of a just state are laws which would have been chosen by any rational man to govern social relationships in a position of initial choice. Kant is not, of course, saying that such a position of original constitutional choice ever existed, but rather that *if* we wish to determine the content of just and impartial laws we should try to work out hypothetically which legal rules *would* have been chosen by a group of rational men forming a society for the first time. Such laws would, in Kant's view, embody both a degree of self-restraint and benefit. Without law a particular individual might well be able to derive more benefits than he would under a system with law, but this will not be true of persons generally, and since no person could know in advance whether he would be able to benefit under a system without law it would follow that it would be in his interest to accept a system of rules which would secure benefits to all men, though in certain contexts keeping such laws is going to require a certain amount of self-restraint. Since any individual derives and accepts the benefits which the existence of law brings, an individual owes obedience to the law as a *debt* to his fellow citizens who equally by their self-restraint keep the laws. If an individual chooses not to pay this debt to his fellow citizens by keeping the law then in Kant's view he is opting to pay the debt in another way — by punishment. If the law is to remain just and impartial it is centrally important to guarantee to those who obey the law that those who disobey will not gain an unfair advantage over those who obey voluntarily. Punishment is a debt to be paid to the law-abiding members of the community, and once it has been paid it allows re-entry into the community of citizens on an equal basis. Only within a theory about the nature of law and political obligation can we provide a basis for the retributive theory of punishment, although it must be said that to justify the theory as Kant does in this way does seem to me to contain some strongly utilitarian elements.

However, it is still arguable that even a theory of this sort does not sanction some of the sorts of remarks typically made by retributivists such as 'one wills one's own punishment', or 'punishment is the criminal's right'. As Morris (1968) has suggested:

> Reaction to the claim that there is such a right has been
> astonishment combined perhaps with a touch of contempt
> for the perversity of the suggestion. A strange right that no
> one would ever wish to claim. With that flourish the subject
> is buried and the right disposed of. (p. 487)

However, it can be argued that while the language of rights in this kind of context is misleading, nevertheless the retributivists are touching on an important problem when they talk in their rather strange way of having willed one's own punishment and having a right to be punished, and once again the issue comes down to what we think is implied by respect for persons. On the view put forward by Kant and Hegel, when we claim to respect someone as a person we

respect his autonomy as a rational moral agent. We may not respect his
character, we may abominate what he does, but we respect him as a
person having in some degree a moral capacity for rational and
autonomous conduct. We respect not the person's episodic desires and
whims, but rather the desires, goals and purposes which he has as a
rational moral agent or *would* have *if* he were a rational moral agent.
We do not necessarily respect persons when we treat them how they
actually want to be treated, but rather in accordance with the ways in
which they *would wish* to be treated if and when they have a rational
view of their situation. Obviously such a view as this would lead us
very quickly to being able to say that punishment is my right as a
rational being. While I may, under the influence of fear, prefer to be
dealt with in a way other than by punishment, to accede to this would
not be to respect me as a rational moral agent. In punishing me and
thus recognising that I am a responsible agent and in sound mind the
State respects me by doing to me what, if I were at that moment
capable of rational appraisal, I would myself wish them to do.[3]

Clearly there are many dangers with this argument and the most
obvious one, interestingly enough, parallels one of the criticisms by
retributivists of the rehabilitative ideal. The retributivist often claims
that in the rehabilitative model the offender is usually thought not to
be capable of a rational appraisal of his position and thus is in need of
therapy; however in the retributive model the individual's desire not
to be punished is equally dismissed in terms of a view about what the
offender would really want if he were more rational than he is capable
of being at the present time. In the rehabilitative case the difficulties
posed could only be solved if we had some objective account of the
nature of mental illness, and some view about the ways in which
the norms of our society embody a standard of social health to justify
the inference that the offender's deviance from those norms is pathological; in the retributivist case the problem is analogous, although
the language is less that of health and illness and more that of
rationality and justice. If we could determine some objective standard
of rationality and the laws which a rational person would choose then
we might avoid some of the obvious dangers in saying that the
offender, if he were rational, would will his own punishment. On this
view I could be shown to have willed my own punishment as a
rational moral agent *if* the laws of my society are the laws which
would have been chosen by rational persons in an initial situation of
choice, and if punishment would have been chosen in that situation as
the means whereby adherence to such laws would have been secured.
My willing my own punishment is thus shown by an argument about
hypothetical rational choice. The issue here is a very central one in
western political philosophy — is it possible to see the coercive power

of the State in such a way as it is the product of each person's rational, though not necessarily current operant, will.[4]

This clearly leads on to the problem of social rather than narrowly criminal justice. And this broader issue is one which is raised in Dr. Bottomley's chapter. In his discussion of the American Friends' report *Struggle for Justice*, he quotes the following important comment:

> . . . the construction of a just system of criminal justice in an unjust society is a contradiction in terms. Criminal justice is inextricably interwoven with, and largely derivative from, a broader social justice. (American Friends Service Committee 1971, p. 16)

This issue is squarely faced by Kant in his theory. The whole Kantian framework depends upon certain conditions being met before laws can be considered just — it would have to be capable of being defended in terms of an argument of the contractual form. The laws are just if they would have been chosen by rational persons in a situation of impartiality. If, however, the existing structure of law cannot be regarded as just in terms of criteria such as these, then clearly the Kantian theory of punishment will fail to apply. This is the great merit of seeing the theory in the wider context of Kant's political philosophy. The retributive theory only stands if it is in the context of laws which can themselves be defended as just. However, there are a number of objections to Kant's enterprise, which has been taken over very largely by Rawls (1972) in his *Theory of Justice*, a book to which many defenders of the justice model appeal. In the first place of course there is the view of legal positivists that it is a mistake to look for some external standard for the justification of law — in this case the social contract. On the positivist view, laws which are enacted according to the proper procedures within a constitutional system are *just* by definition. But, more importantly, it is arguable that it is impossible to derive a substantive theory of just law from *a priori* theory about rational choice in situations of impartiality. Before persons can make choices they have to have information, and choices about laws will have to be based upon information concerning the human condition, but is there any data about the nature of man and his relationship to his fellow beings which can be taken as objective and neutral and thus be able to play a role in a procedure which is seen as providing a firm foundation for external judgements about the just nature of particular laws? (Lukes 1976; Daniels 1975) A Marxist would argue that if the information on which these hypothetical choices are made is based upon bourgeois social science and social theory, embodying assumptions say about the basic competitiveness and aquisitiveness of persons, then we shall end up with a bourgeois theory of justice (Murphy 1973). This is precisely what Marx accused both Hegel and

Kant of doing and what latter-day Marxists have accused Rawls of doing. In his celebrated article on capital punishment Marx (1853) says the following:

> From the point of view of abstract right, there is only one theory of punishment which recognizes human dignity in the abstract, and that is the theory of Kant, especially in the more rigid formula given to it by Hegel. Hegel says 'Punishment is the right of the criminal. It is an act of his own will. The violation of right has been proclaimed by the criminal as his own right. His crime is the negation of right. Punishment is the negation of this negation, and consequently an affirmation of right, solicited and forced upon the criminal by himself.' There is no doubt something specious in this formula in as much as Hegel instead of looking at the criminal as the mere object, the slave of justice, elevates him to the position of a free and self-determining being. Looking however more closely into the matter we discover that German Idealism here, as in most other instances, has given but a transcendental sanction to the rules of existing society. Is it not a delusion to substitute for the individual with his real motives, with multifarious circumstances pressing down upon him, the abstraction of 'free will'. . . ?

What Marx is arguing here is that the theories of both Kant and Hegel presuppose a just society in which the law is seen as a system of rules which free, impartial, rational persons would consider just. However, we lack any clear criteria for determining what free and rational persons would have chosen as just laws. In a manifestly unjust society in Marx's view both Kant and Hegel are forced to ride rough-shod over the real individual with his needs, desires and interests in order to show that if he were rational he would have willed his own punishment in the same way as modern critics of rehabilitation argue that therapists ride rough-shod over the articulated desires and needs of their clients. The rehabilitative ideal has to provide and has lamentably failed to provide a social theory which would allow us to say with objectivity that a particular system of law embodies social health, and that deviation from it embodies pathological features; the retributivist, however, equally has failed to provide an account of just law and rational behaviour. It is the very failure to do this that enables both parties to claim to respect persons while at the same time constructing elaborate theories which enables them to bypass what Marx calls the real person with his existing motives and pressed in by social circumstances.

The recognition, plausible as it is, that the retributive or justice model requires some broader framework of social philosophy, and in particular a theory of social justice to back it up, leads to some difficulties for the model. If in fact all conceptions of social justice are contestable and if there is no single theory of social justice which can command the assent of all rational persons then the claim that criminal justice in a particular society is fair because it derives from a background of social justice is obviously going to be contested just because any scheme of social justice is going to be contestable in a morally pluralistic society. Indeed some influential thinkers such as Hayek (1976) regard the whole notion of social justice as illusory. The moral basis of the justice model is therefore as likely to appear as unsure as the rehabilitative model, at least in a society with any degree of moral pluralism. It is the recognition of this fact that allows the utilitarian theory to regain some kind of foothold. The utilitarian may well argue as follows: if, as is surely the case, a procedural theory of criminal justice is going to require a theory of social justice to back it up and if such a conception of justice is likely to be contestable, then a formula such as that proposed by the utilitarians in which punishment is linked to balancing the welfare of the community against the welfare of the individual offender might be though to bypass these difficult issues about just laws and wider social justice in society. Utilitarianism, so it is argued, begs fewer questions, it is concerned with securing to as many people as possible as much as possible of whatever it is that they happen to want, and punishment has a role only when the actions of an individual conflict in a severe manner with the operation of such a want-satisfying formula. Utilitarianism on this view recognises the facts of moral diversity and different individuals' views about their own welfare, it is only concerned with providing a framework of law and criminal justice which will enable people to pursue their own welfare in their own way. There is clearly some plausibility in this claim and it is true to say that utilitarianism seems to beg fewer moral questions than justice-based theories. To some this is the great strength of utilitarianism and a strength which will always allow it to hold a central place in reasoning about society in general and punishment in particular; others however regard this simplicity as illusory and its failure to consider issues such as justice as a form of tunnel vision on the part of utilitarian social philosophers. Nevertheless in the absence of any philosophically agreed way of securing rational agreement on the substance of social justice, the utilitarian perspective with its central place for deterrence and rehabilitation is always likely to have an important place in reasoning about punishment. A particularly good example of the way in which diversity of conceptions of justice can come to affect issues of punishment is to be seen in precisely the debate which is the subject of this volume. On the one hand the move within criminal justice seems to be away from an individualised approach which attends to the needs (as defined by the therapist) of the offender, and towards a desert-orientated view of punishment, and this seems to meet with the approval of radicals. However, radical theories of *social* justice have always concentrated on distribution of benefits and burdens according to need rather than desert. A society which insists on desert in the distribution of the burdens of punishment and distributes benefits only according to need is likely soon to suffer from moral schizophrenia.

Finally, and more generally, there are a number of difficulties in the return to a retributive theory of punishment, at least one which takes the notion of desert seriously. If we take this notion seriously then it clearly has considerable ramifications for social science. If we really believe that persons have deserts then we have to take the view that they are responsible for those things which form the basis of their deserts, but is this view consistent with maintaining in our social science a search for sufficient causal explanation of behaviour? Would not the social scientist be more likely to want to say with Stuart Hampshire (1972) that we should reject the notion of deserving as having a place in rational and systematic ethics:

> After genetic roulette and the roulette of childhood
> environment a man emerges so equipped into the poker
> game of social competition, within a social system
> determined by largely unknown historical forces.

Yet if we say this don't we have to abandon the notion of respect for persons? Alternatively, if we do not wish to say this we are unlikely to make any progress into understanding the moral basis of punishment until we have worked out what we mean by respect for persons because, as we have seen, both the rehabilitationist and the retributivist can deploy strong arguments to the effect that their views embody respect for persons. Equally, as we have seen, they both seem to manage to neglect the particular outlooks of individual persons.

NOTES

1. The best example of this in Kant is the following: 'Even if civil society were to dissolve itself by common agreement of all of its members . . . the last murderer remaining in prison must be executed so that everyone will duly receive what his actions are worth . . .' (Ladd 1965, p. 331). Here guilt merits punishment even if punishment can be of no conceivable benefit to society.
2. Here I am following Murphy (1970).
3. This is Hegel's argument in *The Philosophy of Right*: Hegel (1821, pp. 99–101).
4. This problem has been central in political philosophy since Rousseau, and has recently been revived by Rawls (1972).

4

Abolition: possibilities and pitfalls

by DAVID DOWNES

The ultimate penal reform is abolition. Thinkers as diverse as Shaw and the Webbs, William Godwin and the anarchists, and H. J. Eysenck and the aversion therapists would at least agree on that. An unlikely consensus, but one which may be a pre-condition for ultimate reforms of the abolitionist kind: the abolition of capital punishment gained this kind of consensus as a goal in the post-war period. But two barriers ordinarily stand in the way of the realisation of such ultimate reforms: first, the route to the reform; second, the alternative(s) to the system which is to be abolished. It is against these two barriers that the energies of penal reformers are spent; it is on the issues they entail that debate customarily centres; it is in the answers reformers give to the questions involved that the sharpest conflicts and disagreements are revealed. For Mathiesen (1974) these barriers constitute the major dilemmas of penal reform. The first classically revolves around the reform versus revolution issue (which has its correspondences in radical politics in general): should short-term considerations take precedence over long-term aims in the struggle for change? Penal reformers typically opt for the former, thereby losing sight of the latter (the counterpart is gradualism in politics). The second entails not only a degree of omniscience and prescience about possible futures rarely if ever granted mere mortals, but also implicitly snares the reformer into an acceptance of system goals: the alternative must meet the same goal as the system it aims to replace. Both have their Catch-22 aspect: the first, by improving the system, reinforces it; the second, by insisting that alternatives be shown to meet system goals in advance of their actualisation, sets impossible tasks for reformers. In combination, and given that the bureaucratic power of the authorities ensures that they are the arbiters in evaluating the case for reforms, the stage is set for penal reformers to end up hopelessly compromised with the system, on the one hand, or condemned to the 'irresponsible revolutionary' role, on the other.

The immense appeal of the work of Thomas Mathiesen on the

71

'politics of abolition' lies in his redefinition of the problems involved, and the solutions that emerge, in and from these dilemmas. In line with a great deal of philosophical work, he does not solve or resolve these dilemmas: he dissolves them. The first dilemma, reform versus revolution, he dissolves by insisting that *both* goals must be pursued. To make this more than sheer word-magic, a certain strategy must be followed, which involves distinguishing between reforms which at least do not strengthen the system — and which therefore can be pursued without detriment to long-term aims — and those which do — which must as a consequence be foregone. The second dilemma is dissolved by refusing to be drawn on the question of alternatives. Activists should press for abolition in its own terms and without becoming implicated in the system demand for a *quid pro quo* outcome. Alternatives are emergent properties of abolition rather than a prerequisite for it. Taken together, these are the theoretical elements in the 'politics of abolition'. The practice is to be catalysed by prisoners themselves. They are to be the prime movers in the struggle for penal reform, and their neutralisation and/or elimination from that process has been the result of previous strategies playing into the hands of the Establishment. They alone can preserve a reform movement from sterilisation. By their influence on reformers outside the walls, who must maintain a sensitivity to their demands, a form of action theory can be evolved which avoids both immaculate theoretical conceptions on the one hand, and token administrative 'practical' changes on the other. The whole strategy is termed by Mathiesen the 'unfinished', a dynamic, open-ended form of praxis which has as its components only the insistence on the need to move towards abolition, and to do so in combination with the 'expelled' themselves.

We are indebted to Mathiesen for providing so full and so personal an account of how he came to evolve this strategy, which coincides with that of KROM, the Norwegian prison reform movement, of which he was chairman throughout its formative years. He (and KROM) began in 1968 to construct a perspective on penal reform little different from that embraced in many respects by the Howard League and many other penal reform organisations in the western world. Its policy was basically treatment-oriented and humanitarian, and it was only when several prisoners (the 'group of nine') contacted them for information about their activities, that the long haul towards radicalisation began. For the authorities refused to allow any contact between KROM and those it aimed to serve, and whose participation it sought. This began a series of confrontations with the authorities over the rights of prisoners to participate in outside organisations of the KROM type, and by implication of their rights to contact with 'outside' on a whole series of fronts, including visits, furloughs, home leave, mail censorship and rights to telephone in privacy, issues which incidentally reveal by comparison the as yet relative mildness of equivalent demands by prisoners in British jails. The keynote to this stage is the relationship between KROM and the authorities, with the prisoners as victim, and the prison staff as the villain of the piece.

The longest single sequence in the book is, however, a record of the Swedish counterpart of KROM and its role in the 'negotiations' which followed the prison strikes of 1970 that emanated from Osteraker. From a stance implying that real concessions would be the outcome of their work, a working group was set up composed of an equal number of representatives from the prisoners and the authorities, with the Swedish KROM allowed a strictly limited advisory role 'backstage' for the prisoners. The tactics of the authorities are conveyed as a masterly exercise in 'divide and rule', with above all their insistence that 'negotiations' (from which results might flow) were in reality 'talks' (from which nothing might come), and with their insistence on the inability of the talks to go beyond strict adherence to possibilities within the current legal constraints. Despite their inexperience in the art of administrative psychological warfare, the prisoners' representatives nevertheless managed to emerge with a few proposals of significance. The package was then put before a large working party, where the inexperience of the prisoners' representatives in drafting proposals was cruelly exposed, and exploited, to whittle down the eventual settlement to one minor change regarding the dates at which prisoners of different kinds became eligible for furloughs. The whole episode, which was born of the gravest risks being run by prisoners in hunger, and in some cases, thirst striking, had been successfully protracted and eventually emasculated by the authorities (with the representatives of the staff vetoing a few concessions that even the authorities had allowed). For Mathiesen, and increasingly of course for those who share his views, this is the type-case of how authorities behave, with the utmost, callous indifference to the interests of prisoners (and the 'expelled' in general): whatever their skills in wrapping it up may be, the reality is one of effectively totalitarian power confronting total powerlessness.

It is important to understand how Mathiesen came to develop his view on the tactics of reform, for — as he makes clear at the outset — it could have been otherwise, if the authorities had reacted differently early on to absorb the reform group by acceptance rather than rejection. For Mathiesen, the emergent quality of the politics of abolition is a paradigm for the emergent properties of abolition itself. Mike Fitzgerald (1977), in his account of the origins and development of PROP (the British prisoners' union), and his analysis of the context

in which that took place, makes much the same point.[1] Both go on to
locate the crisis in the penal system within the class nature of capitalist
(and state-capitalist) society. In such a society, prison is not simply an
anachronistic and muddle-headed 'wasteful' response to crime: it is
part and parcel of the system, and plays crucial functions within it.
Hence, liberal exposés and moral indignation will do little more than
patch up glaring excesses: a radical critique is needed to make the
connections between prisons and class conflict. In line with Gouldner's (1973, ch. 2) critique of labelling theory, the conflict is not simply
between prisoners and prison authorities and staff (the 'caretakers' of
the system): it is ultimately between the 'expelled' in particular, and
the working class in general; and an implacable State which serves the
interests of a capitalist ruling class. Logically, as the crisis in the system
deepens, crime rates, and imprisonment rates escalate; sentences get
longer; the costs of labour-intensive staffing lead to cutbacks in
amelioration; *ad hoc* solutions to stem the tide make matters worse
(e.g. parole); and covert repression surfaces in bureaucratised form
(e.g. control units). Things can only get worse: the only break in the
expansion and intensification of penal control can flow from the
struggle of the prisoners themselves, aided by outside organisations.

The appeal of Mathiesen's strategy for two groups in particular
should be clarified: these are what one might term the 'liberal radicals'
and the 'radical liberals'. The 'liberal radicals' are those who are
committed to a form of libertarian socialism which aims to retrieve
Marxist analysis from more monolithic interpretations. For them, the
'expelled' (dismissed as the lumpenproletariat in conventional Marxist
terms) *do* have a role in the class struggle, and should not be dismissed
as dangerous allies. Orthodox Marxism has tended in many respects
to converge with conservative positivism in regarding 'deviants' in
general, and criminals in particular, as the 'pathological' products of
forces over which they have no control. For libertarian socialists, such
as Mathiesen, Fitzgerald, and the 'new' criminologists (see Taylor *et
al.* 1973, 1975), the struggle of deviants to achieve political voice for
their authentic demands is just as valid as that of other subordinate
groups. Hence, a strategy which links the two more specifically is to
be welcomed. For 'radical liberals', those who do not embrace the
Marxist analysis in general, but who regard more radical measures as
essential if liberal values are to be activated for more than a minority,
the more salient aspect of Mathiesen's work is his notion of the
'unfinished'. Thus, Stan Cohen views this strategy as ruling out the
kind of subtly coercive élitism he discerns in Ian Taylor's interpretation of radical praxis (Cohen 1975). Both groups view the stated
insistence on opposition to State power as basic to any strategy on
behalf of and including the 'expelled'. Indeed, it is the 'State as enemy'

theme which lends Mathiesen's linkage of the politicisation of the 'expelled', and the adoption of an open-ended strategy which is immune to incorporation, its peculiar force.

All of which should make one scrutinise with especial care this notion of the 'unfinished'. Mathiesen's main concern coincides with what Michels (1911) termed the 'iron law of oligarchy', the built-in tendency, as he defined it, for any organisation to stratify, as it expands, to the point where a self-perpetuating oligarchy come to run things, and define the situation their way, increasingly indifferent to the true interests of their mass membership. To avoid this, Mathiesen sees some escape as possible via the process of transition itself, in the metamorphosis from pre-political to organised movement, in the course of which 'negative' reforms should be pursued, i.e. 'changes which abolish or remove greater or smaller parts on which the system in general may depend', e.g. the abolition of forced labour in Norway for vagrants. The converse is to avoid any foreclosing of future possibilities by settling for a fixed plan of an alternative scheme, or by strengthening the system by 'positive' reforms, e.g. adopting 'treatment' strategies. Ultimately, the only alternative lies in the pursuit of abolition itself, 'in an ever-widening circumference' (pp. 198 ff.). The pressures *against* such politics are, as Mathiesen makes clear, immense. They emanate from — *inter alia* — prisoners who think they will benefit from short-term reforms, but who neglect their illusory nature; system representatives who press for 'alternatives'; the whole ethos of our social system, which also demands 'alternatives' of a positive kind; and which as a result of promulgates 'seeming' negations, e.g. the matching of greater internal freedoms by greater perimeter security. Only the constant unmasking of system interests, and the avoidance of system-strengthening reforms, will resolve the dilemma of how to combine short-term with long-term interests.

Possibilities

The possibilities opened up by the adoption of an abolitionist strategy in Britain are perhaps best illustrated by the Scandinavian experience, since the two main attempts to organise on such lines in this country have been so far somewhat abortive by comparison. PROP — as Fitzgerald (1977) describes — was hamstrung for most of its brief history by internal disagreements over strategy, and by a consequent over-selling of its capacity to deliver. RAP has concentrated its energies entirely on the very question of alternatives that in Mathiesen's view should be avoided, and has regarded issues internal to prisons as outside its scope.[2] Assuming, however, that some *rapprochement* is achieved along Mathiesen's lines, what results might follow (assuming more active political and intellectual-cum-academic support than PROP and RAP have achieved so far)?

(i) A much more focused attack on specific targets, which might be expected to attract more widespread support from established reform organisations. In Norway, KROM developed a three-pronged strategy of attacking *existing* controls (e.g. the vagrancy laws and the system of forced labour for vagrants), *defending* such abolitions once they were pushed through, and *resisting* projected controls in their formative stages (e.g. a detention centre planned for young offenders along the lines of the British centres). Also, a 'protectional' school for school-age child offenders was closed down, and a proposal to abolish the entire youth prison system in Norway gained the support of the Norwegian Advisory Council on the Penal System. Pressure for abolition in the adult sector has met far tougher resistance (apart from the vagrancy acts etc.), but the (putative) gains so far are impressive. A similar campaign in the U.K. would probably take as high priorities the abolition of the youth prison sector that has developed as an unanticipated side effect of the 1969 Act, if not the 1969 Act itself; the forcible use of psychotropic drugs in prisons; and resistance to any attempt to introduce new, tougher measures against 'soccer hooligans' and allied forms of youthful delinquency. Ironically, the most spectacular abolitionist case has recently been made out for virtually the entire Borstal system by N.A.C.R.O. (1977a), though whether its recommendations will be actively lobbied for, or quietly shelved, remains to be seen.[3]

(ii) Central to Mathiesen's strategy is the situation of the 'expelled' as a whole, though prisoners as a particular 'group' constitute his main focus so far. A long, visionary passage from a book by Jörgen Eriksson (1970) prefaces his chapter 'Organisation among the expelled', in which the bad and the mad, the vagrant and the forgotten tribes of the elderly lead a surrealist assault on the powerful, wielding bayonets and crutches — the defences of the weak? The organisational principle which Mathiesen recommends is the 'horizontal' linkage of these groups to higher status allies who lack one element in common with the expelled — power. In Britain, the list of the expelled would be even longer, including for a start the immigrant minorities. But the list of putative allies is also longer, producing an embarrassment of riches. What could a British KROM achieve that the N.C.C.L. for example, could not already claim to have achieved or be attempting for such groups (many of whom have their own pressure groups anyway)? The answer presumably would lie in the attempt to connect the expelled by the abolitionist strategy, rather than taking up their individual troubles piecemeal. And certain groups, e.g. dossers, have tried and as yet failed to initiate their own political movement (PROD

— Protection of the Rights of Dossers), an outcome which may have differed had a British KROM been in existence.

(iii) A third possibility is the constructing of more systematic links between PROP/RAP/KROM and the labour movement, a strategy already in process in Norway, but as yet in embryo in Britain. Even quite minor gains here might pay off quite disproportionately in terms of political militancy among prisoners. There would also be the prospect of greater gains for what Mathiesen terms 'positive' organisation in an 'upwards' direction, i.e. the making of a greater economic contribution in terms of prison industry, which yields a built-in contribution which prisoners can withdraw strategically. Mathiesen regards this with some disfavour as a system-strengthening manoeuvre, but on balance seems to come out in favour of it. So far, as Fitzgerald has stressed, British unions have maintained a stony indifference to the situation of prison labour, even when prisoners are used in strike-breaking! *Any* advance here should be an improvement, abolition aside, as prison work remains the most under-developed aspect of the penal system.

(iv) The fourth possibility is that far more pressure would be exerted in the direction of securing certain rights for prisoners as legally guaranteed, rather than as at best somewhat arbitrary privileges, and at worst as non-existent. Both Mathiesen (1974) and Fitzgerald (1977) (and Cohen and Taylor (1978)) as individuals, and KROM and PROP as organisations have produced exhaustive catalogues of what such a 'Prisoners' Bill of Rights' should include. If, as Sparks (1971), McConville (1975) and others have stressed the treatment era is over, and 'humane containment' is (abolitionists apart) the best to be hoped for, then such a strategy seems the minimal denominator common to all reform groups. Greater realism in thrashing out an agreed list of rights for inclusion would be the most appropriate next step.

(v) The work of Mathiesen, Fitzgerald, Cohen and Taylor *et al.* brings sharply into focus, usually as the villain of the piece, the prison staff. The staffing of prisons is almost entirely neglected as an abolitionist issue, presumably because it is assumed that there is no point in attempting to 'improve' a system in need of abolition. But this neglects the process of abolition as a long-term transition, the very point these authors are at pains to emphasise in other respects. It is almost as if the present situation, in which the social system of the prison resembles some colonial outpost, with a District Commissioner, a missionary and a bunch of squaddies holding the natives at bay, is viewed as promoting abolition, since the contradictions of the system are overt and blatant. Crude as this picture obviously is in many respects, the theme that recurs in much of the critical literature is the correlation between the rise in political consciousness of inmates and staff alike. Indeed, a major irony is the denunciation by radicals of industrial action by prison staff, such as work-to-rules, which would be applauded in other industries — naturally, prisoners are the victims of such action. However, unless the prisoners are going to suffer even more as a result of growing militancy activating counter-militancy by staff (and we have Albany, Parkhurst etc. as well-documented instances), then rather greater investment in better trained, paid, even 'treatment-oriented' staff seems a possible implication of the abolitionist strategy.

Pitfalls

It may well be that a strategy evolved in Scandinavia has little hope of successful transplantation to the larger and more heterogeneous societies such as Britain and the U.S. Whilst in the latter there have been dramatic instances of prisoners organising collectively within particular jails, or networks of jails in the case of the U.S., the outcome of the struggles has tended to be tragic and explosive, lacking the steady growth of an abolitionist framework along the Norwegian and Swedish line. KROM claims a membership of almost one-third of the prisoners in Norway. The 1972 prison strikes in Sweden and Britain led Fitzgerald to note that 'the Swedish protests involved over 60 per cent of the prison population; PROP had had the support of less than 25 per cent' (Fitzgerald 1977, p. 158).

Major differences of relevance may be the very position of academics like Mathiesen in small, social-democratic societies, possessing a status not easily imaginable in Britain or the U.S. (The relative cohesiveness of the academic criminological community there, and its stature in the social sciences generally, should also be noted.) And if criminology looms smaller in Britain and the U.S. than in Scandinavia, crime looms arguably far larger, appears both more baleful and intractable a problem, and presents a correspondingly more difficult task for abolitionists. These arguments, however, do not undermine the abolitionist case. They strengthen it: for the larger the prison population relative to the population as a whole, the greater the number of prisoners serving lengthy sentences for relatively serious crimes, the greater the challenge for abolitionists. The pitfalls of abolitionist strategy seem to be of a different order to the sheer *scale* of the task they confront, and have to do with their analysis of that task, and the way they define it.

(i) The abolitionist strategy, by equating 'treatment' with covert control and oppression, and defining it as system-strengthening (by legitimising control measures as medically or therapeutically necessary etc.), may rule out too much. For example, the development of the special unit at Barlinnie Prison, arguably the most promising innovation post-war, comes at a time when 'treatment' and 'rehabilitation' are being written off as useful goals for the penal system. Yet the prisoners selected for Barlinnie were among the most violent in Scottish jails: the concept of a 'therapeutic community' was at the core of the thinking that made the creation of the special unit possible; and the initiative for its establishment came from within the Scottish prison service (see Johnston and MacLeod 1975). Eloquent testimony to the flexibility and willingness to experiment with democratic procedures within the unit has been provided by Jimmy Boyle (1977), himself sentenced to life imprisonment for murder, and scarred by having spent four of his six years in prison in solitary confinement. Subjected to a barrage of criticism for relaxing too many rules, the Unit has not only survived for six years, '. . . it evolves in unforeseeable ways, calling for changes in the behaviour and feelings of prisoners, in the regime of the wider prison service, and in the attitudes of the public at large' (Donnison 1978). The experience of growing trust between inmates and staff, the gradual extensions of freedom within the unit, led Boyle (1977) to describe it as a 'rebirth': 'This is the only place I know of that is offering any realistic hope for guys serving long sentences, or short ones for that matter' (pp. 247, 253). No professional psychiatric or psychological expertise was involved in this transformation, but the 'treatment' umbrella still provided the broad justification for the experiment. Boyle's principal fear is that the political pressures to warp the work of the unit will eventually succeed, and its character will be emasculated as a result, thus demoralising both staff and inmates, and providing grounds for closure. Would abolitionists help fight such pressures, or welcome them as system-weakening? To be placed in the position of opposing or ignoring such developments by virtue of a commitment to abolition seems an unacceptably high price to pay for resolving a dilemma.

(ii) The implication of a great deal of abolitionist writing is that prisons are functional for the survival of a class society, and cannot simply be argued out of existence by superior liberal rhetoric, or substantially reformed or run down by State action. It is difficult to square this analysis with the dramatic reduction in imprisonment in the Netherlands in particular, though a trend towards 'decarceration' more generally has been detected by Scull (1977). Admittedly, it does seem to be the case that rates of *entry* to prison in Holland have not diminished: but that is in the context of their daily population falling to as low as 3,280 in 1971, a rate of 25.4 per 100,000, compared with 37 in Norway, 62 in Sweden and 81 in England and Wales. The figure for the U.S.A. is far higher, 208, but that was in 1965, before the trends analysed by Scull accelerated (see Van Hofer 1975; Cohen 1972; Heijder 1975). The most encouraging inference to be drawn from the Dutch experience is that the decreasing resort to imprisonment, *via* reductions in the average length of sentence, in the 1950–72 period, seem not to be associated with any greater increase in crime rates than had occurred in other countries which did not pursue these policies. 'The increase in reported crime . . . was *lower* in Holland than in Sweden despite the fact that Swedish sentences are traditionally longer, and have experienced a slower rate of decrease in average length during the last twenty years' (Van Hofer 1975, p. 135). There are obviously immense problems involved in interpreting these official data, especially comparatively between societies. But the Dutch experience does seem a heartening one from the abolitionist point of view, if on terms which do not readily lend themselves to the analytical assumptions of the more radical abolitionists. For the prime movers in Holland have been the judiciary, partly facilitated by the powers given to the public prosecutors to waive prosecution (see Heijder 1975; Bishop 1974). In sum, there is a danger of abolitionist strategy ignoring the potential for substantial moves to be made towards abolition by means other than militant forms of praxis.

(iii) For Andrew Scull (1977) also writing from an avowedly 'radical' perspective, the trend in institutional policies towards the 'bad' and the 'mad' is towards decarceration, the converse of, for example, Fitzgerald's view, and at considerable odds with Mathiesen's. Scull discerns the watershed in penal policy as coming in the 1950s, with the capitalist economies facing increasing difficulties in *funding* institutional solutions to crime and mental illness. *Inter alia*, the costs of replacing the prisons and asylums built in the heyday of Victorian expansionism; the growing costs of unionised, labour-intensive staffing; and the escalation in rates of crime and mental illness, combined to push the State towards decarceration. However, the rationale was malign rather than benign: sheerly financial considerations outweighed all else, though the State was quick to latch onto labelling theory and 'community care' as legitimating ideologies. Scull's depiction of the results of decarceration resemble that culled from Norwegian newspapers after the ending of the vagrancy laws (which Mathiesen quotes disapprovingly): the streets and parks 'fill' with derelicts and deviants; deviant 'ghettoes' are created in the inner city to which the decarcerated gravitate, in part because the communities which are held to 'care' mobilise to expel them; the rate of mortality among the 'released' psychogeriatrics exceeds that of those left in hospitals. . . . Scull is scathingly critical of a major abolitionist 'victory', the closure — virtually overnight — of the juvenile reformatories in Massachusetts. The much-vaunted claims made on behalf of this and the related programmes in California are shown by Scull to be at best rhetorical and at worst designed to mislead. The tremendous financial gains (in the U.K., the cost of a prison place is 15 times as high as probation) are not offset against the 'hidden' costs to the community: the uneven and regressive cost of welfare etc. falling on families; the resort (in Massachusetts) to private agencies as dumping grounds for the worst cases; the ghettoisation of deviant populations as respectable communities squeeze them out.

There are many criticisms that can be made of Scull's markedly polemical critique. His case is far stronger for the mad than the bad. In Britain, he notes that imprisonment has *fallen* relative to the increase in indictable crime, but neglects the increasing length of sentences (and the fall is not that marked, a ratio of 25% to 18% of admissions to indictable offence convictions). Nor is his evidence for the malign effects of decarcerating the 'bad' nearly as strong as that for those of the 'mad' — a few excerpts from the *New York Times*. His *forte* is exposing the most overblown aspects of the abolitionists' case especially in the U.S. (Mathiesen's work and the cases of Norway and Holland are not embraced by his analysis). Neither Scull nor Mathiesen addresses himself to the immense variations in the use of imprisonment in capitalist societies, or to the often far more repressive system in nominally socialist states.

It may well be that the forms of decarceration attacked by Scull are quite different from the processes of abolition implied by Mathiesen. But there is little in the latter's work to suggest where those differences might lie. The one point of major agreement between the two is in their argument that modern capitalism is creating and coming to depend on a sizeable 'under-class' for whom it increasingly cannot afford decent welfare in conditions of burgeoning crisis. The burden of Scull's argument is that they are not necessarily helped by abolition, and their plight is conceivably made worse.

(iv) Martin Wright (1975) has noted that 'To demand abolition without proposing alternatives, as advocated by Mathiesen, may well be the best method in some cases; but the tactics he advocates, using the example of abolishing imprisonment for vagrants, would not necessarily apply to offenders who are perceived as presenting a greater risk to the public' (p. 93). The public tend to get short shrift in the abolitionist literature, largely because — one suspects — that reified 'spectre 'public opinion' is so relentlessly exploited by the authorities to veto practically any suggestion for reform that might make headlines of the 'Prisons getting too soft' or 'Residents say no to hostel plan' variety. This does not mean, however, that public reactions can simply be brushed aside. As Scull has made clear, community reactions to deviants are frequently hostile, and abolitionists neglect at certain of the latter's peril that neglected function of imprisonment, the protection of the offender.

(v) Mathiesen's work displays an overriding concern with the dangers of reforms strengthening the legitimacy of the system. Hence, part of the appeal of arguing for *rights* (particularly those of political and industrial bargaining), since this is seen as weakening the power of the system. However, it is not at all clear that the effects of granting rights *will* be to weaken the power of the State, or the system. Arguably, the granting of 'rights' is the ultimate legitimation of the system. If this is so, then a great deal of the energies that abolitionists would expend arguing the 'rights' versus 'improvements' issue could be better spent on pursuing reforms and long-term aims more straightforwardly.

(vi) In the end, Mathiesen's dilemma is the anarchist's dilemma: how far can an organisational framework based on negation be pushed before it adversely affects the structures which guarantee its abolitions? Stray references to the 'cultural revolution' in China and Albania hardly constitute an answer, as Mathiesen himself is obviously aware. The process of metamorphosis cannot be indefinitely prolonged. Either the 'unfinished' means little more than being pragmatic and flexible (which does not rule out resistance to incorporation, the pursuit of abolition, and the alliance with the 'expelled') or it implies working to bring about a society about which one is not allowed to theorise. Suppose one *had* an alternative: should one keep quiet about it? Mathiesen seems to invoke a species of guilt-by-association in his attitude towards alternatives. Because the system makes a great deal of the need to specify them as a delaying tactic, therefore they become a bad thing in themselves. Ultimately, the 'unfinished' can become the nebulous in a profoundly anti-democratic way, since alternatives are never formulated clearly enough for people to make rational choices between them.

Conclusion

In the intractable field of penal reform, the abolitionist strategy of Mathiesen has immense appeal (though ironically, if Scull is right, capitalism is working in the same direction). Its strengths are the refusal to be polarised into either short-term or long-term, reform versus revolutionary, stances; the commitment to abolition tempered by (some) humanitarian reforms; and the centrality of the alliance between inmates, ex-inmates and diverse outside agents. Its weaknesses lie in the obsession with system-strengthening, and remaining 'unfinished' to the point of ruling out 'alternatives', which obscure and even endanger these strengths.

NOTES

1. PROP stands for 'Preservation of the Rights of Prisoners'. PROP was officially launched in May 1972, and called a 'national prisoners' strike' on 4 August 1972. The events of that summer are chronicled in Fitzgerald (1977, ch. 5). Subsequently, PROP split into two locally-based splinter groups, in London and Hull.
2. RAP stands for 'Radical Alternatives to Prison'; it was formed in 1971 out of the remnants of the Prison Reform Council, with which many of those imprisoned during the 1960s anti-nuclear marches had been associated. RAP has been financially linked to Christian Action for most of its history, but is itself not a specifically Christian organisation. For the story of RAP see now Ryan (1978, ch. 5).
3. N.A.C.R.O. is the National Association for the Care and Resettlement of Offenders, formed in the 1960s. It is in receipt of substantial Home Office grants for various hostel and crime prevention projects, and, like the Howard League for Penal Reform (with whom it shares premises) it is generally regarded as a 'reformist' rather than 'radical' organisation, in contradistinction to RAP and PROP.

5

Penology and the crimes of the powerful

by TERENCE MORRIS

There is always a grave danger that in this life the Devil makes a very successful play for the best tunes. That the exposure of the crimes of the powerful should so often be heard as a Marxist folk melody is no exception; it is part of the compellingly attractive way in which the moral putrefaction of our contemporary capitalist society can be portrayed in the context of a social critique that can seem to upstage the moral censorship that was once exercised by Christianity. It is a critique advanced with considerable moral fervour such that it becomes tempting to draw parallels between the Puritanism of the seventeenth century that sought to overturn a modern Babylon and the dialectical materialism of the twentieth that seeks the creation of a new collectivist Jerusalem. There is in their thinking, a simplistic equation of riches with power and from there it is but a short step to the assertion that since the possession of riches is in itself immoral, since it can only have been achieved by exploitation, those who are rich must, imperatively, employ their power in the pursuit of immoral purposes. With a seemingly indefeasible logic there is a further step to be taken, namely that those who are rich and therefore powerful are incapable of virtue. Indeed, the very best that they can achieve is a sort of moral neutrality which naturally debars them from earning any kind of good conduct mark.

Judgement and Natural Law

Now it might be wondered why a chapter on this topic should begin with what appears to be an unequivocal attack upon the views of certain as yet unidentified Marxists, but the reason is quite simple. Some of the most trenchant critics of the moral order — or disorder —

of contemporary society are those whose ideological commitment precludes them from having any belief in a transcendental moral order and the achievement of some ultimate justice from which no wrong-doer can hope to escape; for them, any perfectibility in Man must be realised in this life, for this world and its social institutions constitute the only sanctions that can *ever* be applied to human misbehaviour. I raise this issue, since to me it is one of cardinal importance. The Christian position imposes several constraints upon those who adopt it. In the first place there is the fact that the moral order by which men are bound is not of Man's but of God's making. It permits of no latitude on fundamentals, or at least that is how it seems from any perusal of either the Commandments or the teaching of Jesus in the New Testament. Secondly it binds them to the knowledge that all men are capable of acting virtuously or viciously and to the belief that however narrow the range of choice may be, there are few situations indeed in which when presented with alternatives between one course of action and another men are incapable of making some independent judgement. It is the dimension which must separate Man from the rest of animal-kind. Thirdly, it presents them with the inescapable reality that all men must come to the Judgement, appearing before a Judge from whom nothing is hid. It is this *inescapable* quality of Judgement which, incidentally, makes it possible for the Christian to recognise that the shortcomings of human justice do not lead ultimately to disaster. As the psalmist puts it succinctly:

>Fret not yourself because of the wicked
> be not envious of wrongdoers
>For they will soon fade like the grass
> and wither like the green herb. (Psalm 37, vv. 1–2, R.S.V.)

None of this suggests, however, that the wicked are to be permitted to go their own way unhindered; indeed the need for the laws of Men to reflect the laws of God is an imperative that has been taken all too seriously at times, usually with the result that the latter have been gravely distorted when the State has seen an instrumental advantage in portraying itself as the guardian of true religion. It is interesting to observe that throughout the Old Testament there is a continuous thread of concern about the abuse of power for what are essentially immoral and exploitative purposes, especially the oppression and exploitation of the weak by the strong. Some of the examples that come to mind seem remarkably like some of the 'crimes of the powerful' that are the subject of contemporary concern. Take for example, the great cover-up following the affair between David and Bathsheba; it was not just his adultery with her that was so offensive but the fact that it was arranged that her husband Uriah should get sent into the front line to get killed.[1] David's position may have saved him from the full rigour of the sanction of the Mosaic law, but it did not save him from other consequences. Another instance is found in the story of Ahab and Naboth's vineyard (1 Kings, ch. 21). Originally Ahab had made Naboth a good offer for the property — even the Bronze Age equivalent of what the Department of the Environment would nowadays call an Exchange Land Certificate — but he would not budge. At which point there enters the story Queen Jezebel whose character seems to have been not unlike the wife of some dictator in a contemporary Third World state, determined not to let what she saw as Naboth's insubsordination go unpunished. The murder of Naboth — his liquidation in a manner all too familiar in the modern world — followed inevitably, as did the spoils of his vineyard. But so too did the promised fate of Ahab and his disagreeable spouse. It was C. S. Lewis in his book on the Psalms (Lewis 1961) who made the point that much of the justice in the Old Testament is less like what we understand as criminal justice and closer to our own concept of the civil suit. In other words, wrongs are done by men against each other, not infrequently strong men against weak ones, which demand a kind of compensatory resolution. Such resolution, in the form of damages or injunction, can be clearly distinguished from the idea of penalty in the context of criminal justice. It is noteworthy that the God of the Old Testament reminded his people that vengeance, i.e. retributive justice, was his and his alone. The relevance of this for contemporary penology is that there is a discernible trend towards compensation within the context of the criminal law matched by a movement, or at least pressures towards the 'de-criminalisation' of classes of actions that could be dealt with as if they were merely torts.

Between the sort of jurisprudence that was current among the peoples of the Near East several thousand years ago and that which finally shaped our own criminal and civil law there are so many distinctions that to list them would be tedious. Quite apart from what the Middle Ages picked up at second hand from Roman law (by way of the Canon law of the Church) and from the Anglo-Saxon, there are the effects of political and economic change to be taken into account. Nevertheless, there are certain constants to be observed. The first is the unchanging moral nature of Man himself. Parts of the story of David and Bathsheba are eternal. Queen Jezebel unceasingly grabs vineyards and organises election results to this day. The moral imperatives equally remain in that with the conferral of power there is the corresponding obligation to ensure that it is exercised justly; with the grant of possessions there is the duty of stewardship; that is to say no owner of property can rightly waste his substance if by so doing he deprives others yet to come of its benefits or others who could benefit from that which he had devalued.[2] No less a constant is the defectiveness of human justice and its constant debasement by those who administer it. (By this I have in mind the increasing tendency to treat law enforcement less in terms of the moral obligations of the citizen and more in terms of the instrumental concerns of the State for a 'tidy' administrative order.)

When we are talking of the crimes of the powerful we need to distinguish between actions which are *criminal* and those which, though immoral in the sense of being unacceptable, are not vested with that obloquy which attaches in varying degrees to crimes. When Edwin Sutherland (1949) produced his work on 'white-collar' crime he was accused of seeking to legislate for morality in the sense of seeking to bring within the ambit of the criminal law actions which could be dealt with by administrative tribunals. Now clearly, there are dangers here. Not the least stems from the naïveté of the belief that the criminal law can encompass every class of action that can be morally evaluated and indeed *ought* to do so. That belief tends to result in variants of the disease which afflicted the mind of Anthony Comstock (and still afflicts some contemporary moral entrepreneurs).

This is not of course to say that certain aspects of morality are not quite properly the subject of enforcement by the processes of the criminal law, but it is a case of some but not all. I say this because the categorical imperatives of a divine law are not necessarily incompatible with a degree of moral pluralism, or at least with a degree of tolerance about the shortcomings of particular individuals that, being nut-like, do not always require the application of a legal sledgehammer.

So far the term 'powerful' has been taken as having a given meaning, but before considering the kinds of crimes that the 'powerful' are given to committing it may be useful to consider just what is implied by the word. In the first place it must be distinguished from *authority*, although it is often confused with it. Power consists in the ability to do things, to impress the will, to overcome resistance, to compel. Authority may do any or all of these things, but with the additional component of legitimacy. The nature of that legitimacy, certainly within some forms of the modern state, is not always easy to identify. Some would argue that the authority of Parliament is sufficient if parliaments are elected by democratic means. This presupposes that there is a correspondence between majority and moral rectitude and that there is nothing above the law of parliamentary assemblies. It denies, by implication, the possibility of a Natural Law to which it is itself subject. Sir Ernest Barker (1948) described the Natural Justice which stems from it as:

> . . . a justice which human authority expresses, or ought to express, but does not make. . . . This justice is conceived as

being the higher or ultimate law, proceeding from the
nature of the universe — from the Being of God and the
Reason of Man. It follows that law, in the sense of the law of
last resort — is somehow above lawmaking. It follows that
lawmakers, after all, are somehow under and subject to
law. (312–13)

It will be objected that the idea of a law *de rerum natura* looks
remarkably like the product of faith rather than reason, but it is
possible to show that things are otherwise. Human reason has
endowed mankind with a rather special sense of propriety and
fairness; deep in the consciousness of every child resides the complaint
'It just isn't *fair*'. But more than that, there are certain actions that
produce a sense of moral outrage. Witness the death camps of Nazi
Germany, yet the power by which the atavistic propensities of
National Socialism was translated from the streets to the bureacrati-
cally managed institutions of extermination was vested in Hitler and
his followers by the German electorate. The concepts of 'war crimes'
and 'human rights' *must* derive from a notion of Natural Law;
otherwise the War Crimes trials at Nuremberg were not trials but
merely the puppet show mounted by the victorious allies. The civil
laws of states then, are not merely subject to Natural Law, but ought
to reflect its verities. Otherwise one is left with the possibility that
totalitarian states, claiming that they have 'power from the people',
will employ their packed assemblies to legislate as they please, quite
apart from the fact that in democratic states the propriety of electoral
procedures guarantees neither wisdom nor virtue to the government
which emerges from the process. Whether we like it or not, the
Thomist maxim *lex injusta non est lex* is present to encourage — or
discomfort — us.

Power, then, may be exercised with or without authority.
Without any sanction it is no more than force; with it, it must stand up
to the test of being justly exercised. A good deal of power is exercised
in society which has some minimal sanction, for example the power
conferred upon the stronger participant in a market deal. A great deal
more power is exercised by those who do so in the context of
authority and it is now one of the distinctive features of the
bureaucratic state that there should be an inverse relationship between
the power of the bureaucratic official and his overall social status.
Bureaucracy enables small men to flex the large muscles of the State
and thus enjoy power vicariously.[3] But even the power that is
exercised *with authority* is still subject to the test of its acceptability
under Natural Law. Thus when we are considering the 'crimes of the
powerful' we need to consider the potential crimes not only of the
servants of the State, but of the State itself.

Immunity and Differential Penalties

There are other aspects of power which are of importance here. One is clearly related to access to immunity from the sanctions of the law. The great King David, even before he had arranged the death of Uriah, had earned the penalty of death under the Levitical code for his adultery with Bathsheba. The fact that he was the king meant that there was no temporal authority to enforce the law against him and it was left to the prophet Nathan to inform him of the Divine judgement that had been handed down in his case. Perhaps that is an extreme example. The chances of a person in a powerful position being nowadays able to escape all the rigours of the law for a serious offence are slim, though not entirely absent. The example that comes most readily to mind is that of Richard Nixon whose duplicity in the Watergate affair is an already established part of history. But what is interesting is not so much Nixon's attempts to get himself off the hook but the executive act of clemency on the part of the then President, Gerald Ford, which finally did so. Ford's general absolution was for all offences the ex-President *might* have committed since he had never been brought to trial. Whether this was to protect Nixon himself or to protect the institution of the Presidency, or simply to spare the Republican party from further anguish we shall never know. But within the act of executive clemency there is a fascinating element; the idea that the ex-President's *condition* was in part a justification for his advance gaol-delivery. Bathsheba, it will be recalled sent to David and told him she was with child — and therefore entitled to a reprieve from the death penalty. Nixon's reprieve from the witness stand — and possibly gaol — on the grounds of his mental health is not unlike the pleading of the 'great belly' by women in the days of capital punishment. But it is even more like the plea of benefit of clergy available to the privileged clerks who, when asked if they had anything to say before sentence was passed would then recite what became known as the 'neck verse', the *Miserere mei Deus* of Psalm 51 (see Knowles 1970).

The question of immunity from liability to suffer certain kinds of sentence is historically linked with the question of immunity from prosecution in the civil (as distinct from the ecclesiastical) courts. It was the issue of where the 'criminous clerks' should be tried that became the focal point of the conflict between Thomas of Canterbury and Henry II (Knowles 1970). That Henry lost that round proved eventually to be to the disadvantage of the Church, but only by the time Henry VIII had established himself as head of both Church and State. And then, as a curious offshoot of this Erastianism, the Crown itself became immune from civil suit until the legislation of the Attlee government of 1945–50 removed the anomaly that had made it impossible to sue the Crown if one had been run down by a Post Office van or an army lorry.

There are relatively few situations of immunity like that enjoyed by Richard Nixon and effectively none where there is a form of statutory immunity from prosecution. But in the prosecution process the exercise of executive discretion can still work to the advantage of persons in powerful or privileged positions. There was an instance when Princess Anne was stopped by the Thames Valley police for speeding for the second time in a matter of days; in the normal course of events if a driver had been warned for speeding and was then stopped by police from the same constabulary within a day or so a prosecution would have followed. In this instance none did, and I had the chance to discuss the affair with a Chief Constable in another part of the country in the informality of a social occasion. He observed with a certain practical wisdom 'No police officer in his sane mind would touch a Royal'. Yet on balance there is not much evidence that those in positions of power are protected from prosecution except perhaps for instances of motoring offences not regarded as serious, and even with the 'Royals' things seem to be changing now that Captain Phillips is in jeopardy of losing his licence under the 'totting up' provisions of the Road Traffic Act. And as for those in positions of influence it is notable that not only J.P.'s but more than one High Court judge has been convicted of driving with excess alcohol.

It is still however possible to observe the vestigial remains of differential liability to suffer particular kinds of sentence. In the Middle Ages, and indeed up until the execution of Simon Lord Lovat after the failure of the '45 by means of decapitation, those of high social status, and in particular the hereditary nobility were spared the indignities of a common hanging. Partly because of the comparative barbarity of hanging in the days long before the ingenious Victorian Calcraft had devised his 'drop' and elaborate table of weights and rope lengths, and partly because the sword — of which the axe is a variant — was a symbol of military rank, the status distinction between estates was maintained. It was not, incidentally, any guarantee of celerity since the executioner was often as drunk as the hangman. A last touching gesture of Henry VIII towards his disgraced Queen Anne Boleyn was the promise of a 'swift swordsman brought over from France'.[4] The growth of a system of social classes and the decline of the system of estates had important effects upon the notion of rank, not least in the direction of establishing greater equalities under the law. After the abolition of decapitation as a form of 'noble' execution there followed the ending of the right of the aristocracy to be tried by its peers in the House of Lords. By late Victorian times equality, in the sense of equal liability to suffer particular punishments irrespective of the offender's social status, was well established, Differential *prosecution* naturally resulted in a paucity of high status inmates within the prison system or as candidates for the gallows, but when they did turn up, they took their place along with the poor and down-trodden. It is in fact due to the capacity of some of these high status offenders to write that we have not a few inmate accounts of Victorian convict prisons, such as *Eighteen Months Imprisonment (With a Remission)* by D.-S.[5] Reading Gaol, one of the admired establishments of Sir Edmund du Cane, housed Oscar Wilde, and as far as we know, no significant concessions were made to him on account of his social standing. Similarly one may observe how the staff of womens' prisons during the era of the Suffragettes had the greatest difficulty in dealing with ladies of 'quality' when they were only accustomed to dealing with thieves and whores of the lowest class.

The reform of the prison system, and indeed of sentencing, practicing has changed much of that. Nowadays one can imagine an Oscar Wilde — assuming he could still be convicted — as being encouraged to write the Christmas play by some eager young assistant governor who would paradoxically bemoan the fact that poor Wilde's offence made it impossible for his security classification to be modified so that he could do his time — before his early parole — at Ford or Leyhill. In the days of Jebb and du Cane the mighty when they had fallen fell all the way to find themselves alongside those who were so low in the social hierarchy that they were the companions of men whom they would not even have employed as servants. Offenders of high social status, providing their offences do not disqualify them, are now almost certain to find themselves in open prisons since they are most likely to have committed property offences of a 'white-collar' nature like solicitors and bank staff. Police officers have a tendency to gravitate towards open prisons, and in recent years the staff of open establishments, ever anxious about the fewness of suitable candidates for inward transfer, have looked with some satisfaction upon the various trials of municipal corruption as sources of supply. Because many of these high status offenders have skills of an administrative nature that can be utilised by the prison they are to be found, even if they have not made the verdant comforts of the open establishments, organising prison libraries, Wing accounts, taking tea to the Governor and other like activities. To be doing almost anything, in fact, other than the sorts of menial tasks like scrubbing floors for which there seem always to be numerous alternative candidates.

But imprisonment and its precise nature apart, there is also a discernible reluctance on the part of some courts to use imprisonment as a sanction against offenders of high status. In the matter of length the white-collar offence may not seem to justify a sentence of the gravity which an offence of a more violent nature may attract. One may compare the sentences in two crimes that occurred at about the same time in the mid-1960s, namely the Great Train Robbery and the State Building Society fraud. In the former, violence had been used against the driver of the train, though not fatally. In the Train Robbery the longest sentence was just over four times as long as the longest in the Building Society fraud and the shortest was three times as long. Yet in terms of the sums involved the Train Robbery netted only some £2m compared with the £3m involved in the fraud.

Alternatively, the courts may decide that a sentence of immediate imprisonment is not appropriate and impose one which is suspended. Now a suspended sentence, whatever obloquy may attach to the recipient, is only a threat, not a reality; a whiff of chamber pot and Old Holborn rather than the evil smelling reality. In that the majority of high status offenders have committed offences in very specific contexts rather than at random, the chances of their reoffending within the operational period are not great with the result that the chances of the sentence ever being put into effect are remote indeed. Unlike a probation order, the suspended sentence imposes no constraints upon the offender at all, save that he should be careful not to be reconvicted during the operational period. He has literally been 'let off' and his peers may not be slow to draw conclusions from that as to the imputed nature of his offending. But even more important for our discussion is the use of the fine. Now it would not matter so much if the fine were always related to the offender's ability to pay, but this is not always the case since it is only at the *lower* end of the scale that the courts make any significant effort to take means into account. At the upper end, often in motoring offences, the defendant may not even be in court in person and the tariff system works to his advantage. Some years ago the Magistrates' Association devised a formula for speeding fines where:

$$\text{Fine} = \pounds x + y(\pounds 1)$$

where $\pounds x$ is the amount fixed for exceeding the statutory limit and y equal the number of miles per hour that the driver was travelling in excess of it.

The fines imposed upon Captain Phillips for his last two speeding offences have been £30 and £15. Fines of this magnitude imposed on a person in his financial position can only be regarded as derisory. Certainly they bear no relation to the tariff. The difficulty is that unless there is some system like that of the Swedish 'day-fine' related to income, a large fine may look ludicrous if the offence is comparatively trivial. But there is not the least doubt but that in terms of marginal cost the rich motoring offender does significantly better than his poor counterpart. To quote an instance from life; two offenders are charged with having failed to accord precedence on a pedestrian crossing. The first, a gas-fitter riding a moped, was fined £15. The second, a company director driving a Lotus Elan, was fined £25.

There are other ways in which the privileged may enjoy advantages that they may not deserve. The first of these, perhaps the least important, is the way in which through insurance of a special kind potential offenders may take precautions to mitigate the consequences of conviction. For fairly small sums it is possible to insure against the loss of a driving licence as a result of disqualification. It is arguable that this is little different in principle from the disqualified driver buying his wife a car and paying her as a chauffeuse — except that it may be cheaper. But in that it gives an advantage to the driver who can afford the premium by which the penalty of the court can be mitigated it is equally arguable that the insurance may be a contract contrary to public policy. It is comparable in this sense to the wealthy prisoner being able to have his own food sent into prison rather than having to endure the common fare. The second way is rather more important and that is by means of the Rehabilitation of Offenders Act 1974. The intention of that Act was to prevent the stigma of a conviction hanging like a stinking albatross around the necks of offenders who had paid their debt to society long after they had gone straight. Undoubtedly some offenders have benefited, but on the bandwaggon so to speak have ridden a number of those who have little if any desert in this direction. If, for example, a combination of successful plea bargaining and lenient sentencing has resulted in a white-collar criminal — who may have committed a very serious fraud — receiving a fine or a short or suspended prison sentence then he too, after the minimum statutory period which may be as short as five years may claim the benefits of this generous legislation. The legislation provides, moreover, that he may sue for libel anyone foolish enough to proclaim publicly the fact that he had once been convicted of crime! The workings of the Rehabilitation of Offenders Act is a topic worthy of serious research, if only to discover whether those for whom it was intended are proving to be the principal beneficiaries.

Stigma, strict liability and State Power

We are not, on the whole, unduly troubled by crimes on the part of the powerful that prey upon the lives or liberties of ordinary citizens which cannot be controlled; such things as *droit de seigneur* belong to the past as do the antics of petulant absolute monarchs. What we do have to contend with are the legal infractions of offenders, some private individuals but many corporate bodies, whose failure to observe the law results in consequences for the ordinary citizen that are sometimes very serious indeed. Yet the penalties prescribed as maxima, let alone those actually imposed, may offer little discouragement to the persistence of the offence. Sutherland (1949) in his work on the crime of corporations pointed out that a large proportion of them were in fact recidivists; the position seems not to have changed significantly in the last 30 years, nor does the experience of this country differ to any great degree from that of the United States, save that in this country these are almost entirely matters within the criminal jurisdiction of the magistrates' courts.

A good deal of the problem is undoubtedly related to the growth of strict liability which in turn has been followed by a reduction in the stigma imputed to the offence. It is almost as if the abandonment of *mens rea* has automatically reduced the opprobrium attaching to the offence and reduced it in reality to something approaching the status of a tortious act. Take for example the question of large-scale pollution as the result of the illegal act or omission of a large corporation and its agents. One cannot imprison corporations, but they can be fined. Yet the maxima available and the fines imposed in such cases bear no credible relationship to the amount of harm done. But, runs the counter argument, the matter was one of strict liability; the question of intent (and therefore moral culpability) does not arise. It all begins to look like a matter of tortious negligence, and if there is 'big' money to be paid out it must be in the form of damages.

There is a wide area of action which is highly relevant to the maintenance of the public good which is sanctioned by regulatory legislation of this kind and from what we know from studies of, for example, the Factory Acts, the inspectors are greater believers in persuasion than they are in coercion by prosecution (Carson 1970). Equally, there are some business enterprises like those of demolition contractors, private hauliers, coach operators and taxi firms whose economic marginality encourages them to cut corners all the time. Yet the detection of unsafe loads, worn brakes, defective tyres, dirty diesel injectors making black smoke or drivers working excessive hours is remarkably low and the penalties imposed when conviction does occur do not significantly erode the profit that derives marginally from the deliberate infringement of the law.

Another class of crime that may go very largely unpunished is in the area of the relationship between landlord and tenant. There is no certain way of knowing just how many cases of harassment still occur since the worst days of 'Rachmanism' in which unscrupulous landlords intimidated their tenants by the most violent means. But although there are probably more people now prepared to seek relief in the courts from such duress, there is still the likelihood that there are others who, fearing to lose what shelter they have, are not prepared to take the risk of losing it by making complaints about their treatment or the rack level of their rents. Again, the courts have for the most part employed the fine rather than imprisonment, yet, as with the business operation that involves continuous lawbreaking, the law is a toothless guardian of the citizen if fines do not wipe out the profits of illegal operation.

Just as the growth of strict liability has resulted in the protection of certain offenders from stigma, and the use of the fine from suffering any credible deterrent penalty, so there have been other innovations that have specifically legislated away the rights of the citizen to have recourse to law in seeking relief from his grievances. One of the curses of modern civilisation is aircraft noise, but it is extremely difficult to bring sanctions to bear upon the companies which operate them. One way of doing so in the past would have been for the freeholder over whose property the offending aircraft flew to sue for trespass, since his property extended to the air above. But not since the Civil Aviation Act of 1949 by which this source of relief was statutorily extinguished. It is arguable that if airline companies could be sued for trespass they might have been encouraged to press the manufacturers to develop quieter aeroplanes. It may be argued too that for the inhabitants of the area around Heathrow to suffer the deafening noise of large aircraft landing and taking off is not the same as their being victims of the crimes of the powerful. Strictly speaking, that must be so, just as it is equally true that they do not suffer the trespasses of the powerful, since the act of 1949 changed the legal position. But in practical terms they suffer. As a multitude they suffer in order that a comparative few may be propelled at great speeds from one part of the world to another, and in doing so they may reflect on the way in which a government (which at the time enjoyed a parliamentary majority of 196) increased the power of corporate enterprises at the expense of the increased weakness of the individual citizen. Mention was made early on in this chapter to Exchange Land Certificates issued by the Department of the Environment. They are part of the way in which governments are now able to do through the medium of executive action the sort of thing that Queen Jezebel needed to resort to homicide to achieve. I refer to the acquisition of land by means of compulsory purchase. In recent years the State, many of its agents believing implicitly in their own monopoly of wisdom and virtue, have sought to reorganise the landscape by schemes of urban 'development' and the construction of motorways, both within and between urban areas. The State begins with the principle that what is proposed is not merely desirable but *vitally necessary* and the project cannot be challenged on that score.

Then land must be acquired. Some landowners are naturally loth to yield up what is theirs, not least for purposes which may be aesthetically abhorrent to them, but like Naboth, they find that if they are obdurate and do not negotiate, even if 'exchange land' is offered to them it will simply be taken away. True, there will be a payment, but what is payment for a treasure with which the owner does not want to part in the first place? Put this kind of proposition to an official of one of the Department's Road Construction Units and he will look at first mystified and then offended as he perceives you classify him along with the coveters of vineyards and the enclosers of common land. Yet it is not an unfair question to ask whether the State, in acquiring land for its own use by means of compulsory purchase (other than in time of war or grave national emergency) is behaving in a fashion that is significantly different in a moral sense from the behaviour of those great squires and landowners (who were usually the local magistrates) who abused their superior social and political position to acquire common land and deprive others of its use. After all, Ahab did offer money besides an Exchange Land Certificate.

Part of the mystified reaction to this sort of analysis on the part of those who have become accustomed over the last 25 years to employing statutory powers in the course of large governmental and corporate enterprises derives from their acceptance of the idea that the only kind of law that is worth talking about is the law that is made in Parliament. The idea that parliaments can make laws that are so offensive to the Natural Law that they are no laws at all may not enter their heads. The suggestion that laws made by men that would enable a modern Ahab to acquire Naboth's vineyard not for a vegetable garden but for part of a six-lane motorway (without even being able to challenge the idea that one was even needed) were morally repugnant, could produce a state of incredulity.

Clearly a great deal must depend upon the boundaries of what may be said properly to constitute crime, but in this instance we are concerned with circumstances in which the State removes the rights of ordinary citizens to seek redress that they might otherwise be able to obtain by the processes of civil suit. And from the Christian point of view the notion of wrong must extend further than the narrow limits of crime. The use of the term 'trespasses' — confusing for many generations of children and probably many of their elders — employs in the language of the early seventeenth century a concept that neatly embraces the idea of wrongs done that deserve to be righted. It is consistent with the idea noted earlier that much of the 'justice' referred to in Scripture relates to civil actions rather than criminal prosecutions. And of course every crime has within it the potential of a civil wrong, save perhaps for those offences which may be termed 'crimes without victims'. The modern burglar is charged that 'having entered as a trespasser . . .'.

Simply because the State has concluded that a particular class of action is no longer a wrong if it is done by the State itself, it does not follow that the relatively weak do not suffer from the exercise of power on the part of the agents of the State. Equally, the disadvantage stemming from the actions of large corporations whose illegal acts attract penalties so infinitesimal that they cannot act as a credible deterrent is no less. What is equally important is that in terms of the contribution to the discomforts and miseries of human life the kinds of actions that are nationally controlled by administrative regulations rather than the criminal law may be quantitatively more significant than that of 'traditional' crime. The misery occasioned by the fact that more people die as the result of dangerous, careless and drunken driving than as a result of wilful murder is not lessened by de-stigmatising motoring crime and talking about 'accidents' when there had been instances of wilful and deliberate law-breaking. Moreover, the specificity of many types of criminal offence enables the citizen to take sensible precautions against crime. I can lock up my house against the burglar but there are few if any precautions that I can take against getting food poisoning from a dirty restaurant kitchen. Curiously enough I can get a local authority to enforce the law against itself for having a dirty public lavatory but I cannot invoke the Public Health Act of 1936 against British Rail for failing to do anything about their insanitary conveniences since railway premises are specifically exempted from its provisions!

Yet strangely enough there is at the present time a movement towards further de-criminalisation which would convert many existing criminal offences, most of them subject to strict liability, into contraventions that would be reduced to the status of torts. Whether or not this would be a more effective way of dealing with dirty hotel kitchens, tanker pollution in estuaries, the sale of milk with concrete, drawing pins or cigarette butts in the bottle, short weight in shops, contravention of building and factory legislation and much else besides is not known, but I doubt the possibility unless the consequences of the infraction outweighed the gains of it. To the degree to which an action is divested of its moral character, and in an important sense that character is attested by the gravity of the sanction imposed, it will cease to be controlled by the exercise of conscience and move closer towards a situation in which the potential transgressor in true utilitarian fashion constructs an indifference curve of pains and pleasures relative to the gains and losses of his intended actions. The last thing he will do is ask himself if what he is doing is wrong and whether on that account alone he ought to desist from it. It may be precisely because motoring offences — which some years ago the Law Society argued ought to be dealt with elsewhere than in the criminal courts proper — have been reduced to this position by a combination of legislation, sentencing policy and public opinion that the dangerous or homicidal driver does not consider himself a criminal at all. Parliament in its wisdom has set a maximum of five years imprisonment on the very worst he can do. The comparative lenity of sentences passed by the courts can only encourage the view that these are not serious crimes of violence.

At the outset of this chapter it was suggested that the burden of the Marxist comment upon the crimes of the powerful is in essence contained in the proposition that since power derives from wealth and wealth can only be had by resort to exploitation, power and wealth are totally corrupting. The slogan 'What is the crime of robbing a bank compared with the crime of owning one' really tells us more about the views of those who use it in their emotional responses to the discovery that the distribution of this world's good is unequal than about the morality of ownership as such. But there is also implicit in many so-called 'radical' critiques the notion of a vast and highly complex conspiracy that is prepared to stoop as low as need be to secure the interests of a vast and sometimes shadowy Establishment. The work of Sutherland (1949) on white-collar crime and the crime of corporations and that of those who have followed it up do not satisfy many of these radical critics who dismiss such work as 'exposé' criminology. Yet the evidence from many of the trials of major business frauds and illegal practices by large companies suggests that the offences result from the decisions of particular individuals deliberately to break laws; to be motivated by the same characteristics of greed and duplicity that have marked the character of dishonest men down the centuries. There is a danger in reification, too, in talking about corporate enterprises as if in some wild Durkheimian nightmare a personality had been breathed into their legal framework. Not, of course, that the examples of collectivist societies as we may presently observe them hold out much hope that the corporate fiction of the 'People' will result in a greater degree of moral rectitude in society. If a capitalist society can be criticised for the way in which it permits wealth to be unevenly distributed many socialist societies stand no less firmly indicted for the way in which power is vested in the hands of those who serve the State. To be unfree is to be poor in another sense. Nor do such societies, for all that political education and draconian penalties, combine to make the citizen aware of the sanctity of the property of the State, do much to prevent currency speculation, black marketeering or the theft of State property. One is left with the inescapable conclusion that the moral nature of Man changes not at all, certainly not as a result of his subjection to particular ideologies.

Problems of Policy and Practice

There are practical problems for our own society. Not least among them is the fact that the crimes of the powerful — the dishonesty of the privileged, the contemptuous disregard of laws made for the common good and the corruption of political life through bribery — are *as* important as, and in the long run may be *more* important than, the dreary calendar of crimes committed by working class youths from dreary housing estates or even the spectacular robberies committed by the more competent of our professional criminals. The names of Poulson and Dan Smith are well known; corruption in the North-East which has been legendary to those familiar with its political backwaters. But how many members of the general public know the name of Ernest John Westwood, former Chairman of the Glamorgan County Council Planning Committee, and sentenced to four and a half years; that he is but one of the twelve among the 30 convicted who have been sent to prison following the 20 corruption trials that have taken place in South Wales during the last two years?[6]

The trials post-Poulson went on for some considerable time until a point was reached when, certainly in the view of the Attorney General, there had to be a stop somewhere. But does there have to be a stop? Would the same be true if the police were to have uncovered a network of people concerned to bring in illegal immigrants? Is there any reason to think that the detective drug squad in Operation Julie were content to rest until they concluded that everyone involved had been identified? One might be tempted to think that the result of terminating corruption trials would be to lower the level of political embarrassment. After all a not inconsiderable number of people have suffered it, and it is noticeable that those who have never had anything criminal alleged against them are not always slow to protect their reputations by invoking the laws of libel. Not that it is anything other than their right to do so as individuals; what may be objected to is the way in which the Attorney General has determined a particular view of public policy. In that this kind of corruption, especially as it affects such things as planning decisions and local authority building contracts, is most likely to occur in situations governed by arbitrary bureaucratic rules it is the sort of crime on the part of the powerful that represents a very serious threat to the institutions of government. People do not lose confidence in banks because there are a few bank clerks who dip their hands into the till, nor do they, by and large, lose confidence in the legal profession simply because a few solicitors mismanage clients' money. But the blow the institutions of local government have suffered in public eyes is grievous indeed. Many people simply will not believe that there are not now vast numbers of people in local government, both elected and professional, who are 'on the make'. It is a belief, however unjustly founded, that is encouraged by the sight of conspicuous municipal consumption in the form of large new town halls, multi-storey car parks for the use of council officials, increased expense allowances for councillors and so on.

What prescription might be had to cure this particular malady? The first step must surely be for the nature of the offence to be portrayed in its proper perspective. With power and authority must go stewardship, and in this sense stewardship must include incorruptibility, since those who are set in authority are placed in positions of trust. Every instance of curruption is a betrayal of trust in one who has set himself up as being one who could be trusted by offering himself for election or as a candidate for the Public Service. It is not directly comparable with ordinary cases of trust violation since these are generally committed by employees of fairly lowly rank. The kind of thing we are considering here involves those who have the power to commit large sums from the public purse to others purses but paradoxically, the sums involved may be less relevant than the damage that is done to the image of probity within the institution. In a real sense these offenders are the polluters of the body politic. Only when the prosecution process is maximised to the full, when no more corrupt councillors, chief officers, civil servants and architects and contractors are spared than members of drug rings will the public take the view that perhaps these things are serious after all.

A second step applies not merely to the kinds of offender involved in corruption at the municipal or quasi-governmental level, but to all high status offenders. It is to go some way to redressing the balance of advantage that they enjoy at almost every stage of the criminal justice process. It begins, in many instances, with the presumption that because the offender is a person of social standing then his fall from grace must somehow be temporary, or at least an aberration. Thus: 'It is a tragedy to see a man in your position standing where you do now'. Note that the same magisterial comment would be less likely were the offender to be a young man who had been unemployed for some time. Not so much: 'It is a tragedy to see a young man on the threshold of life wasting his time and losing his good name' but more probably: 'You have been dependent on the State for months now, why haven't you got yourself a job?' But the presumption of basic virtue may have little foundation. People in positions of status do not imbibe virtue at the breast; as creatures of Original Sin they are prey to the same vices as anyone else. To the extent that they are given to greed, to deceit and to abusing their talents they are not likely to be any better than anyone else. Another presumption is that they have a reputation in jeopardy. But there is no reason to think that, if their friends and colleagues take the view that they have been not so much wicked as unlucky, they are likely to suffer any particular loss. This is certainly the case with many business frauds. Montgomery Hyde recounts the story of the rehabilitation of Lord Kylsant nearly 50 years ago. He had been sentenced to 18 months imprisonment for his part in an offence in connection with the accounts of a great shipping company. Not only did his friends refuse to treat him as a criminal but on his return from prison his estate workers pulled his Rolls with ropes up to his front door.

The correction that needs to be applied to offset these imputations and assumptions must originate in judicial education. Unless and until this is done there will always be the possibility of complaints about class bias in the administration of justice and as Professor Griffith has shown there is evidence, if not of bias, then of some ignorance among the judges as to the realities of the world beneath them (Griffith 1977). Unfortunately the problem is complicated by the need to emphasise the gravity of many of the offences involved by the nature of the consequences that must follow on conviction. As Lord Denning put it in his evidence to the Royal Commission on Capital Punishment (1953) almost 30 years ago:

> The punishment inflicted for grave crimes should
> adequately reflect the revulsion felt by the great majority of
> citizens for them . . . (para. 53, p. 18)

Now it does not automatically follow that the great majority of citizens *do* feel a revulsion at the offences of the rich and powerful when they abuse public trust or seem to come off better than ordinary folk as a consequence of certain social assumptions made about their character. But they may. And they are not encouraged to think of them as serious crimes when the social consequences of conviction do not seem unduly harsh. Nor does it do much to produce a feeling in the public mind that the Civil Service takes a very serious view of the matter when after his conviction and sentence in the Poulson affair Mr. Pottinger had half his pension restored to him, notwithstanding that he had been a very handsomely paid man (by the standards of the average citizen), who had still succumbed to the temptation to be greedy. The restoration of pension rights would not matter so much were it not in such stark contrast to the experience of postmen and police officers who are not normally so fortunate. And the pensions of which we are talking, incidentally, are greater than most people's *earnings!*[7]

Not unconnected with the ways in which such things as the restoration of pension rights implicitly suggest that the offence is not so great a violation of trust that it should justify the withdrawal of the rewards that are presumably made in part as a mark of commendation for faithful public service is the preservation of the offender from any permanent public obloquy. It is doubtful whether the Rehabilitation of Offenders Act was ever intended to give further benefit to those who already benefit — often beyond the limits of their desert — as a result of certain assumptions about their moral and social character. It should be possible to amend the Act in such a way that the nature of the offence becomes more extensive as a determinant in deciding who should benefit.

But it is the rehabilitative model of sentencing that produces the greatest difficulties. The kinds of people who are involved in these offences are almost self-rehabilitative should they receive prison sentences. The Civil Service, or the Minister concerned, may be kindly disposed to look after any pension problems. Steadfastly refusing to accept the criminal label, they behave as if what they had done was to have made a mistake, and in this context remorse may sometimes be presented as contrition. But the rehabilitation of such people is a nonsense. What new skills do they need to acquire in the hope of keeping them from further crime? They can scarcely be said to be the kinds of inmate who would benefit from educational classes. They have homes and families to go to, and people ready to give them something to do. Most important of all, they are very unlikely ever to offend again. The rehabilitative ideal is already met, with the result that parole is a foregone conclusion.

As far as custodial sentences are concerned what needs to be considered is the notion of a purely punitive sentence. In fact most sentences *are* punitive, but in this case there is a need for the fact to be explicit. The sentence I have in mind would need to be served in conditions that were rigorous without being unreasonably oppressive, in closed conditions in order that the articulate white-collar inmate would have the fewest chances of manipulating his penal environment to his advantage. The sentence would carry the normal amount of remission, contingent on good conduct, but would not be subject to parole since most of the critical parole variables would be known to the court passing sentence and could be incorporated within it. For both custodial sentences of this kind, and for non–custodial sentences it should be possible for the court to impose certain social disabilities. It is already possible to do this with regard to some offences committed by members of local authorities, and of course in relation to undischarged bankrupts. The kind of things that are possible would include disfranchisement from standing for office or voting at elections, prohibitions on the obtaining of credit, disqualification from following certain occupations, and so forth. The object of the exercise would be two-fold: to express the disapproval of society for the offence in question and to ensure that the sanctions had teeth.

The greater use of civil disabilities of the kind just mentioned would seem to have not inconsiderable advantages over imprisonment which is a blunt instrument at the best of times and ought to be reserved for the most serious offenders. As sanctions they have the merit of expressing the offender's *unworthiness* to enjoy the full benefits of citizenship, besides being rather cheaper than imprisonment which is so often an expensive way of indulging in the luxury of moral outrage.

The device which comes most readily to mind, however, is of course the fine. It is possible in certain cases for fines of a very high order of magnitude to be imposed, but this is, generally speaking, fairly rare. Where such fines are imposed it would be a sensible arrangement if the court were to be able to conduct some form of in-depth statutory inquiry into the offender's means that would be a sensible arrangement if the court were to be able to conduct some form of in-depth statutory inquiry into the offender's means that would include a detailed analysis of his assets. There is already provision for the institution of criminal bankruptcy which could well be modified for this purpose.

In most cases fines will be imposed in respect of offences of a much less serious nature, for example on firms failing to accord with various health and safety regulations, consumer protection legislation, building regulations, and so forth. The matter will often be complicated by the corporate identity of the defendant. There are powers to prevent the continuation of certain activities in case of persistent default, but none, to my knowledge, that would require, for example, that the activities ceased in whole or in part as a constituent of the penalty. Take an instance of a firm operating coaches that has been several times before the courts in various parts of the country and has been convicted of using, for carrying passengers, vehicles that are dangerously defective through lack of maintenance. A fine in the magistrates' court would be limited, but there is in my view merit in the idea of the court being able to make an order 'grounding' every one of the company's vehicles for say one month, and then only permitting them to be used for public service when they had satisfied a duly appointed vehicle inspector as being in good order.

The subject cannot be left without reference to the motoring offender. Leaving aside the question of dangerous and homicidal drivers who would be candidates for the explicity punitive prison sentence, there remain those who persistently offend but for whom the fine is either no deterrent since the offender hopes to get away with his next offence undetected, or derisory since the kind of fine which would bite would need to be so large that it would be disproportionate to the nature of the offence. The solution I would propose would consist in an extension of the provisions for the forfeiture of goods that already exist in relation to customs offences; a vehicle or vessel that has been used to smuggle uncustomed goods may in certain cir- cumstances become forfeit to the Crown. In the case of certain persistent motoring offenders it should be possible as an additional sanction to disqualification to impound the vehicle used in the commission of the offence should the circumstances justify it. Equally, just as it is possible for a magistrates' court to make an order requiring the destruction of a dangerous or vicious dog, so too it should be possible for an order to be made requiring the immediate destruction of a vehicle that was either inherently dangerous in itself, or had been used dangerously. The spectacle of expensive motor cars being yielded up the municipal crusher before the eyes of their rich and sorrowing owners is perhaps a long way off, but in days gone by children who persistently made a nuisance of themselves with their toys sometimes had to endure seeing them taken away. More important than the private motorist here is perhaps the commercial operator. The one-man firm, operating with a single tractor unit worth many thousands of pounds, might be encouraged to see that the trailer he was drawing at great speeds along the highway was not overloaded if he had to consider the prospect of the temporary or even permanent forfeiture of the tractor unit he was probably still buying on hire purchase.

These suggestions are made in the context of the existing distinction in English law between criminal and civil proceedings, and some mention has been made earlier to the possibility of decriminalis- ing certain actions that are now the subject of regulatory statutes and reducing them to the status of matters subject only to civil suit. A primary objection to this course is that the reduction in status would not so much de-criminalise as *de-stigmatise* them, and there is absolutely no reason why selling rotten food or giving short weight, or risking the lives of pedestrians by operating large overloaded or unsafe lorries should be anything but the subject of the most emphatic opprobrium since they constitute among the clearest examples of behaviour by which some men seek their own profitable advantage and are utterly careless of the rights or comforts of others in so doing.

A second objection relates to the manner in which the proceedings might be instituted. In crime we have come to accept that while there is little to prevent the mounting of a private prosecution — in theory at any rate — this is commonly the task of the police to whom society gives a wide area of discretion. Civil proceedings, on the other hand, must be instituted by the aggrieved party, and the question arises as to who is the aggrieved party. In the case of the motorway café selling filthy food the complainant may be the unfortunate diner, but it is conceivable for it to become, eventually, the local environmental health officer. But unless there is a system whereby a complainant may seek a statutory authority to take over the suit it is unlikely that civil proceedings would be other than largely ineffectual. To begin civil proceedings normally requires the services of a solicitor, and later counsel may be needed. Already legal aid in civil matters is highly restricted, and it seems unlikely that those who are outside the scope of legal aid would be prepared to risk money on bringing actions, not least when there is the possibility that even should the plaintiff win the day the other party was without the means to meet the bill for costs. And if responsibility for suits is to become the task of some statutory body or officer, then we are no better off as regards *enforcement* than we are now. The only people standing to benefit are those who as a result of the proposed change would be relieved of even the minimal stigma attaching to the criminal proceedings.

As far as damages go, there are again existing provisions within the law that permit criminal courts to award compensation to injured parties, and there are signs that such compensation is now being awarded not merely to people who have their windows broken, or their glasses trodden on in pub fights, but to people who have suffered a statutory nuisance as a result of a landlord's neglect or who have been induced to buy goods falsely described in a manner contrary to the Trades Descriptions Act.

No comment has so far been offered about the activities of the State. This is a complex issue, not least because in order to abrogate to itself certain powers the State has done so by the processes of law-making so that the actions of its agents, however objectionable they may be to ordinary citizens, are legal in the sense that they constitute no wrong that could be identified in any legal proceeding. Mention has already been made of compulsory purchase, but perhaps more widespread in their scope are the powers that are now given to corporate bodies within the civil state. The list includes not only public utilities that may charge what they please — or what governments tell them to charge — and determine conditions of contract favourable to themselves, but trades unions that through closed shop agreements have the power to deprive members of their livelihood by expelling them from membership. Recent legislation about unfair contract terms may have its effects on the monopolistic practices of some utilities — there are signs, for instance of a modification of the terms of carriage on cross-Channel ferries — but nothing is likely to happen about the exercise of power by unions. The rights of the individual to choose for himself whether or not to belong to a trade union and to seek damages against anyone who sought to persuade his employer to dismiss him for not belonging are now extinguished. As for the right of conscientious objection to member-ship, that seems to be interpreted with the same unsophisticated crudity as it was in the days of conscription, that is, unless the objector belongs to a religious group that expressly forbids his membership of a union the objection must fail.

A Concluding Christian Comment

Having ranged thus far it may now be asked what particular wisdom might be expected to derive from the Christian standpoint on these issues. In summary, the following might be offered.

There is nothing in Christian doctrine to suggest that either the ownership of property or the exercise of power, or a combination of the two is intrinsically wrong. The fact that it may be more difficult for the rich man to enter the Kingdom and perhaps easier for the camel to pass the eye of the needle is no more than a recognition of the fact that the rich may be seduced into thinking that the things of this world are more important and enduring than they are. What is crucial, and it is a point emphasised over and again in both the Old Testament and the New, is that wealth brings the obligations of stewardship and power brings the tasks of ensuring its just exercise and the provision of good example. The Scriptures also abound with examples of the need to ensure a distributive social justice that guarantees an equal minimum to both rich and powerful and poor and weak.

But there is no reason to think that there is any necessary connection between an egalitarian moral order and an egalitarian socio-economic order; the latter is of less importance if the former is guaranteed since there are within an egalitarian moral order sufficient checks and balances to ensure that neither wealth nor power has any capacity to transform the character of actions which are proscribed by vesting them with a permissive legitimacy. In short, all men must be equal under the law if the laws of human society are to reflect the precepts of the moral order that extends beyond temporal experience.

To suggest that the social order, and those set in positions of power within it, must reflect that order does not imply that the powerful are where they are through any 'divine right', merely that there are obligations imposed upon them. The crude debasement of the Calvinist doctrine of predestination led to the assumption that material success was the sign of salvation, and hence the badge of virtue, but that is scarcely acceptable as a basis for believing that vice and virtue are other than randomly distributed in the population.

The major difficulties that arise in attempting to constrain the actions of the powerful and privileged are connected in part with the admiration for the 'effective' — the instrumental, often rudely utilitarian solutions to social problems whether by the State, private corporations or individuals — and in part with the uncritical acceptance that majorities must be 'right'. One can imagine my suggestion that certain motoring offences might be dealt with by forfeiture or destruction of the vehicle being called 'unworkable', and therefore not worthy of consideration. (In reality, it would be thought *unpalatable.*) The decline in the use of imprisonment, particularly its restriction by legislation and its mitigation by the introduction of parole, have come about because of a desire to empty prisons, not from any conclusion that prisons are less justified as a means of dealing with offenders. In the example of the parole system the end has come significantly to justify the means. But if, in the light of careful consideration, imprisonment may still serve a purpose then the fact that there are not enough prison places is not sufficient justification for eschewing its use.

But probably the most important point that might be made is that the Christian viewpoint makes unambiguously clear the proposition that all men are as capable of virtue as they are of vice; the choice, ultimately, is theirs, just as their salvation itself rests upon their own choice. Thus there can be little doubt that 'Christian princes, kings and governors' have both the right and the duty to suppress crimes and actions which harm the interests of others, and to the extent that they permit or encourage the development of special classes of exemption they fail in their duty to do justice to their fellow men who are less privileged but together with whom they must appear at a final Judgement. Yet at the same time they have no mandate to anticipate that judgement in its finality. There is a tendency in Christian social thought to envisage the message of the Gospels as a kind of blueprint for some kind of transcendental Welfare State with the result that the very idea of 'punishment' is thought to be old-fashioned. The danger is that it leads on to the idea that men maybe are saved by their deserts — an idea which is mirrored in the positivist contention that people commit crime because of their social condition and what has been done to them, rather than because they choose to do so.

It is not in fact a Welfare State but an 'equal opportunity' state, a condition in which men are equal before the Law that is above human laws. Those set in positions of privilege, should they fall, must of necessity fall further since they have been set higher to begin with; any attempt to cushion that fall in order to preserve some vestige of their former privileges and advantages constitutes an interference with the moral order of equality. If benefit of clergy has long since gone in one sense, it remains in another in that the white collar is the modern equivalent of the tonsure. To the extent to which its existence is justified by those who shape and manage the criminal justice system they erode the credibility of justice in the eyes of ordinary men.

NOTES

1. See 2 Samuel chs. 11 and 12. It also effectively precluded David from taking any action — as he should have done — after the rape of Tamar: *ibid.*, ch. 13.
2. The notion of stewardship is embodied in legal concepts such as entail, which prevent the dispersal or break-up of estates intended to be handed down, and to various interpretations of the concept of 'waste' preventing those who have a life interest from damaging the property, e.g. by cutting down woodland, or draining lakes of fish.
3. The *petit fonctionnaire* who meets the claimant at the counter in the office of the welfare agency, or the minor local government official ordering his private empire, are familiar examples.
4. Anne clearly knew what sorts of things could happen. Not long after, the ageing Countess of Salisbury was chased round the scaffold in terror by her clumsy executioner.
5. This particular work by a 'late Captain of . . . Regiment' was published by George Routledge and Son in London in 1883.
6. In sentencing Westwood at Cardiff Crown Court, Mr. Justice Watkins is reported to have said, *inter alia*, 'Greedy and avaricious men cause more damage to the community than a hundred or more thieves with whom we pack our prisons' (*The Times*, 25 February 1977).
7. Pottinger is not alone in being the recipient of clemency in respect of pension rights restored to former public officials; what is notable is that the group does not include significant numbers of former postmen and ex-police officers.

6

Social theology and penal theory and practice:
the collapse of the rehabilitative ideal and the search for an alternative

by RONALD H. PRESTON

A theological contribution to a discussion of penal policy must begin by recognising that Christians as such have no special access to the details of criminological problems unless they happen to be professionally or voluntarily engaged in the activity of the apprehension, trial and treatment of criminals (as of course many Christians are), in which case they have their own experience on which to make a contribution to public discussion. But all Christians have the duty as citizens to share in the communal responsibility for criminal policies, for this is a test of the quality of our communal life and insights. This chapter therefore makes no claim to expertise in the field of penology beyond that of the concerned citizen.[1] In an effort to reflect responsibly on the issues it must rely to a considerable extent on the expertise of those who have specialist knowledge and experience. This includes the experience of those involved in legal processes, the whole complex of prison services (including that of prisoners), and experts in relevant fields of study such as law, psychology and sociology. Expert evidence has to be examined critically, partly because experts often differ, and partly because value judgements will be explicit or latent in it and need to be assessed. In the last resort, however, expert evidence will not settle the matter but the policies which the moral judgement of the public will support or at least not actively oppose. We must try to make it as informed and sensitive as we can.

In the present context we are told that the rehabilitative model for the treatment of offenders is in the process of breaking down, and that the growing awareness of this is producing something of a crisis in British penology. I do not doubt that there are differences of opinion on this matter among criminologists (no academic discipline is without them); but this chapter assumes that the breakdown has been substantially established and agreed, and attempts to reflect on this collapse, using insights from the Christian tradition. It will also consider in view of the breakdown of the rehabilitative model, the justice model which is offered as an alternative to it. Further the chapter seeks for some common moral ground on which social policies can be built, a task which cannot be avoided in our increasingly plural society.

Problems in Making a Theological Contribution

In a plural society it cannot be assumed that the nature and limits of a theological contribution to a discussion of penal policies are commonly understood. In particular two difficulties arise, the first out of the position of the Christian faith in this country, and the second out of the nature of the faith itself. Because of our long Christian tradition we have inherited in Britain the remains of a 'Christendom' situation which less and less corresponds to the reality. For centuries the Church was influential and a broadly Christian understanding of life was accepted and publicly assumed. A country where this is still the case is Eire. For centuries Christianity and commonwealth went together, and Christians were deeply involved in penal policies and institutions. Now, however, Christians have become in this and most traditionally Christian countries what Peter Berger (1971) calls a 'cognitive minority'. When it comes to questions of public social policy they can no longer assume that common ground exists, and they have to search for it with those of other faiths and ideologies, including a considerable number of humanists who have absorbed much of the classical–Christian ethical tradition. Among other things the contribution of moral philosophy must not be neglected in the effort to clarify moral issues involved in public policy. The question is what are the penal institutions and practices which our highest common moral insight requires, and what sort of society do we need to sustain them? How far can distinctively Christian insights contribute to this? How can we work towards such a society? And at any given moment, how far can the State go in such a penal policy and still carry the support of the man in the street or in the Clapham omnibus?

The second difficulty arises from the nature of the Christian faith itself, which is not focused directly on the institutions of civil society but derives from the ministry of Jesus and his teaching on the Kingdom or Rule of God. The ethic of the Kingdom of God is paradoxical by the standards of commonsense morality because it is non-reciprocal, and transcends embodiment in social institutions whilst also challenging them. The teaching on forgiveness is a key example in our present context. When the disciples suggest that seven times is the most that any human being could possibly be expected to forgive an offender, Jesus puts the whole question in a different dimension by demanding forgiveness 70 times seven.[2] The basis of this demand is that this is the way God in his graciousness treats us, so this is the way we must treat one another.[3] The Gospel ethic starts with the graciousness of God as its fundamental presupposition, which means that hope arises from faith or trust in this God, and both are expressed in love. The Christian gospel is that the gracious and loving God, whose paradoxical way of ruling the world Jesus believed himself to embody in his life and in his teaching on the Kingdom of God, goes on forgiving the crimes and follies of man 490 times, that is to say without limit.

At one level there is a realism which some would call pessimism in the Christian faith because of its understanding of human wayward-ness ('sin' is the theological term[4]). Nor does it think that a Christian has been translated out of this double condition of great moral possibilities and tragic failures. Rather it sets his face in the right direction, assures him of renewal and forgiveness, and that God has set no limits to what he may achieve. Nevertheless he remains in Martin Luther's words '*simul iustus et peccator*' (at one and the same time 'justified', i.e. forgiven, and a sinner); he is still prone to do what he ought not to do and leave undone what he ought to do. This is especially the case because the more subtle sins are not the flamboyant ones — the ones most likely to get one into a criminal court — but those which are the corruption of good qualities, such as the pride of the 'unco guid'. The Gospels are thus as much concerned, if not more, to expose a taint in the motives of the 'good' as they are to rebuke the 'bad'. This is not because they take in a simple sense either an optimistic or pessimistic view of Man, but that they expose Man as he is in his mixture of good and bad, and rejoice in God's graciousness towards him despite it. The sting of the situation is that the good are not as good as they think themselves, and the bad are not as bad as the good think them.

This teaching is in the setting of one-to-one relationships. How can it be related to social relationships and social policies? The problem of corrective justice is not raised in the Gospels, because the problems of ongoing civil society are not the focus of attention. Jesus' mission was other than that, and of perennial significance transcending any particular embodiment in civil society. The fact of the State, and that it has legitimate claims is admitted (Mark ch. 12, vv. 13–17), indeed stressed, but how to work out what is God's and what is Caesar's and what related to both, is not gone into. From the time of the earliest

Christians, such as St. Paul, until now that problem has remained with the Christian community. The radical gospel insights are not related to the details of social problems in the Gospels themselves, and cannot be related directly to the problems of penology. Nevertheless they must not be allowed to become irrelevant to them.

In practice this is precisely what has happened. Radical Christian insights have been bypassed. There have been two characteristic ways of doing this. The first has been to make a separation between the moral precepts incumbent on all, and the counsels of perfection to which a few are specially called (and these are termed 'the Religious' with a capital R). The second has been to make a very sharp distinction between the Two Realms, that of the Church and that of the State and civil society, and in effect not to allow the radical Christian writ to run in the latter.[5] But that is not the whole story. At their best Christians have wrestled with problems of justice — including penal justice — and tried to see how they are related to love (with varying emphases and varying success[6]). They found in the Greek ethical tradition an understanding of justice as 'rendering to every man his due' (*suum cuique*), and in the Old Testament a witness to God's concern for social justice and for the vindication of the poor and oppressed. The love of which the New Testament speaks was seen to require not less than these two even though it goes beyond them. The story of Christian reflection on justice in society is long and complicated, but in general it has led to a stress on the coercive authority of the State under God for the common good. Classical Protestantism has talked of the State as an 'order of Creation'; and classical Catholicism of it as expressing man's social nature. Nevertheless they have an even stronger doctrine of the Person as in the last resort transcending the authority of the State, not least because in the Christian view the Person has an eternal destiny.

In the course of dealing with the problem of justice and the State, Christians have joined moral philosophers in elaborating retributive, reformative and deterrent theories of punishment, though as a rule they have seen dangers in going along unequivocally with any one of them. At their worst Christians have so let go of their radical insights that they have discussed penal questions on society's own terms and shared in its inveterate self-righteousness. In particular they have supported current social institutions and structures of authority uncritically. 'Throne and altar' became a byword. It is this attitude which is being increasingly criticised amid the political stresses of the twentieth century.

The danger for Christians is therefore of having a radical ethic which is neutralised in practice. The problem is how to bring at any given time an ethic so radical as to transcend the possibility of complete empirical embodiment alongside current theories and institutions, and to make a creative contribution to current problems. This means calling the current situation into question in such a way that possibilities of creative change are enhanced without what is advocated being so far ahead of current opinion as to be impracticable, yet doing it in such a way that the further challenges of radical Christian insights are not forgotten. In doing this the Christian finds himself in an ambiguous relation to the history of his own past. He has the problem of distancing himself to some extent from its unsatisfactory features whilst affirming its deepest insights. It is not surprising that in a plural society he is frequently misunderstood, and may indeed find it hard to get a hearing. At all events if it leads him to a sense of the provisionality of what he says and the avoidance of all pretension in relation to his own tradition, it is likely to lead him to be sensitive to all pretensions in the discussions of penological issues and to the provisionality of practices proposed. Indeed this may be a significant contribution he can make to the public discussion of them, but it is not easy to achieve. There can be a temptation to criticise everyone else from a 'perfectionist' Gospel stance which in effect evades the responsibility of tackling the immediate problems. More common, perhaps, is that the realisation of the complexity of making a Christian contribution leads in effect to a silence on the matter, of which the upshot is to give an irresponsible, because tacit and unthought-out, support to the *status quo*.

Rehabilitation, Retribution and the Christian Tradition

The breakdown of the rehabilitative model is presented by some with a certain amount of zest as the overthrow of an idol which had pretensions to knowledge which it could not sustain, which led to a coercive form of reformation hidden under the guise of concern for the person, and which resulted in grave injustices in the treatment of different persons who were convicted of the same offence. It means the exposure of institutions (such as prisons) which are incapable of fulfilling some of their alleged aims. There is no reason for the Christian to cavil at the exposure of pretension in institutions or theories. Indeed more traditional theologians such as Brunner (1945) pointed out the dangers of leaving prisoners relatively at the mercy of would-be reformers (pejoratively referred to as 'do-gooders'), who were free to decide if and when they were rehabilitated and suitable for release. In particular, without being obscurantist, Christians will be glad that the mystery of the person has proved elusive to those social scientists who thought that the antecedent causal conditions of criminal behaviour, whether in the psyche of the criminal himself or in his social environment, were so established as to be an 'objective' scientific matter. They will also be glad that the hidden value judgements in rehabilitation have been called in question. If one asks rehabilitation in terms of what?, the answer must presumably be the norms of society as incorporated in its legal systems. Yet while some of these norms may be (and indeed are) acceptable, a good number at any time may well need questioning. Infringement of them may even be praiseworthy. In any case there is cause to raise objections to custodial sentences, indeterminate within wide limits, where release depends on the prisoner showing himself to have been rehabilitated in the eyes of experts whose expertise is itself under scrutiny, and may indeed differ. For it is not uncommon for practitioners in different behavioural sciences to work with incompatible theories, or indeed for different practitioners in the same discipline to do so.[7]

Yet from a Christian point of view there is a certain element of tragedy in the breakdown of the rehabilitative model. A great deal of Christian idealism went into it, a great deal of care for the offender and of courage in defending him against philistine public attitudes. This itself was a reaction against what was felt to be an excessive Christian insistence on retribution among the three traditional justifications of punishment.

Christian partiality for a retributive view was on three grounds. First, assuming that the criminal code reflected God's moral laws, offenders against it ought to be punished. Second, a retributive code avoids sheer vengeance by setting public penalties for crimes. Third, in its concern for justly deserved punishment such a code does justice to man's responsibility for his actions and therefore to his dignity. His punishment — assuming that he is correctly convicted and is responsible for his actions — is itself a witness that he is treated with proper respect. Augustine, Aquinas, Luther, Calvin, Hooker and Butler — to name six very different key figures — are on the same side in this respect. The theological backing for this preference probably lies in the classical Christian view that although God shews himself as signally gracious and forgiving in the ministry of Jesus, the fruit of forgiveness must progressively issue in right moral conduct; for in 'the end', at the 'last' judgement, God can no longer continue in this way but will judge every man according to his works, and human penal justice must do the same and give every man his due, which in the case of a sane, properly convicted offender, is punishment.

However there have been other strains in Christian theology, and one in particular has grown in the last centtury or so. This holds that a Being (God) who is both good and rational cannot inflict punishment for the sake of retribution and nothing but retribution. If God cannot be thought of as doing this, men must not do it either. It is those who take this view who have been sympathetic to reformist theories of punishment, and more critical of the institutions of civil society and aware of the ambiguities of the State. Many of them have been active in the prison service — one obvious name is that of Alec Paterson. Nevertheless although it is clear that the influence behind the rehabilitative model in the last 20 years or so owes much more to the theories of social scientists than to Christians, the breakdown of the model represents a tragedy for much not altogether uninformed Christian idealism, which often shewed real care and concern even if it did not pay enough attention to the warnings of more retributive-minded theologians, especially concerning the elements of paternalism and injustice in efforts to reform a person who is in a coerced situation.

However if the model has broken down, facts must be faced. We must not ignore evidence, if it is clear, and allow ourselves to be buoyed up with false hopes. On the other hand we need to be sure that the model has not been given up too easily; that with more care there are not elements of value in it; that it really is the case that any element of coercion in the situation frustrates the possibilities of success from the start. Indeed what is meant by 'success' needs careful thought unless we are working in purely mechanistic terms. A religion which has a cross at its centre is at least alert to possibilities of evaluating success and failure which might ask questions of commonly accepted criteria. When Jesus told us to love our enemies he did not suggest that by this means we should always win our enemies over and have none. We cannot give up a rehabilitative concern because its success is much more doubtful and the conditions it requires are much more subtle than we thought. What Christians must not give up is a critical concern for the needs of offenders, nor a concern for a social order which works towards the fulfilment of person-in-community rather than hinders it, one which tends to foster rather than frustrate the common good.

A Critique of the Justice Model

The critics of the rehabilitative model are in different ways mostly advocates of what may broadly be described as the justice model, but they appear to fall into at least three main and incompatible groups.

(i) Liberal humanitarians or radical liberals. They stress the oppression of individuals under the practice of the rehabilitative model, and are particularly concerned with justice as fairness.[8]

(ii) The radical Left or liberal radicals. These stress the oppression in all pre-socialist societies. Many of them are libertarian Marxists verging on anarchists and almost all are utopians. Some would hold that what the liberals are concerned with is only 'formal' justice, characteristic of imperfect societies. When the perfect society comes it will be irrelevant. In any event even now proletarian justice is more important. Sometimes the Chinese form of communal correction is favoured, with the minimum of formal law (Pepinsky 1976).

(iii) Those of the political Right. Not many of these as yet have realised the breakdown of the rehabilitative model. For one thing they have had little or no sympathy with it. When they do realise its breakdown they will press for longer and harsher sentences in the interests of law and order, and rejoice in the collapse of what they regard as mostly sentimentalism which is more bothered about the criminal than his victims. In this attitude they will represent the majority of the electorate. Critics of the rehabilitative model need to realise that they are playing with fire, and their exposures of it need to take account of this.

A number of the advocates of the justice model seem to me — though I may misunderstand them — to try to 'bracket out' the divergent attitudes of the critics of the rehabilitative model by making punishment as much as possible a regulative and technical matter. Of course they realise that there must be some moral-political base to it, and they sometimes refer to a minimum 'social contract' theory of the State. This is akin to the attenuated version of the traditional Natural Law theory of society as presented by H. L. A. Hart (1961). This refers to the minimum level of common agreement to enable human society to survive, to moral rules which any state must enforce if it is to be viable. It includes restrictions in the use of violence and bodily harm, a system of mutual forbearance and compromise as a basis of legal and moral obligation, a limited requirement of altruism, a minimal form of property (not necessarily private), the recognition of promise-making as a source of obligation, and some system of sanctions to ensure that those who obey these minimal requirements are not sacrificed to those who do not.

In this view the law sets out in rationally articulated rules the basic conditions for human life and co-operation to be possible. Criminal activity therefore presupposes the human co-operation on which the law insists, and the criminal has secured an unfair advantage by undermining the system which secures to everyone (himself included) basic goods necessary to human corporate life. Punishment, therefore, redresses the balance of advantages which the criminal has unfairly swung in his favour (Hegel 1821, secs. 90–103). So far so good (though it is doubtful how far the Marxist will accept this view of society and therefore of punishment).

But there are difficulties in this position which in my view need further thought. An impression can be given that punishment is verging on being seen as a purely regulative matter like the 'sin bin' in ice hockey, or library fines, or (perhaps) the growing attitude to shoplifting. At first the obvious point occurs that the State is a very different institution from ice hockey, in that one cannot get out of it whereas no one need take up ice hockey. That is to say the State is much more morally significant. If one were to take a purely technical view of the juridical system one would have to take an even more minimal view of the State than Hart's attenuated Natural Law approach, a view such as that of the sociologist Bryan Wilson who refers to society as being held together 'by non-human mechanistic forms of control such as the conveyor belt or parking meter' (Wilson 1976). But this may not be what is presupposed, and we can leave Wilson's remark aside as a rhetorical exaggeration. Nevertheless Hart's view and the minimal social contract view is a very 'thin' view of the State. Its heyday was the break-up of the old mercantilist system and the early stages of modern industrial society. It was the foundation of a *laissez-faire* view of the State and its tasks which had serious theoretical and practical defects. It is not suitable to enlarge upon them in this context, except to say that it gravely underplayed the corporate and organic as against the individualistic aspects of human life, and in my view is quite inadequate as the basis for an advanced industrial society. Is it wise, then, to base a view of punishment on such an inadequate view of the State? We cannot be content to think of the State as being concerned with no more than the question of how we can make the necessary technical arrangements to survive together; it must be concerned with richer, more common, human values than this.

Moral considerations also enter into the justice model of punishment in connection with the boundaries and the range of severity of the fixed penalties which are imposed. Crime and sin are not identical. There are many sins (and the most subtle ones) which are not crimes and there are crimes which are not sins. Nevertheless crime and sin do overlap. Obviously the area and scope of penalties reflects a preference for order rather than anarchy. But beyond that they may be more or less related to a particular social order which is more or less worth defending. A concern for human fulfilment must not be lost in concern for the justice model. It remains legitimate to raise the question in connection with any law and penalty for infringing it, 'In whose interests is this being enforced?' Frequently it is the common good that is involved. Not infrequently, however, as the history of social reform shows, the law needs criticising in the interests of a wider common good; it is too tied up with the interests of a particular class, or race, or group. It is not hard to think of instances where disobedience to law may be a moral duty, a way of bringing creative moral criticism to bear on the social order.

Again legal penalties must be exacted humanely. This brings prison conditions under scrutiny. In this connection we may mention those criminals thought to be sufficiently dangerous in one way or another as to require incarceration for a long period or permanently. It is evident that there are such, but that it is not at all easy to establish with accuracy who they are. The evidence is that the tendency is to put many more into this category than is necessary, perhaps in order to err on the side of protecting the public, which is understandable. Moreover the breakdown of rehabilitative theories of human conduct casts doubt on the adequacy of the theories by which permanently dangerous criminals are classified as such. There is thus a moral challenge both to improve methods of classification, and to administer this 'prisoner-of-war' type of imprisonment for dangerous offenders as humanely as possible. 'Out of sight, out of mind' is the temptation of society as far as they are concerned. If classification cannot be improved society has to face the problem whether in order to be sure of locking up those who are dangerous it will agree to locking up perhaps twice as many in addition who will not be dangerous, for lack of any means of identifying which is which.

Although society is prone to oversimplify penal questions (a point to which I shall return), it is surely right in thinking that much crime is morally blameworthy, and that the criminal deserves punishment. (I assume in saying this that he is properly convicted and is properly held responsible for his actions.) This brings back the 'classical' retributive element, and is an indication that the area within which crime and punishment can be treated as primarily a technical and regulative matter is limited.

Prudence, Proportion and Theories of Punishment

Nothing that has been said so far seems to me to remove the necessity of wrestling with the three traditional models of punishment, retributive, deterrent and rehabilitative. Indeed much of it requires us to do so, as does the ideal of 'respect for persons'. (The traditional wisdom is that it is unwise to follow any one of them to the exclusion of the other two.) Christians have come to encapsulate their concern for human beings in the phrase 'respect for persons', and adherents of other faiths and ideologies often agree with them. In doing this they realise that persons must not be seen as isolated individuals but as persons-in-community. They also realise that this concern relates to all three common theories of punishment but cannot be satisfied with any one of them alone:

(i) Persons must be treated as responsible, the onus being on those who wish to qualify this in particular cases. If they offend, punishment must be deserved and legitimate (retribution). But once paid society should wipe the slate clean, something it signally fails to do.

(ii) In certain cases the common good of persons-in-community may require an element of deterrence. I state this with caution because of the inveterate tendency of the public to exaggerate the deterrent effects of punishments. In most cases we have no deterrence except community attitudes. Deterrence, however, is not the focus of attention in this chapter and I shall say no more about it.

(iii) Because of the ambiguities of society in causing crime and in punishing it, a rehabilitative attitude is needed. That is to say that punishment on solely retributive grounds with no other consideration in mind will not do. An intention actively to promote the good of the offender is also required. This should not mean adding a further and indeterminate length to a retributive sentence purely for rehabilitative purposes and under coercive conditions.

In this connection it is suggested that rehabilitation should be available to the criminal but entirely on a voluntary basis, with no explicit or implicit coercions in the shape of a hidden threat such as 'if you don't accept treatment you won't get parole'. Those who refuse to have anything to do with it would be free to ignore it. A partial analogy with Alcoholics Anonymous has been suggested. There would seem much to approve of in these proposals. They are certainly compatible with many Christian ideas and insights. There is less pretension, more mutual respect, greater readiness to recognise 'solidarity in sin', and that what human beings have become is something to be discovered together rather than announced by the 'good' to the 'bad'. It is also more realistic to recognise that many do not choose to be 'cured', at any rate by this means. One would like to see a serious effort put into a scheme of voluntary rehabilitation. It will certainly not require less resources than the present system. It would need to guard against the same kind of coerced 'soul transformation' which it has criticised in the rehabilitative model, but its advocates seem quite aware of this.

One of the main problems will be the attitude of society. In my view the bulk of the electorate has never accepted rehabilitative policies let alone realised their collapse. Reformers in the Home Office, often accused of obtuseness, have pushed ahead of public opinion. This remains appallingly self-righteous and revengeful, amounting at times to the view that we should do to others at least what they have done to us, if not more so. There is much hypocrisy in punishment. Is it not significant that the vast majority of those in prison (perhaps 90%) come from the social classes four and five, whilst white-collar crime, like fraud, embezzlement and bribery is liable to escape prison? We are often keener to deter offences against property than against persons. Moreover all the traditional theories of punishment have been advocated in simplistic ways. High-sounding retributive theories are put forward in a society which fails to fulfil its side of the theory and pervasively discriminates against prisoners once the penalty has been paid. Similarly advocates of rehabilitation have overlooked the fact that it involves what amounts to experiments on human subjects in a milieu of coercion. Advocates of deterrence have had an unfounded belief in the deterrent effects of fierce punishments. Candour forces the Christian to admit that he finds many examples of these distorted attitudes in members of the Christian community, and that is a reason why any comment he makes must be made with due modesty.

Clearly the traditional virtues of prudence and proportion are required in threading one's way through the intricacies of penal policy. They are the virtues of practical wisdom. Prudence relates basic insights to the weighing up of the pros and cons of different theoretical and practical considerations, each of which has to be allowed for, but never to the exclusion of others. Proportion considers the details of each proposed policy in relation to the weight of the various considerations embodied in it. For instance mandatory sentences appear indiscriminate, and discretionary ones appear arbitrary. Is there not a cleft stick between consistency and discrimination? Does this not indicate that one must not be pursued too far without reference to the other? This is one of several questions which could be put to the advocates of the justice model.

Hopes, Aims and Policies

I turn in the final sections of this chapter to the wider question of the nature of the society within which penal policy operates, and to some suggestions for changes in policy which Christians should support. They will require a great effort by men of goodwill if they are to carry public support. Human justice in the Christian view corresponds neither to the paradoxical justice of God now, as Jesus affirmed it, nor to the ultimate judgement of God (however this is understood[9]) but is between the time of these two, and therefore provisional. Its task is to restrain the 'natural' justice of aggrieved individuals and groups by institutional procedures, to see that the procedures themselves are just, and that the State which sets them up pursues personal and social justice. The Christian understanding of justice makes it necessary to speak relatively of the penal system. Punishment will always be ambiguous because persons and societies are always ambiguous, and will be short of the parousia.[10] In particular what are suitable punishments, and the relative seriousness of different offences are relative matters.

However this ambiguity is no reason for not attempting to improve things. The Christian in one sense is pessimistic in that he expects neither a perfect society nor a perfect penal system, if only because success can be a subtle source of pride and therefore of corruption. After all it was a combination of flagrant and subtle sins that brought Jesus to a cross. On the other hand the Christian is an optimist because he is not prepared to set any limits to what might be achieved by a humanity which is alert and sensitive. He has a large hope, and that allows him to hope against hope when provisional hopes are dashed.[11] Indeed if God and the world are as Jesus said they are he must needs hope, because the nature of things is with him. He can understand, because he shares, disappointment that the rehabilitation models have not worked. He will not be surprised at the breakdown of what is provisional, and he will not seek to put his hope in an illusion. He will look for fresh initiatives. At the same time he cannot give up hope for the criminal, not even for those in long-term or permanent confinement for security reasons. He will seek what is possible for their full humanity for them too. He cannot allow society to forget the criminal in the process of dealing with his crime.

It should be evident that hope does not destroy critical powers. It can even enhance them. It should encourage a cold eye to be cast on the element of pretension in punishment and on the social conditions which encourage crime. Some recent theorists suggest that a strengthened sense of neighbourhood and community is the best hope of diminishing crime. It seems very likely. But this is an immense task which no advanced industrial society has solved: it is as much a problem to the U.S.S.R. as to us. Community has become a catch-all word which has to be unpacked (Plant 1974). Demands for it reach us on all sides, witness the growth of community development or community work concerns in the last decade. Two achieve an improvement here requires the co-operation of a variety of different people with different skills, theoretical and practical. Perhaps it is worth noting in this connection that the churches have a large number of full-time paid agents and potential part-time voluntary ones, and a lot of plant (although much of it is the wrong sort) which could be very useful, if the struggle to keep them going at a time of inflation could be sufficiently successful to allow concentration to move from the needs of the immediate worshippers to those of the neighbourhood in which the worship takes place.

Mention of neighbourhood and community leads to a consideration of the nature of the wider society within which penal practices operate. At the end of his critique of John Rawls' (1972) *A Theory of*

Justice, Brian Barry (1973, pp. 166–8) says that there are three basic models of society — hierarchical, liberal–individualistic and altruistic-collaborative. I think he is right. Many are advocates of one model only, but just as the Christian faith relates to, and asks questions of, each of the three traditional theories of punishment, it does the same with respect to these three models of society. It relates to the hierarchical one because there will always be a division of interest between the givers and the receivers of orders, between the managers and the managed, in any society. It is the mark of Utopian thinking to suppose otherwise, however greatly methods of participation in decision-making are devised. It is necessary to work for power structures that are just and humane, that provide for checks on the abuse of power, and in particular to be actively concerned for those who are less powerful or powerless. The Christian faith relates to the liberal–individualist view because self-interest must be harnessed yet controlled for the common good. It relates to the altruistic-collaborative model because men and women need to give as well as to get, and are only truly themselves in a community which expects and encourages mutual giving and receiving. The task is to achieve the best 'mix' of these elements at a given time, and it requires both a critical and a sustaining role from the Christian community. The third one needs fostering because it is the weakest of the three. Human sin favours the first two. A continually renewed vision is required to strengthen the third.

This vision has to be married to practical steps which are capable of being realised, in the sense of winning enough public support, or at least tolerance. In the immediate context there are some things which it is certainly worth working for:

(i) An attempt to deal with as many convicted offences as possible by non-custodial penalties, which is one of the aims of some advocates of the justice model. The evidence suggests that as many as 80% of those in prison at present ought not to be there. It does not protect the public and it actually harms rather than improves those imprisoned. The system is unfair and inefficient, indeed monstrous. It will not be easy to shift public opinion on this, but if I were an Old Testament prophet I would feel like saying 'Thus says the Lord; cursed be a society which tolerates this prison system; away with it; it is an abomination to me'.

(ii) Efforts to make claims on an offender, in terms either of personal restitution or of community service, as being suitable to his dignity as a responsible person and fellow citizen. I do not think that the charge that this is paternalistic cuts much ice. It is possible that such a practice might prove reformatory but that would not be the reason for adopting it. Vigorous pursuit of this might also help the public to see that there is concern for the victims of crime and not only for the criminal, which is a widely held view.

(iii) Beginning a system of voluntary rehabilitation, as has already been mentioned.

(iv) Scrutinising more closely the crimes of the powerful with the aim of securing as much attention to them as to those of the less powerful.

(v) Continuing to wrestle with the problem of containing the 'mad' and the 'bad'. Not only must containment be humane, but efforts at restoration must not be given up even if they are unpromising.

To return to where this chapter began, we note that in advocating these policies and in general discussions of penal policy the Christian will seek to relate himself to an ongoing public discussion, especially among those with the greatest concern and with special expertise. He will hope that their ideas will not be a denial of his own even though they cannot achieve all that he would wish for in penal policy. He will be prepared to use relevant arguments devoid of any special Christian basis, though they may accord with Christian insights. One of these is the attempt to get the public to see beyond the immediate facts and short-term interests to the secondary consequences of actions and long-term interests. This is on the basis that the Lord needs to use any suitable weapons that he has available to coax or propel men into more humane ways of behaviour. It is aptly expressed in the prayer which ends 'save Lord, by love, by prudence, and by fear'. Positively the Christian will hope to extrapolate from common human experience and see how far he can take it in public policies. Thus it is only the very unfortunate who have no experience at all of what it means to be unconditionally loved and forgiven in family life or its equivalent. The Christian gospel takes this experience, however fragmentary it may be, and expands it to cover the whole dimension of the ways of God with men. It is not Utopian to hope that there can be sufficient understanding of it in society at large that glimpses of it may illuminate penal policies and practice.

At times it is the hopeful side of the Christian understanding of life which speaks most powerfully, at others the realist; it depends on the context. It is not easy to express both together. W. H. Auden and Louis MacNeice (1937) do not quite achieve it in these lines, but they do express a good deal of what I have been trying to say of the way Christian insight may be brought alongside contemporary problems of penal theory and practice and illuminate them:

> And to the good who know how wide the gulf, how deep
> Between Ideal and Real, who being good have felt
> The final temptation to withdraw, sit down and weep

We pray the power to take upon themselves the guilt
Of human action, though still as ready to confess
The imperfection of what can and must be built,
The wish and power to act, forgive and bless. (p. 258)

NOTES

1.   This chapter arises out of group and individual discussions with my colleagues, and with Professor A. E. Bottoms, and among these I am particularly indebted to Principal Michael Taylor of the Northern Baptist College Manchester; but none of them is committed by my argument.

2.   Matthew ch. 18, vv. 21 ff. Of course there is much more on forgiveness in the Gospels, not least the necessity of those who would be forgiven being ready themselves to forgive, but it does not affect the main point made in this chapter.

3.   Of course only a man of faith sees this. Jesus appealed to the weather (the sunshine and rain, Matthew ch. 5, vv. 43 ff.) for evidence of God's graciousness. A sceptic could draw a different conclusion. The evidence is ambiguous. But Jesus was a man of faith. Subsequently, Christians, as men of faith, have appealed to the life and death of Jesus himself as a true indication of the nature of God and his way of ruling the world and dealing with human sin.

4.   The classical expression of this is the doctrine of 'original sin', which amounts to saying that there is no element in man's nature, not even his reason, which is not 'fallen' because he is born into a sinful society; hence the persistence of his self-centredness and his continual need of renewal. Many have held that this is the one Christian doctrine which is empirically verifiable! However it has become so caught up in the classical western Christian tradition with St. Augustine's views of sexuality that it is exceptionally difficult for the enquirer not to misunderstand it. So acute a theological moralist as Reinhold Niebuhr gave up using it for this reason and tried to state, as does this essay, what the term implies without using it. (cf. Niebuhr's Gifford Lectures of the 1940s, where he used the term, with the 1965 introduction on 'Changing perspectives' to his *Man's Nature and His Communities*; Niebuhr 1941-3; 1965). The doctrine is too often interpreted in an individualist way when in fact it basically refers to the corruptions in society which affect the growing person from birth.

5.   The first tendency has been specially characteristic of Roman Catholicism, the second of Lutheranism.

6.   Some have held justice and love to be identical, some that they are antithetical, and the majority that love presupposes justice but points beyond it. The first says that justice is love distributed as soon as more than two people are involved; the second restricts love to I–Thou relationships and thinks of it as warm, spontaneous and personal while justice is impersonal, cool and deliberate; the third says justice prepares for love and expresses it but cannot exhaust it.

7. One thinks for example of S. Freud and B. F. Skinner in psychology, both of whose theories have been widely reflected in penal practice.

8. For the most part they have not related their thought to the major theoretical work of John Rawls (1972), but there are significant links.

9. I am avoiding the technical vocabulary here of eschatological (meaning the 'last things' in the sense of those of ultimate significance, which Christians hold to have already been disclosed in Jesus), and apocalyptic (meaning the last things in chronological time). The Christian looks in some way for the final triumph of the former at the latter.

10. Another technical term; it refers to the 'return of Christ', and is a way of expressing the triumph at the end of time (however conceived) of what he embodied.

11. There does seem a tendency for secular humanism to ricochet from an over-confidence in men and in 'science' to despair when things do not work out as expected. H. G. Wells was a notorious example in my youth. Now we have Arthur Koestler (1978), who has verged for a long time on insights which if not explicitly Christian are consonant with Christianity, but has never quite achieved them, adopting in his recent book *Janus* a deeply pessimistic view of man. His brain is alleged to have evolved too fast, so that he is only now coming to terms with an inherent sickness and paranoia of character which is bound to destroy him. There could be a similar pessimistic rebound when the failure of the rehabilitative model is realised. The Christian has resources in his faith which guard against this, and he will need to deploy them for the good of all involved in penal policies.

7

The future of imprisonment in Britain

by FREDERICK McCLINTOCK

> Men make their own history but they do not make it just as they
> please; they do not make it under circumstances chosen by
> themselves, but under circumstances directly encountered, given
> and transmitted from the past (Karl Marx 1852)

The subject of this chapter is the *future* of imprisonment in Britain. At
the outset it is important to recognise that forecasting — or the science
of 'futurology' — is a hazardous undertaking even in the best of
circumstances, as, for example, in demographic studies where one is
dealing with precise data with a limited forward projection; the recent
inaccuracies and contradictions in attempting to assess the future
school population of this country over the next ten to 20 years have
admirably demonstrated this. How much more difficult is it then to
depict with any confidence the possible future of such complex
institutions as the two prison services, that of England and Wales, and
that of Scotland.

At the time when John Howard (1777) published his famous
prison survey, nobody could have forecast the fundamental changes
that occurred during the nineteenth century; or, at the time of the
report of the Gladstone Committee (1895) on prisons, the developments that took place in the early part of the present century. Coming
nearer to the present day we already find that the penal ideas and ideals
of rehabilitation and reformation of the '20s and '30s — which inspired
so many innovations and improvements through to the 1960s — have
a quaint and rather old fashioned ring in the contemporary context of
penological agnosticism (McClintock 1976; Radzinowicz and King
1977, ch. 9; Home Office 1977b). Few, again, could have forecast the
Mountbatten Report (1966) and its aftermath, or even the rapidity
with which the serious contemporary difficulties, as regards prison
staff, would have arisen with the adoption in the late '60s of a penal
ideology of management.[1] On this showing, perhaps the most that
one can safely predict about the future of imprisonment is that it is not
likely to have many of its present-day features.

126

It is the uncertainty as to the future of the penal system, coupled with a disillusionment as to the recent past, which has created the tension, dramatically proclaimed as the current 'crisis' in British penology, and which has given rise to the Manchester conference and the present volume. Some would describe the situation as a lack of *confidence* in the *present* and a lack of *faith* in the *future*: a moral and spiritual crisis of which the penological predicament is a derivative. Whether such a perspective is acceptable or not, there is little doubt that, in order to understand contemporary issues in British penology, it is necessary to consider the penal system in a wider cultural and social context.

The Prisons Dilemma: the Wider Context

Clearly, it is not possible in this chapter to deal in a detailed and systematic way with the wider contextual framework relating to the contemporary prison system. All that can be attempted is to state a few of the salient issues relating to the current dilemma.

First: the prisons, except in a narrow administrative and technical sense, cannot be fruitfully considered in isolation from the substantive criminal law, the criminal justice process, sentencing principles and practice, and the nature and purposes of the various non-custodial measures. It is only in this context that it is worthwhile to consider the aims and organisational arrangements (i) for putting people into custody; (ii) for dealing with people in custody; and (iii) for releasing people from custody (see McClintock 1978).

Second: the prison service is part of the State bureaucracy, and the prison staff, as servants of the State, exercise power in a highly concentrated and intimate form over those citizens who have forfeited their liberty so as to become prisoners. The executive side of imprisonment consequently plays a part in the very important balance between freedom and authority, which is fundamental to modern societies. Prison affairs are therefore part of the political process and cannot be divorced from the theory of the State. 'Scientific Penology' has attempted to make such a separation through questionable assumptions based upon a positivist outlook (Lopez-Rey 1964). This has created considerable confusion as regards theory, policy and practice in the penal field.

Third: the methods and practices of the prison service cannot be understood in isolation from the theories and explanations that are made as to criminal, or deviant behaviour. These need to be examined at the policy level as well as among the practitioners in the penal system who often mistakenly profess that they adhere to no theory of criminality. The recent divergences in criminological views — their conflicting and frequently irreconcilable tenets — have contributed significantly to the confusion and malaise amongst prison staff and penal administrators. For example, the one-time partnership between the authorities responsible for penal affairs and criminologists of the traditional school has been under sustained attack from those of radical attitude. The school of criminologists dedicated to social engineering on behalf of liberal goals has been severely criticised both as regards its assumptions and its academic status. Furthermore, a sociology of change which emphasises the importance of prediction and control through the development of the social sciences is regarded as highly questionable. As with the penal process, a sociology of deviance cannot be isolated from its political lines of thought. The wider social context in which prison staff carry out their everyday tasks has become very much more complex and problematic with the breakdown of consensus in criminology.

Fourth: the ambivalent nature of 'objective' history and the resultant disputes over historiography have also contributed to the uncertainty as to the future, in relation to the past and present, of the penal system. Prison history has always had its official writers who, in a descriptive way, gave an account of the development of its institutions (e.g. Fox 1952). Such accounts today are regarded as social compositions in which the past is *re-created* in order to *explain* the present and *prepare* for the future. In this context the possibilities in the future are usually limited by a conservationist's perspective, while more radical alternatives are rarely considered. Analytical history widens the whole dispute from an exclusive consideration of the penal system to include the interrelationship between the economic, social and ideological changes (Rusche and Kirchheimer 1939; Foucault 1975). Thus it can be claimed that:

> The protection of society is the aim of all punishment, or penal treatment, no matter what form it may take. . . . The social values which are given the protection of the law, the rules which are enforced by the political power of the state because they are embodied in the criminal code, are those which are deemed desirable by those social groups within the state who have the power to make law. . . . (Also) the character of punishment is inextricably associated with and dependent on the cultural values of the state that employs them. (Thorsten Sellin, Foreword in Rusche and Kirchheimer 1939)

A consideration of these fuller contextual issues clearly indicates the highly problematic nature of making any accurate forecast of the future of imprisonment in modern society. Two possible alternatives may be anticipated: (i) a modification of the present system; (ii) the abolition of imprisonment as a penal sanction.

The Present Prison System and its Possible Modifications

As already mentioned, England and Wales have a separate prison system from that of Scotland, each of which receives prisoners from separate and distinctive courts of criminal justice. But as the legislation governing the two systems is enacted by the same parliament, and as there is considerable contact between the administrative and prison staffs, a large number of the salient features of the two systems have developed along parallel lines. It is notable, however, that the Scottish prison system serves a criminal jurisdiction relating to five million inhabitants, whereas the English system relates to a population of 49 million. The latter service is consequently run by a much larger bureaucracy with a greater amount of differentiation in the classification of institutions and in roles and duties of prison staff. However, the principles behind the classification of prisoners and of training programmes are similar in the two systems.

In the English system there are more than 130 institutions whereas in the Scottish there are 24; the daily average prison populations are 42,000 and 5,000 inmates respectively, while the corresponding prison staffs amount to 21,000 and 2,500. The annual cost of the English system is over £200 million and that of Scotland over £20 million; the cost of keeping an inmate is the same in both, approximately £4,000 per year. This is not the occasion to make a detailed comparison of the two prison systems.[2] It is sufficient to note that both are complex bureaucratic organisations involved in a large number of different activities, that each employs thousands of staff, and, like most man-management organisations, their costs are high. The penological enterprise of detaining nearly 50,000 citizens in custody in Great Britain is a significant feature of our State system. It should also be added that, as a large number are detained for only short periods of time — on remand, in default of fine or short-term detention — the number of *different* citizens therefore undergoing detention for some period during a year is probably in the region of 200,000. Another important feature of the contemporary scene is the heavy increase during recent years in the number of receptions into prison and the rapid expansion of the daily average inmate population; this is in spite of the fact that of those sentenced by the courts the *proportion* given custodial sentences has been declining.[3] The prison systems are faced with a rapid rise in population, overcrowding, lack of resources, staff shortages, together with increasing overall costs and costs per inmate. For the penal administrators one of the pressing practical questions is how to reduce the prison population or at least keep it steady, and a considerable part of the impetus to find alternatives to imprisonment springs from motives of economy rather than of ideological zeal (House of Commons 1978). This is not to suggest that no good humanitarian reasons can be put forward to justify not only the grant of bail as against an order for remand in custody, but also the use of short prison sentences, the extension of parole eligibility, or more frequent resort to non-custodial alternatives; but that from the direct financial savings entailed those reasons gain greater weight in bringing about such changes (see Bean 1976, esp. Ch. 6; Bottomley 1973, esp. Ch. 5; Young 1976).

In dealing with a large proportion of their charges prison staff are solely concerned with custody and security whether it be external or internal. These are also primary considerations for dealing with other prisoners, but in addition the staff are expected, during the period of detention, to encourage and assist the inmate to lead a good and useful life (Prison Rules 1964, Rule 1). This requirement is seen as part of the reformative or rehabilitative ideology which has in recent years come under severe criticism and which has precipitated what some regard as the current *crisis* in British penology. Coupled with this, penological research has been unsuccessful in establishing any positive differential outcome from rehabilitative institutional programmes in the reduction of individual recidivism (Brody 1976). Furthermore, with the development of non-custodial measures as the principal method of disposal, it is permissible to question whether imprisonment has any useful function at all in terms of rehabilitative stimulus. On the whole the answer has been a negative one, and consequently the morale of prison staff and the satisfaction gained in the discharge of their duties has suffered accordingly.

The debate on the 'rehabilitative' model *versus* the 'just-deserts' has been considered in detail in other chapters. The question that needs to be considered here is what kind of role would prisons have in a penal system based upon a 'just-deserts' model. Would they not be reduced to fulfilling a purely punitive function, and would this not mean turning the clock back and running the risk of their developing in the future into a new barbarism in criminal justice? The answer that is given to this question is that imprisonment, while not being directly reformative in aim, would through *humane containment* provide facilities on terms acceptable to inmates and not, as at present, on authoritative terms as part of a correctional programme. Rehabilitation as part of the paternalistic social-welfare ideology, which has been used to legitimise the authority of the State, would be replaced by tutorial facilities for social education and self-help, of which prisoners could avail themselves if they so wished. Prison staff would genuinely be able to encourage and assist inmates to lead a good and useful life; but the meaning of 'a good and useful life' would be defined by the inmates, providing, of course, that it was within the law. Prison staff would act as non-coercive social educators; and some would regard this as a much more challenging and rewarding task than that of correctional personnel attempting to operate a modified model of therapeutic control within the penal system.

What is being suggested is that, while the criminal justice system would maintain *a right to punish*, the decision-making process as regards penal sanction — whether of a judicial or executive nature — would be concerned solely with 'just-deserts' criteria; but that the State, either within or outside penal institutions, would be under *an obligation to provide resources for the education and for the treatment of those convicted*. 'Treatment' in this context is restricted to the provision of medical and psychiatric attention.[4] The extent to which the resources were utilised would depend upon the free choice of the offender and would have no bearing upon, nor be affected by, the sentence, or its termination.

The merit of Sir Alexander Paterson's campaign in the 1930s — and that of Sir Lionel Fox and other penal reformers later — was to emphasise, in addition to the *right* of the State to punish, the *obligation* of the State to provide facilities for education and treatment on grounds of humanity and social justice. The shortcoming in their aims — and the weakness that lies at the centre of the present debate — is that they coupled the ideas of education and treatment of prisoners with that of crime prevention, in the belief that this would be an important way of reducing individual recidivism. This inevitably introduced education and treatment, or training, into the coercive regime prescribed by criminal justice.[5] They overlooked its coercive nature because at the time the assumptions underlying the paternalistic social-welfare ideology had not been subjected to systematic critical scrutiny, especially when associated with the criminal justice process. If today a decision is reached to separate the *obligation* to provide educational and medical treatment facilities on a voluntary, i.e. non-paternalistic, basis, from the *right* to punish, then a new and challenging vista would be opened to the staff of penal institutions, when faced with meeting and handling prisoners on an egalitarian basis, instead of on the custodial terms now prevailing. Moreover, the former independent role of prison chaplains would be re-established for the 'educational workers' in penal institutions.

Trends in this direction of greater respect for prisoners as *persons*, treating them as equals, and providing facilities and help in self-development are beginning already to emerge in some penal settings. But social workers, doctors, psychiatrists and chaplains would be part of the control system; they would be available at the request of prisoners. The implication for the dual role of prison officers — discipline cum education — has not as yet been considered in any detail, but in relation to prisoners' rights and facilities there would be a pressing need for an independent inspectorate as well as a formally constituted appeal procedure (Morris 1978).[6] Parole, as a privilege granted after examination based upon casework reports and interviews, would have to be abolished, or perhaps replaced by a judicially oriented model along the lines developed in the Netherlands (Hulsman et al. 1978). After-care would have to be provided by the local social services and not, as now, at the hands of a member of the probation service.[7] Given a greater clarity as to the purpose of imprisonment, together with a specification of the facilities provided in prisons under a 'just-deserts' model, it is to be hoped that there would be a drastic reduction in its use as a penal sanction, especially when costs and the provision of non-residential alternatives are considered.

Towards the Abolition of Imprisonment as a Penal Sanction

Most people regard the idea of society without a prison system as quite preposterous, and yet prisons as places of punishment have only existed as an important or central feature in State control for a comparatively short period in the history of human societies. Throughout history few societies have had imprisonment as a penal sanction; consequently it may be not entirely unreasonable to consider the possibility of its gradual disuse and eventual disappearance. The non-rehabilitative model, discussed in the previous section, is a move, it is suggested, in that direction as it reduces the formal use of imprisonment to the infliction of punishment on a 'just-deserts' basis, or perhaps to the fulfilment of society's desire to protect those citizens regarded as dangerous (see Advisory Council on the Penal System 1978; Bottoms 1977). But from a more radical point of view its abolition entails the drastic curbing or even total destruction of the criminal justice system as a primary measure of social control.

One way of reaching a comprehension of the current debates on penal process is to analyse what is being said in terms of 'moralism' (blaming the offender, the victim or others in society), 'causalism' (explaining in terms of individual characteristics, social circumstances, social structure or the political economy), and 'legalism' (controlling by embodying the one or the other, or both, in legal rules and sanction). The debate can then be seen as a vicious circle of alternatives in criminal justice: 'rehabilitation' *versus* 'just-deserts' introduces little that is new, and can be explained in terms of change from consensus to pluralism. The 'collapse of the rehabilitative ideal' becomes inevitable when the paternalistic social-welfare ideology, legitimising the authority of the State, is seriously challenged. A way out of the vicious circle of 'moralism' and 'causalism' is drastically to curtail or abolish altogether the criminal justice system and prepare to solve in other ways the issues that it now deals with: for example, to regard 'criminal events' as accidents or conflict mistakes. If such a radical change occurred, then there would be *no* need for prisons and *no* need for a probation service. Changes of such magnitude, however, are not easy to bring about, especially as the criminal justice and penal systems are supported by strong bureaucracies (Young 1976).

Is the idea of abolishing the criminal justice system, and with it the prisons, as unrealistic as the majority of opponents claim? It certainly is, if no other changes in society take place, particularly if the role of the State persists in relation to its control in communities or neighbourhoods. But a change in that direction can be envisaged if the styles of law and other kinds of social control are developed along lines already discernible in society. In a report to the Council of Europe, in 1972, on 'The phenomenological and contextual analysis of criminal violence', I suggested that part of an increase in criminalised violent events was due to the breakdown, in urban areas, of forms of social control that had previously been operative (McClintock 1974). That line of thought can be carried further and we can modify the proposition of Donald Black (1976) in his provocative book on *The Behaviour of Law*, and state that the quality of *Criminal law* varies with the quality of other forms of social control, whether formal, informal or legal.

It is suggested that the styles of control in social life generally have their corresponding styles of control in law. The penal and compensatory may be classified as *accustorial* styles of social control (see *Figure 1*). There are contestants, winners or losers; with punishment or nothing, payment or nothing, as the outcome. In contrast, the

FIGURE 1: *Four Styles of Social Control*
(derived from Black 1976)

	(1) *Penal*	(2) *Therapeutic*	(3) *Compensatory*	(4) *Conciliatory*
Standard	prohibition	normality	obligation	harmony
Problem	guilt	need	debt	conflict
Initiation *of action*	agent of group	deviant	victim	disputants
Identity of *Deviant*	offender	patient	debtor	disputant
Solution	punishment	help	payment	resolution

therapeutic and conciliatory are *remedial* styles of social control; the aim is social repair, assistance for people in trouble, amelioration of a bad situation and so on. While the goal of therapy is 'normality' that of conciliation is 'social harmony'.

The criminal law, and consequently the nature of sanctions imposed, has during the present century spread out from Style 1 (Penal) into Style 2 (Therapeutic) and Style 3 (Compensatory). What is suggested in the above argument is that the penal law should be restricted to Style 1 and that other forms of social control should be dealt with by different institutions in society, including the civil law. Such controls should not be the business of the criminal justice system as such. This does not mean that society provides less social welfare, medical services or education. What is being proposed is that these should be provided in a different way, outside the criminal justice system. In Sweden there are current discussions in a similar vein for the social services to be separated from judicial control, i.e. the abolition of probation as such; already in Holland the probation service has moved away from being *a service for the courts* and is now primarily *a service for the clients*. The proposal for restricting criminal justice, and the developments in the Netherlands and the Scandinavian countries, connote more than merely transferring a set of formal controls to another agency; the importance lies *in changing the way the issue is defined, which changes the very nature of the issue*. Also, an analysis in this form leads to a reconsideration of the ways in which issues are dealt with, or are prevented from arising because of the strengthening of the informal processes of control. On the basis of this analysis it becomes possible to have *a serious discussion that calls in question the need for a criminal justice system at all*, and *a fortiori* the need for a prison system. But for those who favour the maintenance of criminal justice and its prisons the argument becomes not merely one in terms of expedients to cope with an overloaded system and service — such as adopting diversion tactics and proliferating alternatives to penal institutions. Rather they must deal, in terms of the principles of punishment, with the nature of conduct to be prosecuted and with reasons for establishing penal institutions to contain certain categories of offenders.[8] 'Why criminal justice?' and 'why prisons?' return as cardinal points of debate for the philosopher, the lawyer, the criminologist and the penologist.

Those who accept the implications of abolition recognise that it cannot be achieved immediately without the unlikely event of a revolution which would result in the withering away of the State. For the innovator therefore the immediate question for the future revolves around curtailment of the powers of the criminal justice system, along with the injection of some transformingly humane ideas. Decriminalisation can clearly be one part of the process; but diversion and depenalisation act as a hybrid process that might merely consolidate the *status quo* as regards criminal justice. A second way of reducing criminal justice control is to remove the therapeutic, social welfare, and compensatory processes from its sphere — the latter being developed through the civil law or insurance schemes. Then, by breaking the link between criminal justice control and training and treatment in penal institutions, and only providing educational, social welfare and medical facilities on a client-oriented basis, one will restrict the legitimisation of the use of institutional sanctions, a step that would herald the end of their present use.

A great deal of criminological effort in the past has been expended in attempting to demonstrate the various ways in which criminality is related to the criminal justice and penal systems. The outcome is usually to emphasise the complexity of the connection. Today, a small group of writers suggest that the best hypothesis for both research and social action is to assume that they are unrelated other than in producing delinquency amplification and human suffering without behaviour modification (Hulsman 1978). One may hazard a guess that such writings are likely to have an impact on changing the nature of imprisonment as well as leading to its drastic curtailment.

NOTES

1. The ideology of management was initially seen primarily in terms of the management of prisoners, especially in relation to the development of prison industries and production. It is somewhat ironic that industrial disputes with prison officers should now have precipitated a crisis and necessitated the setting up of an urgent inquiry into the United Kingdom Prison Services, under the chairmanship of Mr. Justice May (November 1978).

2. See the annual series entitled respectively *Report on the Work of the Prison Department* (England and Wales) and *Prisons in Scotland*, both issued by H.M.S.O. as Command publications. See also Home Office (1977b).

3. See the table in the introductory chapter by Bottoms. These features of the contemporary situation are related to the large increase in known (or recorded) crimes and the consequent increase in the volume of cases resulting in conviction: see McClintock and Avison (1968), esp. ch. 9.

4. See the reports by Nils Christie (1977) and F. H. McClintock (1977); also Gunn (1977) and Gunn *et al.* (1978).

5. Philip Bean (1976) argues that 'training' involves less of an intrusion into an offender's life than 'treatment'.

6. The Home Office has now accepted that the question of an independent Inspectorate of prisons shall be considered by Mr. Justice May's committee

(above, note 1): speech by the Home Secretary to the Annual Conference of Boards of Visitors, 21 November 1978.

7. The recent Swedish Commission on Criminal Justice has recommended such a separation in its final report: personal communication from Professor Alvar Nelson, one of the Commissioners.

8. Some consideration was given to the use of imprisonment for certain categories of offenders by the House of Commons Expenditure Committee in its report on the prison system (House of Commons 1978).

8

The future of the community treatment of offenders in Britain

by KEN PEASE

What the Crisis is Not

Tony Bottoms, in his introductory chapter, identifies the putative crisis at the theoretical level as follows:

> There is a serious likelihood of a vacuum in penal thought following the coming certain collapse of what I shall call the rehabilitative ideal.

There is a danger of interpreting this view as being equivalent to the defeat of good by evil on the battlefield of penal affairs, the defeat anticipating a sharp trend towards harsher penalties, the reintroduction of the death sentence and a crash programme of prison building to house the criminals who have now been identified as intractable. There is in fact precious little truth in the view that, in recent times, it has been the rehabilitative ethic standing between the offender and the full rigours of the law. This is most clearly evident in the use of imprisonment (the treatment of which is not my brief), where the notion of rehabilitation justified the use of long rather than short sentences, and of indeterminate sentences rather than determinate ones. As recently as 1974 the European Committee on Crime Problems could argue:

> For several decades, penal administrators and criminologists have been concerned with the problem of short-term imprisonment. This is due to the fact that this form of punishment is regarded as having all the long-deplored drawbacks of imprisonment without providing for the offender to be observed and treated with a view to his social rehabilitation. This objective is regarded as essential under modern penal legislation. (p. 11)

and later that short-term imprisonment is 'insufficiently long for reconstructing the offender's personality or even for complete

137

vocational 'training'. The Advisory Council on the Penal System's (1977) Interim Report, *The Length of Prison Sentences*, suggests that the rehabilitative ideal lengthened prison sentences:

> The principle of rehabilitation was to have an important effect on the length of sentences courts thought fit to pass, the emphasis shifting from consideration of what might be the appropriate penalty for the offence to consideration of the need to reform the offender. It followed that if the principal role of imprisonment was to reform, short sentences were at the very least unhelpful for that purpose. . . . At sentencing seminars, first established in the early 1960s, judges were advised to avoid passing very short prison sentences. The cumulative effect of the theory and the advice of penal reformers to which it gave rise may well have been to increase the length of prison sentences across the board. (pp. 2–3)

Among non-custodial sentences, offenders' preference for the community service order over the much more explicitly treatment-oriented[1] probation order (Flegg 1976) gives further evidence that the decline of the rehabilitative ethic does not necessarily redound to the disadvantage of the offender. The most recent publications of the Home Office, which acknowledge the collapse of the rehabilitative ideal, do not argue for increased harshness of penal sanctions. For example, the Home Office of Criminal Justice Policy in 1976 argues:

> Longer sentences seem no more effective than short ones, different types of institutions appear to work about equally as well, and rehabilitative programmes — whether involving psychiatric treatment, counselling, casework, or intensive contact and special attention, in custodial or non-custodial settings — appear overall to have no certain beneficial effects. (Home Office 1977a, p. 49)

But the same report states as a particular preoccupation of policy the aim 'to reduce the size of the prison population and the proportionate use of imprisonment as a court disposal' (pp. 3–4) and to meet that need advocates 'the provision of an increasingly wider range of alternative forms of non-custodial disposal' (p. 5). Whether the continuing liberality of approach is a function primarily of expediency (given the pressure on the prisons) or of simple humanity (contrary to popular imagination it is blood and not engine-oil which courses through the veins of most Home Office officials) is not evident. My own belief is that central government thinking is much more influenced by judicial theories of sentencing than it is by the view of the probation service or of academic criminology, and that, notwithstanding the views expressed by the Advisory Council, it is very easy to over-state the importance of considerations of rehabilitation in judicial thinking. Cross (1975), writing under the heading 'Sentencing aims', quotes the following with approval:

> In passing sentence the court may have one or more of a number of objectives in mind: to make it clear to the offender and the public that offences cannot be committed with impunity; to impose some penalty or obligation which may discourage others from committing offences; to make clear the seriousness with which the courts, on behalf of the community, view the offending behaviour; and to prevent the individual concerned from committing offences in the short term, whether or not he can be induced to stop in the long term. (Advisory Council on the Penal System 1974, para. 151)

Cross comments, 'Quite rightly, it is submitted, there is no reference to reform in the above passage' (p. 130). Cross also comments that the quoted extract is consistent with Morris' principle that power over a criminal's life should not be taken in excess of that which would be taken were his reform not considered as one of our purposes. (See N. Morris (1974) for a full working out of the principle.)

Of course, the relative importance of reform and other factors in determining what sentence should be passed is a matter for debate. As far as non-custodial sentences are concerned, the pattern suggests that the sentence traditionally identified with the rehabilitative ideal is not of overwhelming importance in numerical terms. Probation orders are now made on fewer than one-tenth of offenders aged 17 or over convicted of an indictable offence. In contrast fines are imposed following well over one-half of such convictions. Although there has been a decline in the use of probation over the last ten years, even at the beginning of the decade probation was given after less than 15% of convictions for indictable offences and the use of fines has only dropped below the 50% level once in the last ten years. The Home Office handbook for sentencers (Home Office 1969) suggests 'in deciding between a fine and a probation order the court will wish to consider whether or not the offender needs the continuing attention that could be provided by the latter' (para. 13). That the court regards such attention as necessary in only the small minority of cases suggests that the change in the offender which it seeks to bring about is more in the nature of individual deterrence than rehabilitation, or alternatively that individual change is not wholly the primary consideration.

To this point I have argued that the decline of the rehabilitative ideal does not of itself mean that penalties will tend to become harsher. In fact, the lessons of history suggest that the converse may be true. I have suggested that a major reason why the changes in overall sentencing pattern resulting from the demise of the rehabilitative ideal may be slight is that that ideal never completely permeated sentencing policy (certainly as far as non-custodial sentences are concerned).

What of course may be true is that treatment agencies, and this primarily means the probation service in the non-custodial setting, may change the nature of the sentences they administer. Thus what is experienced by the offender on a probation order may change dramatically to be much more directed towards containment in the community than towards rehabilitation. There is some evidence that this kind of holding action can be successful (Sinclair 1971; Berntsen and Christiansen 1965) and as Bill McWilliams has pointed out to me, the emphasis is not inconsistent with that applying in the case of parole supervision by the probation service. There are suggestions that the most innovative probation and after-care services may move in this direction (see, for example, Thomas 1978).

Why Not Lock People Up?

In the first section of this chapter I argued that the use of non-custodial sentencing was not likely to decrease on the basis of the demise of the rehabilitative ideal. A question that was evaded is why have non-custodial sentencing at all? Arguing from a position which takes crime prevention as the primary aim of sentencing, there is quite simply no justification for the non-custodial sentence. Research on the effectiveness of sentencing suggests (Home Office 1969) that penal treatments do not have different effects in terms of reducing reconviction, but this is really done by methodological sleight of hand. A typical reconviction experiment compares reconvictions *during time at risk.* Thus, for example, a comparison between a group sentenced to imprisonment and another group given a non-custodial sentence measures time at risk of the imprisoned group from the date they leave prison. If reconviction rates were measured from the date of conviction then imprisoned groups would always show a lower reconviction rate than a group given a non-custodial disposal. Further, commonsense assumptions about general deterrence would suggest that prison is useful in crime prevention in this second way. Against this, of course, must be weighed the cost of prison in human and economic terms, and the fact that although rehabilitation has been discredited as an achievable aim of treatment, rehabilitation in the sense of reduced convictions is a likely result of the passage of time. To put it a bit more simply, age cures crime. In 1976 one 17-year-old male in 15 was found guilty of an indictable offence, compared with less than one in 100 men between the ages of 40 and 50. Thus the crime prevention function of imprisonment is less than one might expect on the basis of an extrapolation of the criminal records of those who have been before the court. For example a 29-year-old man with at least one conviction each year for the previous ten years will be regarded as certain to be reconvicted within one year on the basis of this record. However, *on the basis of his increasing age,* the probability of his reconviction is declining.

I raise the kind of consideration above because, although I believe that the effect of the demise of the rehabilitative ideal will be small on the use by the sentencer of non-custodial alternatives, the real crisis will appear if and when it becomes possible to make sensible estimates of the effect of imprisonment as a preventer of crime. Studies which are the first steps to producing estimates of this kind are already in hand. These are known as studies of incapacitation. Put simply, incapacitation studies examine criminal careers and set out to calculate how many and what kind of crimes particular sentencing policies would prevent. To take a silly example, focusing upon all murders committed in a given year, if all murders in that year were committed by men who had a conviction for a criminal offence in the five years before the murder took place, then a sentencing policy which locked up everyone found guilty of a criminal offence for a period of six years would have prevented all the murders in the year concerned. It is thus conceivable that, if all serious crimes were committed by people with recent criminal convictions, incapacitation research, allied to a better understanding of general deterrence, could provide the empirical basis for changes in sentencing practice. It will be a source of pleasure for the liberals amongst readers that research of this kind done up to the present time has suggested that the increase in sentence lengths would have to be pretty stupendous to produce a significant level of prevention of serious crime (see, for example, Van Dine *et al.* 1977). Nevertheless, these are early days and I would persist in speculating that incapacitation studies and studies of general deterrence could provide a much greater threat to the use of non-custodial sentences relative to custodial sentences than does the decline of the rehabilitative ideal. Even assuming research findings justifying greater use of custody, it would be some time before they were translated into judicial action.

Current Non-Custodial Sentences

It is perhaps appropriate at this stage to describe some of the more frequently used non-custodial sentences as a backcloth against which to consider trends and possible developments.

Discharges

These are appropriate when the court 'is of the opinion, having regard to the circumstances including the nature of the offence, and the character of the offender, that it is inexpedient to inflict punishment and that a probation order is not appropriate' (Home Office 1969, para. 8). A discharge can be absolute or conditional. If conditional, the court specifies the period during which the condition applies. The condition is that the offender does not commit another offence. Unlike the suspended sentence, a conditional discharge implies no presumption of the way in which a court will act on a breach of the condition or indeed whether the court will act on the breach at all.

Fines

For offenders of all ages and both sexes, the most frequently given sentence is the fine. To give an example of the numerical prevalence of the fine over other sentences, we can take people aged 21 and over sentenced to indictable offences (and thus excluding the more trivial motoring offences for which fines are virtually universal). Fifty-four per cent of people of this kind in 1976 were given fines. This is over four times as many as were given the next most frequent sentence, namely immediate imprisonment. A fine seems to be a sentence of default in the sense that positive reasons for fining rather than dealing with someone in another way are not typically given. The relationship tends to be expressed in the other way, for example, the court 'will wish to be satisfied . . . that neither the interests of society nor those of the offender require that he should be detained in custody' (Home Office 1969, para. 13) and 'if the offender cannot pay . . . he may ultimately have to be committed to prison in default *and the attempt to avoid a custodial disposal will have failed*' (Home Office 1969, para. 13, italics added).

Probation

A probation order requires an offender to be under the supervision of a probation officer for a specified period of not less than six months nor more than three years, during which time he will periodically be visited by, or visit, the officer. The frequency of such visits typically decreases as the order progresses, eventually taking place perhaps once every three weeks or a month. The Home Office (1969) specifies that an *a priori* case for the use of probation exists when:

(a) the circumstances of the offence and the offender's
record are not such as to demand, in the interests of society,
that some more severe method be adopted in dealing with
him;

(b) the risk, if any, to society, through setting the offender at liberty is outweighed by the moral, social and economic arguments for not depriving him of it;

(c) the offender needs continuing attention, since otherwise, if condition (b) is satisfied, a fine or discharge will suffice;

and

(d) the offender is capable of responding to this attention while at liberty. (para. 23)

Conditions may be attached to a probation order, for example to reside where directed, to undergo treatment for a mental condition, or to spend 60 days learning social skills in a day training centre.

Suspended Sentences

A suspended sentence is in law a sentence of imprisonment and in fact a non–custodial sentence. After a suspended sentence the offender leaves court essentially free, but if he is convicted again during the period over which the sentence is suspended, the court:

is required to order the suspended sentence to be executed in full unless the court is of the opinion that it would be unjust to do so in view of all the circumstances which have arisen since the suspended sentence was passed, including the facts of the subsequent offence. (Home Office 1969, para. 161)

The evidence is clear that suspended sentences are not always used where an activated prison sentence would otherwise be imposed (Bottoms 1979).

Other Sentences

The sentences set out above are numerically the most important. However, a number of recently introduced alternatives may be mentioned in passing. The first is the *community service order*, by which an offender of age 17 or over convicted of an offence punishable by imprisonment can instead do work for the community supervised by the probation service for between 40 and 240 hours, as specified by the court. Instead of sentencing immediately upon conviction, a court may *defer* sentence for up to six months, after which circumstances relevant to sentence may have changed. In addition to sentencing an offender, courts may order an offender to pay *compensation* for personal injury, loss or damage resulting from a criminal offence (Powers of Criminal Courts Act 1973).

Trends and Possible Developments

Tony Bottoms described, in his introductory chapter, trends in sentencing practice over the years between 1938 and 1975. Of these the most remarkable was the rise of the fine to account for over half of the sentences imposed for indictable offences in 1975. Taking a rather shorter time perspective, perhaps the most striking development of the last decade in criminal justice has been the rise in recorded indictable crime, and in the face of that fall in the proportionate use of active imprisonment. Recorded indictable crime has increased from 1.2 million in 1966 to over two million in 1975 and 1976. Active imprisonment has fallen from 18% in 1966 and has hovered around 10% during the last two years. Among non-custodial sentences, emphatically the most striking trend has been the reduction in the use of probation orders. For those aged 17 and over, probation represented 12.5% of all disposals in 1966, and was down to below 8% in 1976. Since suspended sentences were introduced by the 1967 Criminal Justice Act, clearly their development, to account in 1976 for over 10% of people aged over 21 convicted of indictable offences, is a noteworthy feature of the last decade. Another remarkable development has been the swiftness of the rise in community service orders. These have increased in number very rapidly since the end of their experimental period in 1975 to number over 9,000 in 1976. Another minor miracle has been the increased use of compensation orders since 1972 (Tarling and Softley 1976; Softley 1977).

What do the trends mentioned above and the longer-term ones outlined by Tony Bottoms amount to? I would suggest that they are consistent with the ascendancy of two related themes. The first is that of reparation, and the second is that of responsibility, i.e. the notion that an offender's actions are self-directed.

Reparation was identified as a theme in Tony Bottoms' chapter. What the community service order, compensation order and arguably the decrease in custodial sentences have in common is the desire to exact from the offender some contribution either to the victim of his offence or to society as a whole. Such an emphasis is not consistent with the extensive use of custodial sentences since the original offence is likely to preclude compensation (Softley and Tarling 1977) and the original offence is compounded by the use of the most costly possible sanction, imprisonment, where such a sentence can realistically be avoided.

The importance of the principle of reparation in the development of community service orders is evident from the Home Secretary's introduction to the second reading debate on the Criminal Justice Bill of 1971, which included the following:

> I was attracted from the start by the idea that people who
> have committed minor offences would be better occupied
> doing a service to their fellow citizens than sitting alongside
> others in a crowded jail. (H.C. Deb. vol. 826, col. 972)

The Howard League (1977a) report, entitled *Making Amends*, is another recent expression of interest in reparation. Here it is concern with the needs of the victim of crime that is the major justification for reparation. As to the offender responsibility theme, Tony Bottoms in his introductory chapter suggests that an approach to our present situation could be 'to work out a purely regulatory scale of penalties . . . of which the fine is the most obvious example'. One could argue that the theme of reparation, and the consequent pressures towards the treatment of issues like compensation in the criminal courts is a way of conceiving the relationship of victim and perpetrator of crime as responsible people in conflict. Another argument derives from the massive growth in the use of the fine. Those offences which are dealt with almost universally by means of a fine are, one could argue, those which involve the least suggestion that the offender is not as other men are. The most obvious example of this is motoring crime. Here, although sometimes the consequences are equivalent to murder, the fine is overwhelmingly the sentence of choice (Bottoms 1977, pp. 83–4). Unless special arrangements are made for the enforcement of fines (for example the making of a money payment supervision order), it places the responsibility on the offender to pay and not on the penal system to change him. A third argument is based on the nature of new or newish sanctions which have proved popular. The suspended sentence is a recently introduced sanction which implies that the offender is responsible for his actions, being capable of changing his ways if he so chooses after weighing the probability of having the suspended sentence activated. Community service orders too suggest the self-direction of the offender by characterising him as a source of work rather than a source of problems.

None of these thoughts is remotely persuasive taken by itself, but taken together, they may represent a breakdown of received wisdom about what criminal behaviour has reasons and what simply has causes, in the direction of allowing more criminal behaviour to be reasoned choices. It may be that the rehabilitative ethic will persist longest with those offenders whose reasoning we find most difficult to represent to ourselves, and these groups would probably be the impulsively violent and petty persistent offenders (see Bottoms 1977, p. 75).

If reparation and responsibility are the principles which increase in importance, what are the developments in non-custodial penalties which we can reasonably anticipate?

(i) The continuing development of community service orders. Community service is administered by the probation service, and if probation continues to decline at its recent rate, community service orders could provide the bulk of the work of the probation service coming directly from the courts before 1990. There may also be a move to make community service orders available to offenders aged under 17 and presumably this would imply a renewal of interest by the probation service in offenders in this age group. The only danger that one can foresee to the continuing growth of community service orders is that they may become probationised, with the choice of work and enforcement of attendance at work based more on offender needs and preferences than on considerations of the task in hand. It is easier for academics to say that the rehabilitative ideal is doomed than to persuade those probation officers who have hitched their wagon to the star of rehabilitation that it was all in vain. If the community service order falls into the hands of those who administer it on the basis of their hopes of effecting rehabilitation, then community service will come to be discredited in the eyes of the courts. Dissatisfaction with 'punitive' community service has existed in the probation service since the beginning of the scheme (Pease *et al.* 1975). Even the most superficial discussion of community service with probation officers now makes it obvious that these reservations still exist, and the trend to decentralise the administration of community service from a central office within each region to ordinary probation offices places the community service administrator in a climate which may be hostile to community service considered as a reparative rather than a rehabilitative sentence.

In what one fears may be a prescient article, Willetts (1976), writing from the standpoint of the year 2000, describes the history of the last quarter of the twentieth century as follows:

> The discredited probation order became less frequent, and discharges and fines more frequent. The greatest rise, however, was in the number of community service orders. . . . However, as you may recall, the community service order was administered by the probation services. Soon the tasks ordered became 'looking for a job', 'discussions with probation staff' and so on. In other words, the community service order became, in effect, a probation order. Thus our predecessors triumphantly reasserted the caring role. (p. 24)

(ii) Compensation orders will increase in frequency, particularly in cases of offences of violence, where they are currently under-used. However, compensation orders on those given prison sentences will become less frequent, on the basis of the extreme difficulty of the enforcement of such orders (Tarling and Softley 1976).

(iii) Schemes which provide victims with emotional support and with practical help and advice will increase in number. The probation service may involve itself in such schemes. Victims of crime may be given the opportunity of asking offenders on community service to do work for them which has priority over other work supplied for the scheme.

(iv) Consideration will be given to circumstances where the victim and perpetrator of a crime can meet (see Howard League 1977a).

(v) As much or more use of the fine will be made.[2]

(vi) Periodic or weekend imprisonment may be reconsidered (see A.C.P.S. 1970a).

(vii) The parole scheme may be revamped to allow release on licence after one-third of sentence. The only condition of the parole licence (other than those requiring the offender to keep in touch with his probation officer) will be that no further offence is committed. Such a development would have the additional advantage of guaranteeing the future of the probation and after-care service, and in a way consistent with its current increasing commitment to after-care work (Home Office Statistical Department 1977).

The Limits of Reparation

The Advisory Council on the Penal System (1970b) in its report on reparation distinguished two alternative concepts of reparation which were very difficult to reconcile:

> One is that of the criminal courts, where the decision and the assessment are entirely within the court's discretion and the victim has no legal rights. This method produces quick and practical orders within a limited range of cases. The alternative concept is that reparation is another form of civil damages to be applied for and enforced through the civil courts on the initiative of the victim, who at best will get his damages after some delay but many have nothing to show for his litigation but his solicitor's bill for costs. (para. 84)

As recently as 8 April 1978 in an article on compensation in *Justice of the Peace*, it is stressed that 'the High Court has said repeatedly that in a great majority of cases the appropriate place to deal with the extent of the loss is in the appropriate civil proceedings' (Anon. 1978). The only major extension of financial reparation within the criminal courts which the Advisory Council seems to have regarded as possible is one which would involve a fairly basic restructuring of the limits of criminal law. In such a restructuring findings of guilt would be followed by some assessment of damage in which victim and offender would have a right to be heard. Sentence would then be reached on the basis of a fully argued decision about appropriate compensation. The costs to the victim in such a system would have to be borne by the State.

A strong advocacy of 'victim-oriented' courts is made by Christie (1976). He argues that in such courts:

> The first stage will be a traditional one where it is established whether it is true that the law has been broken, and whether it was this particular person who broke it. [In] the second stage . . . the victim's situation was considered [with] detailed consideration what could be done for him, first and foremost by the offender, secondly by the local neighbourhood, thirdly by the State . . . only after this stage was passed, and it ought to take hours, maybe days to pass it, only then would come the time for an eventual decision on punishment [i.e.] that suffering which the judge found necessary to apply *in addition* to those unintended constructive sufferings the offender would go through in his restitutive sufferings *vis-à-vis* the victim. (pp. 18–19, italics in original)

Christie's scheme is interesting in illustrating the degree of change from the traditional mode of operation of criminal courts which would be necessary to give fullest expression to the principle of reparation. It is a degree of change which is not likely to take place in the foreseeable future. Even the most modest increases in compensation predicted above are limited by the difficulties of the criminal courts in relating the money exacted from the offender realistically to his means. This difficulty is very clearly specified in the Report of the Advisory Council on the Penal System (1970a) on Non-Custodial and Semi-Custodial Penalties when discussing the applicability of the Swedish day-fine system in the United Kingdom.

Given that the restructuring of the courts to allow the principle of reparation its full scope is unlikely, are there more indirect means by which the principle of reparation could be made manifest? In my view, the incorporation of the principle of reparation into the criminal justice system is circumscribed more by the structure of the system and other practical difficulties than it is by the will to incorporate it. Perhaps one should therefore try out new ways of putting the principle into effect. One avenue which could be explored is the role of the insurance companies. The role of the insurance industry (from the viewpoint of the insured) is to make good loss. Would it be possible to link the efforts or money of offenders to a scheme of insurance in such a way as to subsidise the insurance premiums of potential victims? If, for example, all money paid in compensation were set against the commercial costs of crime insurance, then this would provide an incentive for insurance protection, certainly against property crime. This is, of course, only the bare bones of an idea but it does seem to me to have one critical advantage. Potential victims of crime, notably of property offences, would have their premiums calculated on the basis of the extent to which they fail to protect themselves against crimes committed against them. Certain kinds of crime not associated with victim precipitation would have no insurance premium associated with them. If the degree of subsidy from compensation in the courts was sufficiently high, it could also be the case that premises protected as completely as is possible against crime would thereby get free insurance.

Is the Rehabilitative Ideal Really Dead?

Having progressed thus far on the basis of tacit acceptance of the premise that the rehabilitative ideal is in fact dead or dying, it is probably perverse to start questioning it now. However, that is what I propose to do, since the rehabilitative ideal seems to me to be a remarkably lively corpse. Taking the probation service, even the most cursory examination of recommendations of probation made in social inquiry reports, or a reading of the journal of the National Association of Probation Officers, *Probation Journal*, or a conversation with most experienced probation officers makes it abundantly clear that rehabilitation is not a lost cause in the probation service. Even a very recent book about the probation service (Haxby 1978), which makes thoughtful and intelligent proposals for the future of the service, nonetheless proposes that it will 'have a responsibility to promote a range of services designed to assist in the rehabilitation of offenders and the prevention of recidivism' (p. 90). In the 1976 Report of the Work of the Prison Department (Home Office 1977d), a whole chapter is devoted to the topic 'Treatment and training'. Therein we read:

> For many prisoners a proven inability to benefit from either treatment or training has led to their being in prison, and it is against this background that the 'treatment and training provided' should be measured. (para. 55)

The Prison Department thus emphasises the difficulty of treatment and training rather than acknowledges its irrelevance to the chance of a subsequent good and useful life by the prisoners. The parole system remains based (officially at least) in part upon its rehabilitative component. The Report of the Parole Board for 1976 (Home Office 1977c) includes the sentence:

> Through his parole licence [the prisoner] may receive the practical help and discipline which will enable him to

survive the first few weeks of freedom without resorting to crime. Supervision in this sense may be the only hope for rehabilitation. (para. 18)

This hope is a vain one if the relevant research (Nuttall *et al.* 1977) is to be believed. In a report on community service (Morgan 1976), Judge D. Watkin Powell argues that community service 'combines punishment with rehabilitation in the fullest sense of the word' (p. 44).

In short, the language of rehabilitation is still with us. The fact of rehabilitation is probably sincerely believed by many. I would like to suggest that the implication of this is that developments in the penal system in the next few decades will occur in a context from which the rehabilitative ideal has not been wholly removed. The rehabilitative ethic may still powerfully influence the direction of the penal system.

I would go further to express the view that the influence of the Rehabilitation Rump will be on balance an unfortunate one. It will be to introduce new sources of injustice and perpetuate old ones. For example, my experiences of community service include cases in which men working together for the same amount of time have been credited with different numbers of hours on the basis of treatment considerations. The parole system will continue to be a source of frustration to prisoners and to liberal outsiders so long as the inscrutability of its process is justified by a rehabilitative ethic. Offenders will continue to be incarcerated or not on the basis of their supposed susceptibility to probation treatment as expressed in social inquiry reports. Victim schemes may wither because of an emphasis on 'treating' victims of crime to the neglect of offering practical help.

In Conclusion: In this chapter I have tried to argue the following points:

(i) The rehabilitive ideal is less dead than the evidence warrants.

(ii) The demise of the rehabilitative ideal does not necessarily imply harsher treatment for offenders.

(iii) Rehabilitation is not the major purpose of sentencing and the demise of the ideal should not produce spectacular changes in sentencing practice, although it may substantially change the administration of particular sentences.

(iv) Themes which are in the ascendancy are reparation and personal responsibility. Consequences of their further development may include the extended use of compensation orders, community service orders and possibly fines. Periodic imprisonment may be reconsidered, and the parole system restructured.

NOTES

1. The word 'treatment' tends to be used in two quite distinct ways. In the first its necessary ingredient is the *intent* to rehabilitate. Treatment in this sense is usually contrasted with punishment. It is used in this sense in this chapter. In the second sense, treatment is anything that the criminal justice system does to an offender.
2. There is a potential for irony here. The fine is popular on grounds other than its reforming effect but it is the only sentence for which there is evidence that it may reduce the number of subsequent convictions (Home Office 1969). This evidence has been fairly criticised by Bottoms (1973) but if the 1969 data were ever to be reproduced (and no one has yet tried) it would be the case that a sentence lacking in rehabilitative intent was the only one to have rehabilitative effect.

9

Some considerations concerning crime and social policy

by ELIZABETH E. BARNARD

In this chapter, my purpose is to put the debates over the practical and theoretical problems in penal policy into the context of the concerns of social policy generally. At a practical level, there is parallels in resource problems, personnel difficulties and the setting of realistic objectives, while theoreticians are similarly concerned with challenges to erstwhile-dominant ideologies. In examining these issues, I shall pay particular attention to the changing definition of social policy; to the ways in which penal and social policies have been related in the past; to the implications for social policy of current theoretical arguments about penal policy; and to some current developments in social policy.

The Definition of Social Policy

Social policy has been defined in many ways, and students of social policy have been broadening their scope in recent years. Perhaps the broadest definition would be those institutionalised actions purposively designed to promote the welfare of others or of the collectivity, rather than of the self. In this formulation, the actor could be an individual, a group, the State or even a supra-state organisation. Thus, an interest in social policy is a concern with altruism and collectivism, and with their strength relative to egoism and individualism, in social order. Such a definition leaves open, as issues for empirical analysis and ideological debate, how welfare is and should be defined, whether the actors or the others do and should determine the criteria for such action, and the form it takes. Narrower definitions of social policy tend to restrict it to issues facing particular societies at particular points in their history. Thus, within capitalist countries, social policy has often been defined as those State policies which seek to counteract the allocation of resources by the free play of market forces, thus excluding non–State action such as charities, friendly societies, etc.; it has even been restricted to institutional sectors, such as health, education, the personal social services and so on, which represent relatively new State interventions and involve collective provision, rather than also including, for example, fiscal benefits.

From a broad definition of social policy, conceptually distinct criteria of social welfare and strategies for its attainment may be specified. It is useful to distinguish political philosophies in terms of their central value commitments or standards of social welfare. For a conservative, the prime requirement is order, for a liberal it is freedom, and for a socialist it is equality. Actual political parties propose compromises of these, and none more so than social democrats, whose chief claim is that these standards need not conflict, but can be promoted simultaneously. A task for social theory is to help us to know which strategies of social policy are going to achieve the chosen welfare goals. Social theories and political philosophies need to be compatible, unless one is prepared to accept a radical pessimism and abandon policy-making.

Penal policy may be seen as a strategy, or set of strategies, in the promotion of welfare, and the appropriateness of a particular penal policy will be judged in terms of its contribution, in the context of social policies as a whole, to a particular standard of welfare. A crucial question for theoretical and empirical analysis is whether penal policy is merely the ultimate means of enforcement for a set of social policies, i.e. the stick behind the carrot. In this view, the criminal law embodies ideals for conduct, which may be promoted in a variety of ways, but the threat of punishment for non-conformity is always present, and symbolises the importance of those ideals. The choice of penal policy, though not necessarily of a particular type of penal policy, would not, then, be a directly utilitarian one; it would not be a matter of asking whether punishment was an effective means of promoting welfare, but, rather, if a given state of affairs was desirable enough to be promoted, then policies for its support must include penal elements. Other views of the role of penal policy within social policy either allows for the possibility that for every welfare objective there may be choices of strategy, so that in some circumstances penal policy may be the most effective, or increase total net effectiveness; or consider that penal policy is appropriate for some objectives (such as, perhaps, the maintenance of certain types of order or the preservation of certain liberties) but not others (such as, perhaps, health, prosperity or substantive equality).

As well as considering objectives and strategies, however, we need to ask how these become institutionalised. Traditionally, practitioners in both criminology and social administration have implicitly believed that social change could occur through the action of enlightened and informed agents of authority, and have concentrated on influencing and joining elites to contribute to policy-making. More recently, however, in line with other shifts in their thinking, their involvement in policy-making has often been at a different level, taking the Marxist emphasis on class struggle or the 'appreciative stance' of a subjective identification with the powerless as their starting-point.

It is a truism that penal policy necessarily involves individualising, in the sense that only selected persons directly experience punishment, whereas other social policies *may* be directly applied to individuals, both selectively and generally (personal social services, many health and education services, financial benefits and so on), but *may* alternatively supply a general good, without direct impact on selected individuals (armed services, lighthouses, roads, sewerage and so on). The distinction is principally concerned with the means rather than the goals of policy, but it is important to stress that whether the goals of penal policy are seen as promoting a general good (such as the protection of all members of society from harm, the general deterrence of harmful acts, or the declaration of universal standards) or as having a more particular purpose (such as the correction of the criminal's attitudes and behaviour, or making him suffer for his sins) the means are always individually focused. It is also generally taken for granted, but nevertheless worth stating, that penal policy is State-controlled, though it may involve non-State bodies — as licencees, in effect — whereas other social policies include wholly private measures. In looking at the relationship of penal and other social policies, the differential involvement of State and non-State agencies and of general and personalised provision, should be given particular attention.

A Brief History of English Social Policy

The sixteenth century is generally recognised as the time when penal policy in England was at its most harsh. The Tudor State is associated with the growth of a central administrative apparatus, of foreign trade and of manufacturing, while the dissolution of the monasteries and enclosures of common land reduced the resources of the poor. Beggary and vagrancy were obvious outcomes, and they were dealt with largely in penal terms initially. A new institutional measure, the House of Correction, which entailed coercive control, and the Elizabethan Poor Law, which established a localised responsibility for poor relief, were later policies. Interpreting these developments, it would appear that a problem of disorder was generated by policies which promoted the concentration of wealth, that this problem was reacted to in penal terms initially, later reinforced by other measures.

With the industrial revolution, paternalism and localism were increasingly eroded; communities with mutual obligations were transformed into societies where the free, mobile individual sold his labour power in the market place and became personally responsible for his own welfare and that of his family. In the eighteenth century, new statutes created more opportunities for the imposition of harsh penalties, but mitigation could be obtained by using networks of patronage (Hay 1975), giving an appearance of justice tempered with mercy. In the early nineteenth century, physical punishments were largely replaced by imprisonment, under increasingly central and bureaucratic control; the impersonality of the market place was reflected in the reformed administration of criminal justice. The Poor Law Amendment Act of 1834 completed a social policy system based on deterrent principles to support a free market and personal responsibility. As the able-bodied were only eligible for poor relief if they entered workhouses, and as workhouses were required to provide worse conditions than existed outside, this policy was successful in reducing the cost of poor relief and in forcing labourers into the market place. The 'burden' of dealing with non-participants in the labour market was increasingly removed into specialised institutions — asylums, hospitals, orphanages, schools, workhouses, prisons — but the 'less-eligibility' principle, in deterring people from freely resorting to such institutions, encouraged them to develop private and mutual resources for dealing with misfortune. As the economy prospered in the mid-nineteenth century, sections of the working class were increasingly able to do more than live from day to day, and friendly societies developed. The rigorous public system was maintained, however, by two strongly held sets of beliefs among the politically powerful classes. Moral defect was seen as the principal cause of social misfortune; some had prospered by hard work and enterprise was free, after all. Ironically, the other set of beliefs, the iron laws of political economy, implied a structural, albeit unalterable, basis for poverty; among these laws were Malthus' theory of population growth, which held that any surplus over subsistence needs would rapidly be absorbed by extra people, and Ricardo's theory of wages, that they must always tend to subsistence level, and that poor relief keeps wages low, both by reducing work incentive and by draining the resources of the economy. Thus, it was believed that the long-term interest of the working classes was served by reinforcing labour discipline, in factory, workhouse and prison.

But, almost as soon as this system of social policy, with its negative public interventions, had been established, other elements in public social policy began. Some were of the 'general good' kind, such as municipal sewerage schemes, often promoted by the same people, such as Owen Chadwick, who had been proponents of the deterrent poor law. Others involved concern for the well-being of selected individuals, such as women and children in mining and textile industries; and, from the 1830s, State regulation of working conditions and hours began, though for a long time it was applied only to exceptional cases.

A more detailed analysis is required, but it appears that the transition from feudal to capitalist social relations, which involves shifts in what is considered the good society and the good citizen, and what a citizen may reasonably demand of others, was stabilised by penal policies (in which the deterrent principle and the institutional mechanism were increasingly dominant) and subsequently reinforced by other social policies. Social policy in the twentieth century shows a shift from deterrence and competitive market relations towards a new concern with mutual aid, which is now achieved at the societal level, through State intervention and specialised service rather than resting on traditional communal ties of mutual obligation and personal service. The post-war welfare state is built on State aid to the market economy, which is expected to build up the resources, whose distribution will be modified by State intervention. Under welfare capitalism, the penal expression of this concern is the rehabilitative ideal, which has developed from soul-saving to scientific treatment, but other expressions include (roughly in order of emergence) the compulsory social insurance system, which spreads and shares the risks of illness and accident, to which all are thought to be vulnerable; compensation for disadvantage, which may spread from disability allowances through to recent schemes of positive discrimination, such as educational priority areas; and recognition of social rights to goods and services irrespective of market power, in health, housing, education and even leisure pursuits such as sport and the arts. In the first phase, State intervention does not involve a rejection of market patterns of distribution, but it becomes clear that the limited redistribution of insurance policies cannot ensure adequate minimum standards for all, let alone equalised provision, and if standards take precedence then the insurance basis becomes notional. The residual model of State social intervention is justified by the argument that resources are scarce and should be devoted to the most needy, but, while market moralities remain, this creates a stigmatised 'dependent' population, perceived as a drain on those who 'stand on their own feet'. However, the collectivist model, giving all citizens access to public services, may reinforce the inequalities of the market place, most notably in such opportunity-creating sectors like education, especially if the distribution of its resources are linked to perceived market needs.

As Abrams (1978) has recently pointed out, when market

moralities are combined with highly-organised services and an escalation in recognised needs and rights of citizenship, personal responsibility for social welfare is minimised. A fiscal crisis is likely to result. The penal system is not alone in experiencing resource problems; it is an inevitable consequence of a welfare state, for needs are virtually limitless, and the specialised welfare bureaucracies become competitive interest groups. Indeed, economic growth, which may be advocated as a solution to the resource problem, stimulates newly-sensed needs.

Alongside the rehabilitative ideal in penal policy, crime reduction has been cited as an objective for, or a criterion in, the measurement of the success of social policies such as slum clearance, the abolition of selective secondary education, the promotion of youth clubs and the reorganisation of the social services. For example, the Report of the Committee on Local Authority and Allied Personal Social Services states that:

> This was the immediate point of origin of the Committee: a
> concern at the increase in officially recorded delinquency,
> the need to concentrate resources and a belief that
> preventive work with families was of cardinal importance
> in this context. (Seebohm Report 1968, p. 17)

A common objective of penal and other social policies has been the creation of attitudes and circumstances which would be congruent with a social ideal, a society which offered all its citizens opportunities for a full life. Penal policies would be emphasised by those who believed that ours was such a society but that some citizens had a defective understanding of this, from personal inadequacy or by chance or choice or marginal system failure, so they required re-education. Other policies would be emphasised by those who believed that the ideal had not been attained; however, in the phase of social policy when compensation for disadvantage was emphasised, and the State's role was seen as providing residual services, notably in the 1950s and 1960s, penal and other social policies were similar, for the focus was on selecting individuals for special treatment and it was assumed the Beveridge-inspired (Beveridge Report 1942) welfare state had made the social structure essentially just. There were a number of problems with this view, however; it assumed that there was a fundamental consensus on what constituted a full life, and that none of its features was essentially scarce, rationed or competitive. Furthermore, it assumed that any remaining defects in the organisation of our society were marginal, capable of solution through minor technical adjustments, rather than fundamental aspects of the core structure, which would need radical change to overcome. Thus, there was considerable emphasis on influencing patterns of child-rearing, locating the source of deviant life-styles and the critical element in the cycle of deprivation in the family. The persistence of poverty was interpreted as a problem at this level in the social structure rather than at the political or economic level.

In the late 1960s, innovation in social policy included programmes of positive discrimination, directing central government resources selectively to areas of greatest need. Among these, the Community Development Projects are especially interesting for they were launched by the Home Office and explicitly modelled on American experience (Marris and Rein 1967), which had included local programmes financed under the Juvenile Delinquency and Youth Offences Control Act of 1961. The British programme, like its model, rested on the conviction that better co-ordination of official services and their linking with local voluntary action would prove both more effective and less costly than the general pattern of universal provision through specialised agencies. But its practice demonstrates:

> marked discrepancy . . . between fieldwork activists, who
> want to redistribute power and opportunity, and
> governments, who want to show maximum concern at
> minimum costs in ways that cannot fundamentally alter
> society. (Meacher 1974, p. 7)

The programme began in 1969 and entailed designating about a dozen areas for special attention. These were spread throughout the country and all were seen as presenting extreme problems of deprivation in income, housing, employment, education and other indices, but rural, urban and metropolitan areas were included. Action and Research teams were appointed, and funding was provided by both local and central government. It was clear that social work standards of well-being were to be the basis of evaluation. Local workers in the projects have had some success in helping individuals obtain personal rights in claims on the official welfare services and in asserting a local case in planning decisions, especially over housing. But their experience in working with people living in deprived areas had led them to move increasingly from a model of personal inadequacy towards one of structured inequality, and hence they have become involved in conflicts with local government bureaucracies, private employers and other entrenched interests:

> Confronted with the wider canvas of population
> movements, employment and housing changes, local
> teams have increasingly questioned and moved away from
> the original 'social pathology' assumptions of the
> experiment. They have begun to develop perspectives
> which better account for the unequal distribution of both
> private and public goods and services, and provide

explanations for the powerlessness of Community
Development Project populations to influence these
distributions. (Home Office 1974, p. 23)

The fiscal crisis of the 1970s has extended the pattern in social
policy of official subsidy to voluntary action, which was spread cost
and localised activity, but, as Women's Aid exemplifies, this may
strengthen the organised challenge of those who had previously been
considered marginal inadequates, not only for a fuller participation in
citizenship but for rewriting the rights and duties of the citizen. The
language of rights, expressed directly by the disadvantaged, is
increasingly replacing the language of needs, expressed on others'
behalf by professional diagnosticians. The arguments in the debates
on penal policy, concerning offenders' and victims' rights and
just-deserts, rather than the treatment needs of criminals, is, therefore,
a reflection of broader trends on thinking about welfare. However,
deserts and needs should not be considered contradictory concepts,
although the former is frequently associated with a view of man as a
free and morally responsible agent and the latter with a determined,
non-responsible imagery of human nature; another way of referring
to needs-based policies would be to say that they recognise needs as
constituting deserts, that people deserve certain goods and services
and, indeed, rights, because they need them. Furthermore, needs may
be subjectively defined and negotiated, rather than necessarily
objectively definable by professionals in official roles, as has been
characteristic of the welfare state.

The Justice Model and Alternatives

Other chapters in this volume have considered the justice model in the
context of penal theory, policy and practice. I shall examine its
implications for social policy generally, both by reference to the
explicit arguments of its proponents and by drawing on the preceding
analysis of trends in social policy. The justice model is not
homogeneous, but has drawn on both left-wing and right-wing
critiques of recent penal practice.

In *Struggle for Justice*, the authors commit themselves at the outset
to the belief that a just penal policy depends on a just society. They
refer to the:
        impossibility of achieving more than a superficial
        reformation of our criminal justice system without a radical
        change in our values and a drastic restructuring of our social
        and economic institutions. (American Friends Service
        Committee 1971, p. 12)

To this, they add:

> The quest for justice will necessarily be frustrated so long as we fail to recognise that criminal justice is dependent upon and largely derives from social justice. (American Friends Service Committee 1971, p. 13)

and:

> To the extent that equal justice is correlated with equality of status, influence and economic power, the construction of a just system of criminal justice in an unjust society is a contradiction in terms. (American Friends Service Committee 1971, p. 16)

They are, therefore, committed to socialist values and to the necessity for social policies other than penal policies to achieve them. One of their major attacks on the rehabilitative ideal is that it mystifies, disguising social injustice and so contributing to its perpetuation. The main part of their text is devoted to exposing discriminatory features of actual penal practice, and their principal recommendation is to make criminal justice agents responsible within strict confines of law; thus, their emphasis is on formal, rather than substantive, criminal justice, embodying primarily liberal values, incorporated in a utilitarian calculus, that:

> a criminal justice system should be evaluated by cost-accounting theories that give substantial weight to the values of individual privacy, autonomy, equality of treatment, individual dissent, and cultural diversity. As the administration of criminal justice inevitably involves the impairment or denial of such critical values, its heavy cost can be justified only if:
>
> 1. there is compelling social need to require compliance with a particular norm.
>
> 2. the law and its administration can be applied equally . . .
>
> 3. there is no less costly method of obtaining compliance,
>
> and
>
> 4. there is some substantial basis for assuming that the imposition of punishment will produce greater benefit for society than simply doing nothing. (American Friends Service Committee 1971, p. 66)

Now, this position begs a number of questions, notably the definition of a 'compelling social need'. They would clearly like this to be determined through democratic processes, but hesitate to trust 'the people' yet, for:

> a fair, equal and rational system of criminal justice can only

be achieved by a society of such sufficient maturity and
self-confidence that it no longer needs to use criminals as
scapegoats upon whom it loads its angers and frustrations.
(American Friends Service Committee 1971, p. 60)

Their attack on our present discontents is empirical as well as
ideological, but they have little to say of the nature of social policies to
complement their minimalist criminal justice system, though it is
strongly implied that it should be non-coercive. Their analysis can
hardly give them much confidence that the relatively privileged will
suddenly see the light and voluntarily relinquish their power. The
ambiguous prescription that:

criminal sanctions be imposed only when other remedies
have proved inadequate (American Friends Service
Committee 1971, p. 145)

is presumably not intended to refer to spuriously non-coercive
attempts to change the attitudes and behaviour of offenders, but rather
to problem-solving which does not involve blame-allocation. Such
problem-solving need not be limited to State-initiated and State-
controlled policies; indeed, many of the items referred to in their list of
critical values imply an expanded role for individual and group action
rather than State action. Whether the 'last resort' principle of criminal
justice should also mean that in the short-run, while society remains
unequal and, therefore, unjust, under-privilege should be a recognised
mitigating factor in the application of the criminal sanction is also
unclear. Von Hirsch (1976) considers this is a possible element in a
deserts-based system of criminal justice, but rejects it on feasibility
grounds, especially as it would reintroduce discretionary powers, and
concludes that:

the sentencing system may simply not be capable of
compensating for the social ills of the wider society. (Von
Hirsch 1976, p. 147)

However, the concluding paragraph of this study recognises force-
fully that there must be policies to deal with such problems directly:

But it should be only small comfort that our theory of
punishment deals somewhat less unfairly with deprived
persons than traditional utilitarian theories do. As long as a
substantial segment of the population is denied adequate
opportunities for a livelihood, any scheme for punishing
must be morally flawed. (Von Hirsch 1976, p. 149)

It is noteworthy that both the American Friends Service Committee and the Committee for the Study of Incarceration (Von Hirsch
1976) recognised the dictum that criminal justice is dependent on
social justice, yet the former uses utilitarian arguments for the
selection of policies, while the majority of the latter rejects them; and

the former's standard of social justice entails equality, while the latter seems only to demand a basic minimum, so we cannot infer a common platform of social policies.

J. Q. Wilson has a more hard-headed approach, grounded in his explicitly pessimistic view of human nature. In his introduction to *Thinking About Crime* he asserts that:

> the proper design for public policies requires a clear and
> sober understanding of the nature of man and, above all, of
> the extent to which that nature can be changed. . . . Man is
> refractory enough to be unchangeable but reasonable
> enough to be adaptable. (Wilson 1975, pp. xi, xvi)

Later, he scorns the view that:

> the only morally defensible and substantially efficacious
> strategy for reducing crime is to attack its 'root causes'
> (Wilson 1975, p. 43)

at any rate as a basis for public policy. His conception of the crime problem involves the existence of two problematic groups in the population, a finite, identifiable 'pathological and predatory' (Wilson 1975, p. 5) criminal class, for whom an incapacitative policy is recommended, and rational economic man, for whom a deterrent policy is appropriate. Therefore:

> What the government can do is to change the risks . . . and
> the rewards of alternative sources of income for those who,
> at the margin, are neither hopelessly addicted to thievery
> nor morally vaccinated against it. (Wilson 1975, p. 177)

One consequence of this view is that deterrent penal policies may be reinforced by appropriate social policies, though these receive relatively slight emphasis:

> Anti-crime policies may be frustrated by the failure of
> employment policies . . . but if criminal opportunities are
> profitable, many young persons will not take those
> legitimate jobs that exist. The benefits of work and the costs
> of crime must be increased simultaneously. (Wilson 1975,
> p. 202)

With this one exception, he generally favours a separation of penal and social policies, i.e. that penal policies should be concerned with minimising crime and reassuring the law-abiding, whereas social policies should not be judged by their effects on the crime problem. Thus, he stated:

> our society has not done as well as it could have in
> controlling crime because of erroneous but persistent views
> about the nature of man and the capacities of his
> institutions. But I do not believe that, were we to have
> taken a correct view and as a consequence adopted the most

feasible policies, crime would have been eliminated, or even
drastically reduced (Wilson 1975, p. 198)

and also that:

Reducing poverty and breaking up the ghettoes are
desirable policies in their own right, whatever their effects
on crime. (Wilson 1975, p. 203)

In comparing the left-wing and right-wing arguments for a justice
model in penal policy, we find some interesting contrasts. There is a
tendency for the left (American Friends Service Committee 1971; Von
Hirsch 1976) not to expect penal policy to contribute to crime-
reduction and to reject this criterion for penal policy, yet to believe,
though without substantiation, that society can be improved and
crime reduced, by other means. On the other hand, the Right (Wilson
1975) would retain the purpose of crime-reduction for penal policy,
while doubting the viability of social change to reduce crime, which is
seen as a product of wickedness and calculation among criminals,
rather than of social structures and the unfair distribution of society's
resources, including the power to define crimes.

The failure of left-wing justice-model theorists to spell out more
fully the implications for social policy of their reformed penal policy is
due to more than a pragmatic concentration on exposing present
injustices. They suggest that desert criteria should be primary for
penal policy, and imply that penal policy can be insulated from other
social policies, where, perhaps, need criteria could be dominant, but
this view may be more appealing than plausible. If one takes the
view that penal policy is only one of the means of social control,
albeit its most extreme form, it must maintain the same values as
other means of social control, such as criteria of eligibility for social
services.

Justice-model theorists share the liberal mistrust of the State, and
agree that a reformed criminal justice system must minimise
discretion by State agents, especially those claiming a professional
expertise. This view of the State is problematic for those with a
concern for structural changes to promote social justice, for under
welfare capitalism it has been the power of the State which has been
the means of preventing gross inequality. If the State may coercively
change social structure, then its powers are ultimately penal in
substance if not in form; there are already problems in distinguishing
fines from taxes in some instances, other than by the form through
which they are levied. If, however, society is to be made more just
without using the State, then two principal alternatives are offered —
an extension of the abolitionist emphasis on dismantling State
apparatuses, or class struggle.

The abolitionist stance shares with the justice model opposition to the discretionary powers of professionals in the criminal justice system. The justice model advocates:

> a greater mechanisation of justice because we have not achieved either the individual love and understanding or the social distribution of power and property that is essential if discretion is to serve justice. (Von Hirsch 1976, p. xl)

This recognises that we live in mass society, in which bureaucratic organisation, with formally and impersonally administered rules, is the most appropriate manner to run many aspects of our lives. Abolitionists favour a more radical approach, amounting to a destruction of mass society and its bureaucracies; instead of trying to limit the power of the State through a more rigorous application of the principle of the rule of law, they would break up the State itself.

Christie's solution is an example of this approach, the polar opposite of the advocacy of a limited social contract between the individual and the State, with the predictability of a formal system. He argues that the role of the criminal justice system should be *expanded* and *localised* (Christie 1976). He seeks a recreation of personal encounters and community responsiveness in the reparation of interpersonal conflicts. A court case, in his view, should involve four stages, in strictly separated order. The first would be a traditional trial. The second would seek to readjust relations of victim and offender, and would involve both having a direct say, without restrictive rules of evidence nor professional representation; where the victim's legitimate needs could not be met by the offender, the local community, or, as a last resort, the State should do so. The third stage would consider what punishment the offender should experience, in the public interest, given knowledge of the arrangements made to recompense the victim and in a fuller understanding of their respective moral responsibility, as revealed in the second stage, which may modify the view of legal responsibility produced by the first stage. The fourth stage would consider services for the offender, meeting his needs from community resources, but strictly *after* guilt, compensation and punishment have been fixed. This model proposes *integration* rather than *insulation* for the relationship of penal and other social policies. Whereas the justice model would extend the trend to impersonal administration, Christie's model would reverse it. Furthermore, where the justice model stresses the *individual* responsibility of the offender, Christie's model partially *collectivises* both needs and deserts.

This programme for penal policy is part of a wider emphasis on reinterpreting human welfare in terms of personal relationships rather than the notion of standard of living grounded in mass consumption which has been the dominant point of reference in the welfare state and a major determinant of the proliferation of bureaucracies. It involves a scaling-down of societies, and of the division of labour into technically distinct activities, and a withdrawal of deference towards science and the claims of professional expertise (Schumacher 1973; Illich 1977).

Since State intervention and bureaucratic forms have been the means through which rights have been established and needs met, the abolitionist case implicitly accepts the loss of these benefits, such as they have been, for the rediscovery of personal and communal responsibility. If the State apparatuses were dismantled without changes in the scale of economic activity, then individuals and communal groups would be powerless, but if they organised into larger groupings, then they would risk losing the personal revitalisation which was the purpose for which the State was abolished.

From a Marxist point of view, the abolitionist solution is utopian, and the justice model is an embodiment of capitalist ideology's individualism. A Marxist perspective gives primary attention to the method by which social changes are to be achieved, i.e. class struggle, rather than a blueprint of a better system. Neither the justice model nor the abolition model would contribute to the development of class consciousness, and the working class should strive to protect and enhance its power base, including State welfare measures, rather than be concerned with abstract concepts of justice.

Some Implications for Social Policy

Arguments for decriminalisation pre-date the justice model, but are an essential part of it, for if discretion is outlawed and a liberal society is to exist, then there must be a lot less criminal law to enforce. But decriminalisation is not a unitary concept and it needs to be examined in some detail before we can decide how it can become a matter of practical policy.

Advocates of the 'scientific' rehabilitative ideal are far from unsympathetic to the notion of decriminalisation, but for them it is *persons*, not *acts*, that should be decriminalised, and such persons could nevertheless expect to be regulated. As critics stress (Kittrie 1971) this is name-changing, and removes due process more than it removes stigma, but this is what deriminalisation has meant for children (Bottoms 1974) and other marginal deviants. The rehabilitative ideal has been particularly strongly attacked (Kittrie 1971) when it has operated, in formal terms, outside the penal system, such as in mental hospitals.

In the justice model, it is *acts*, not *persons*, that should be decriminalised, while for those acts which remain criminal, the moral opprobrium attaching to them should be strengthened, countering the informal decriminalisation of under-enforcement, paltry penalties, strict liability, and so on. This argument is particularly important for those who reject the utilitarian justification of punishment, but it appeals also to those concerned with the effectiveness of policy. It has been shown (Carson 1970) that criminal law enforcement is not the normal response to criminal law violation in many circumstances, such as factory safety, and that persuasion, advice and warning may be preferred where an offender is thought amenable, irrespective of the seriousness of the criminal conduct. In such matters, the criminal law is of greater symbolic than instrumental importance (Gusfield 1963), which is unsatisfactory to both moral and utilitarian viewpoints. It has been suggested (Wilson 1975) that the criminal law has acquired this overreach partly because democratic influence on policy is greatest at the legislative level, so that passing a law, without responsibility for its effects, is the best that politicians can do to appear to respond to demands to do something about problems which worry citizens.

There is little evidence of substantial success for decriminalisation arguments. Indeed, the recent growth of regulatory and reparatory processes *within the criminal justice system,* as noted in other contributions to this volume, may be seen as tendencies in the opposite direction. Much conduct which is formally criminal is dealt with, if at all, by virtually fixed financial penalties. Would there be advantages in transferring much of this to civil courts, converting the State's role from prosecutor to plaintiff in some cases, perhaps, and extending civil legal aid to enable victims to become plaintiffs, in others? This would recognise some of the ways in which the State's interest may be different from that of society or of individuals.

If decriminalisation is to be set in motion seriously, there are many stopping-places before total non-regulation is reached, such as the civil law of torts; selective licensing, taxation and other controls available to the State; and controls available to individuals, groups and organisations within the State, such as insurance and physical self-protection, direct retaliation and exclusion. Such alternatives for social control have been seriously debated mainly in connection with so-called victimless crimes (Schur 1965) and the partially-overlapping field of self-destructive acts (Vallence 1975).

The arguments for alternatives are principally utilitarian — what state of affairs should be brought about? What action is most likely to produce it at least cost? But before the utilitarian choices can be examined, it is usually necessary to assert that the act in question is not a blameworthy one, or at least that the use of criminal law to control it leads to acts of greater blameworthiness (though this latter argument would be unacceptable on a Kantian view of justice that wrongful conduct must be punished with no regard to utility). Campaigns to decriminalise drugs, abortion, homosexuality and suicide illustrate this (Wolfenden 1957; Schur 1965; Duster 1970). Thus, in this area at least, reversing the *Struggle for Justice* dictum quoted above, it is when criminal sanctions are perceived as inadequate that other remedies are given a chance. Is this simply a feature of the inertia of social institutions? If so, we should expect that it might also be the case that alternatives are explored before new criminal laws are passed, if the penal option is thought to be the last rather than the first resort. Broadly, this seems to be the case for 'crimes of the powerful' or when everyday actions of 'respectable' citizens, such as driving motor vehicles or smoking cigarettes, are threatened with regulation. But it is also at least partially the case for the actions of the less respectable, such as squatters, football 'hooligans', pop festival fans and others.

In recent years, there have been many useful studies (Gusfield 1963; Carson 1974) of the emergence of forms of social regulation in various contexts, and they point to the importance of command of ideology. If a given pattern of behaviour can be conceptually normalised, then there is a greater chance that remedies for its unwelcome consequences will be sought without the allocation of blame to those who practise it. For example, substantial investment in road improvements may be advocated to reduce traffic injury rather than heavy penalties for bad driving; the language of 'accident' rather than 'violence' is a conceptual normalisation which makes the criminalising reaction appear inappropriate.

Further scope for decriminalisation could be achieved by considering aspects of the relationship of criminal and social justice. Critics of the rehabilitative ideal (American Friends Service Committee 1971; Bean 1976) have emphasised its consequences in punishing the weak more than the strong, but the differential impact of the criminal law is not exclusively the problem of that model of justice. Despite legal rhetoric, which may justify law as limiting the powerful and giving protection to all citizens equally, it is clear that law is frequently one of the means through which power is preserved. Changing the distribution of power should, therefore, include changes not just in the administration of justice, and in social policies outside the system of justice, but in substantive law, in the rights it recognises and protects. For instance, is it feasible or desirable to remove the protection of the criminal law from corporate owners of property, so that they would need to bear their own costs to protect it instead?

There are some signs that self-protection, rather than reliance on State-protection through law enforcement, is gaining greater attention. One response to realisation of the ineffectiveness of the penal system in dealing with crime is to look for measures which will reduce opportunities for crime. Among these have been architectural and physical planning features (Newman 1973) and direct physical security (Reppetto 1974; Mayhew *et al.* 1976), as well as the expansion in security service personnel. While these policies are intended to reduce the likelihood of criminal acts, they may have diversionary rather than preventive consequences, if practised on a small scale, and an emphasis on purely physical security may also escalate the seriousness of crime, from thefts to burglaries, for example (McIntosh 1975). Advocates of environmental modification (Spence and Hedges 1976) may go beyond the purely physical to a concern with changing patterns of social relations, particularly increasing neighbourliness, which, in combination with environmental measures, would be expected to reduce the amount of crime, the fear of crime and the seriousness of the consequences of victimisation.

Another strategy for dealing with crime involves the insurance principle, though, by mitigating the consequences of victimisation rather than reducing the odds of victimisation, it may actually increase the incidence of crime, unless it were controlled by recognising contributory negligence. In private cost-effectiveness terms, it is probably the best action the individual citizen can take, although our knowledge of victimisation patterns (Sparks *et al.* 1978; Hindelang 1976; Skogan 1976) suggest that on an actuarial basis, the poor would not necessarily be charged the lowest premiums. State intervention via insurance to protect citizens from misfortune has been far more noticeable in other fields than crime, and this is closely related to the differences between blame-allocating and other forms of problem-solving. That crime is conceptualised as non-accidental misfortune, as far as the offender's responsibility is concerned, is not much comfort to the victims, however, for whom it is particularly ironic that criminal, but not civil, justice assumes the responsibility to be wholly one-sided.

Some consequences of the renewed interest in victims shed further light on alternatives to penal policy for dealing with crime. The extension of the powers of the criminal courts to make orders for compensation and restitution and the creation of the Criminal Injuries Compensation Board are the major official recognition of the needs of victims, but victim support schemes that are being developed by voluntary organisations are an example of non-State contributions to social policy.

Victim support schemes come in many shapes and sizes, but they share a commitment to expressing solidarity with the victim, recognising his needs as legitimate and unmet by penal policy and social services. Some schemes are envisaged as experiments, demonstrating a need and the means to satisfy it, with the intention that the statutory services should take over the responsibility and provide universal cover. Others see this as an appropriate field for voluntary service, to express a grass-roots community feeling, and would resist its incorporation in statutory welfare bureaucracies. In Britain, the National Association for the Care and Resettlement of Offenders has been associated with pioneering schemes, notably in Bristol, so demonstrating that victim support is not necessarily inimical to offender support, although in some quarters the expression of concern for victims may be a metaphor for the belief that offenders have received excessively benevolent attention. Some victim support schemes, most obviously the rape crisis centres, are a response to highly specific dissatisfactions with the way victims are treated by the criminal justice system. Victim support schemes usually deal mainly with stranger-to-stranger serious crime and rely on the referral co-operation of the police, so they may increase public consciousness and fear of such crimes. The service they provide is fairly heterogeneous, dependent on the subjective needs of victims and ranging from a brief contact, showing someone cares, through factual advice and referral to specialised agencies like solicitors, doctors and social security, to long-term emotional support. They have highlighted the extent to which victims of property crimes may have a strong sense of personal injury.

Another feature of interest in victims has been the recent growth of victim surveys, which are now often used as a resource for the evaluation of policies whose objectives include the reduction of crime. The original purpose of victim surveys was to provide a different basis from the official statistics from which to calculate crime rates. Despite recognition of the problem of the 'dark figure' of unreported, unrecorded and unsolved crimes, the emphasis on offenders' characteristics in both criminology and penal policy was such that the victim had become invisible and it was not until the 1960s that sample surveys, a common feature of social research in many fields, were used to investigate criminal victimisation in the general population. The main focus of victim surveys had been on the amount of crime that is recognised as crime by a victim but not reported to the police, and studies agree (United States 1967; Skogan 1976; Hindelang 1976; Sparks et al. 1978) in finding that this is overwhelmingly accounted for by two reasons, that the crime was not serious enough to bother and/or there was nothing the police could do about it. These reasons raise some interesting, but under-investigated, questions: what are victims' other resources for dealing with crime? How important are they, compared with official action via the criminal justice system, in providing victim satisfaction? Do victims alter their life-style as a result of the experience of victimisation? If so, does this reduce their chances of future victimisations? Little research on these issues has yet been carried out, and the results so far are inconsistent — but a promising line of enquiry has been opened up.

Surveys of public attitudes to crime and punishment, often an adjunct of victim surveys, are also beginning to provide evidence which is relevant for social policy. It is frequently found (Sparks *et al.* 1978) that fear of crime, and attitudes towards criminals and towards penal policy are related at least as strongly to the respondent's own social circumstances, particularly the degree of involvement in family and neighbourhood networks, as to personal experience of victimisation and the actual rates of crime locally.

Research and action in these new directions suggest realignments in the objectives and strategies of social policy. There is less optimism and enthusiasm for 'curing' crime, and more attention is being given to learning to live with it with least suffering.

A common theme in debates over social policy is the idea of community. Social theorists have been united in identifying a decline in community values and personal ties and the growth of impersonal relations in modern, large-scale, urban, industrial societies and this analysis has informed many explanations of the growth of crime. They disagreed on the causes and remedies of this process. Some, like Max Weber, were pessimistic, expecting further increases in bureaucratisation; the rise of the justice model fits Weber's characterisation of social trends (see Rheinstein 1954). However, other theorists thought large, complex societies could regain communal values, and these provided ideological support for the emergence of the welfare state. The rehabilitative ideal is one expression of this aspiration, and the crisis in penal policy is part of a wider crisis as the welfare state is increasingly seen not to have produced a welfare society (Robson 1976). So new avenues to recreate communal values are explored and recent initiatives in social service focus on the *local* community. As well as growing evidence (Young and Willmott 1957; Frankenberg 1966) that local communities were not extinguished by industrialisation, mobility, and centralisation of government, there have been attempts to stimulate new community ties. These have included sectarian and other communes (Abrams and McCulloch 1976); mutual-aid and self-help groups, like tenants' associations; and, at a professional level, the growth of community work and decline of exclusive reliance on individual and family casework. The idea of community is so popular, indeed, that it is sometimes difficult to detect much content of meaning in its use. As Scull (1977) has strongly argued, 'community treatment' as an alternative to the institutionalisation of offenders, the mentally handicapped and others may mean neglect of their needs for care; this analysis of this policy trend leads him to conclude that:

> . . . This whole enterprise is built on a foundation of sand. The contention that treatment in the community is more effective than institutionalisation is an empty one. There is massive ignorance about what 'community treatment' actually involves, and about the likely effect of abandoning institutional controls. . . . Excluded from the more desirable neighbourhoods by zoning practices and organised community opposition, the decarcerated deviants are in any case impelled . . . to cluster in the ghettos and the decaying core of the inner city. . . . Decarceration thus forms one more burden heaped on the backs of those who are most obviously the victims of our society's inequities and it places the deviant in those communities least able to care for or cope with him. (Scull 1977, p. 1)

The focus on the local community in many recent social policy initiatives has overestimated the significance of locality as a basis of shared interests in modern societies; Abrams suggests that:

> We should be paying more attention to kinship ties and to the moral communities of religion, race and occupation as possible contexts for basic social care, and less to the supposed communities of locality. (Abrams 1978, p. 87)

Despite justified scepticism about community as slogan, some initiatives deserve serious consideration. The Community Planning Project in a council estate in Widnes, managed jointly by the National Association for the Care and Resettlement of Offenders and Social and Community Planning Research, is an example of how these new trends in thinking about social policy are being implemented.

The starting-point of the project was an interest in crime-reduction; vandalism was the focus, and:

> The theory under study is that environmental improvements which are (and are seen to be) in line with the needs and wishes of residents will involve people more with their surroundings. If they are more involved they are more likely to take care of their environment (perhaps to the extent of helping to improve it) rather than destroying it. (N.A.C.R.O. and S.C.P.R. 1976, p. 1)

The project team surveyed the population and consulted them in various ways, engaged the co-operation of the local authorities and other official bodies, promoted new local organisations and ventilated channels of communication between people and officials. No additional public resources were to be devoted to the area. They believed that local apathy disguised potential resources for self-help and that teenage vandals' motivation arose from boredom and frustration; in both cases, the project was conceptualised as a catalyst, releasing the 'natural' goodness of the people. After two years, impressionistic reports were optimistic (N.A.C.R.O. and S.C.P.R. 1978), but among the official agencies, only the police and the housing department had changed their policies towards the area by becoming less impersonal in their dealings, and perception of the crime problem had changed without any impact on the official statistics of crime. Indeed, victimisation may fall and official statistics increase (Skogan 1976). Closer interpersonal relations within the estate were perceived as relevant in promoting a sense of confidence and well-being, for earlier:

> . . . when teenagers were causing a nuisance or smashing
> things, nobody dared go out and tell them to stop. Now
> they are not afraid to, and the reasons they give are that they
> know the teenagers individually and they can rely on their
> neighbours to come out and support them. (N.A.C.R.O.
> and S.C.P.R. 1978)

There is a danger that the emphasis on community will neglect critical issues for social justice, in that power cannot be satisfactorily understood at that level, which deals only with its most visible signs (Lukes 1974). Similarly, we would not expect Christie's model for criminal justice (Christie 1976) to be satisfactory for controlling crimes of the powerful which are on a national and international scale, and whose victims may not have perceived themselves as such.

For social policy generally, as well as for penal policy specifically, we need to recognise bureaucracy and communalism as contradictory principles. Our experience of the welfare state has been that they cannot be integrated successfully. Rather, we must determine which matters are more appropriately handled in the bureaucratic mode, and which in the communal mode.

10

Possible theological responses to apparent criminological confusion

by DAVID E. JENKINS

Part I: The Possibility of a Theological Response, the Case for it and the Methods of it

> Crime and punishment is an eternally fascinating subject. Fanned by the similarly misleading concept of law and order, it has evoked and continues to evoke more facile and nonsensical views than any other social issue of our times. Much of the responsibility for that sad state of affairs lies with the criminologists.
>
> These academicians, whose writings are now legion, have wholly failed to convey to the public (including a Press that seeks only to sensationalise) the message that there never has been a causal connection between the two concepts, and that penal policies have failed miserably to effect any kind of alleviation of this century's relentless growth of crime.

So Louis Blom-Cooper begins his laudatory review of Lady Wooton's (1978) *Crime and Penal Policy* in *The Observer* of 27 August 1978. The passage provides a helpful jumping-off point for a theologian and Christian believer, to attempt to ease himself into the discussion on penal policy going on among criminologists and others directly concerned with the present policies and practice of criminal justice in our society.

Firstly, Blom-Cooper, in what is doubtless a salutary way, puts criminologists in their place. Incidently and not very importantly, this is encouraging to a theologian as he ventures into one more field of expertise, controversy and social uncertainty. It gives him a fellow-feeling with 'academic' criminologists, for he too is always being put in his place, being rebuked by believers for not helping them to believe and by unbelievers for asking them to believe what is either unbelievable or irrelevant.

173

But more importantly than providing a basis for fellow-feeling, the rebuke to criminologists also helps to confirm the impression which a non-expert gains from the material presented at, or referred to in, this consultation. This is that in the fields of penal theory and penal practice theories are not working and they are 'not working' in a two-fold sense. On the one hand practices (based on or implied by whatever theory) are not producing the practical results that are needed or expected of them. As Blom-Cooper puts it, punishment of offenders does not prevent rises in the crime rate. As much of the consultation material argued, rehabilitative treatment does not rehabilitate criminals. On the other hand, people are at present largely unable to produce coherent and convincing theories which link together such matters as what society treats as crime, what humane people would want to justify as responses to crime and what practical measures are available or inventable to implement these responses in society as it now is, or as it should be changed into being.

The whole field seems heavily charged with negativity. What goes on (in the field of criminal justice and penal practice) does not seem to be producing what is *desired* (usually assumed to be the control or the reduction of crime). Secondly, there are strong grounds for holding that both the practices and aims of what goes on are not, in any case, *desirable* (imprisonment degrades to no purpose and can do nothing else; imprisonment is inflicted disproportionately on certain types of people for certain types of offences and the selectivity is related to class and social prejudice and to arbitrary decisions exercised within the scope of those prejudices; and so on). Thirdly, there are no very clear views and, certainly, no views which are clear, comprehensive and widely accepted, about what *ought to be desired* in reconstructing or redirecting the fields of criminal justice and penal policy. (Proposals range widely up to the abolition of the concept of 'crime' and the abolition of the practice of imprisonment. The arguments and theories which support these proposals are not always convergent, there is much controversy about them among the experts and there is clearly a very wide gap between them and public opinion.)

Hence my conclusion that my task is to attempt to outline some possible theological responses to 'apparent criminological confusion'. One such response which I shall later develop will argue that such confusion is not necessarily a bad thing and certainly not wholly a bad thing, still less evidence of incompetence and failure among criminologists. If society or a society is moving in a period of general uncertainty and if it is sufficiently clear that various societal attitudes, practices and institutions can validly be called in question then clarity and certainty among experts can well demonstrate at least incompetence and at worst actual human betrayal. But I shall return to this.

First, I wish to return to Blom-Cooper's review and extract a second main point from it which is relevant to easing theology into the criminological discussion.

The review not only helps to confirm my impression of 'criminological confusion', it begins to indicate how far-reaching are the questions which have to be faced if this confusion is to be clarified, interpreted and lived with constructively. Blom-Cooper points to a popular and slogan-like linking of 'crime and punishment' and of 'law and order' and to the further linking of these two compound concepts together by the assumption that the normal purpose of and justification for 'punishment for crime' is that it will contribute to 'law and order' in the sense of causing a reduction in the growth of crime. As he points out later in the review these assumptions and linkages are highly questionable. He writes 'There is an assumption, of which we should be promptly disabused, that some carefully selected penal sanction will produce a downward trend in the commission of crimes'. Further on he writes 'You do not have to be a Marxist to observe that the causes of crime lie deep in the economic and social structure of society or to be a Benthamite to know that punishment of offenders is unlikely to reap any lasting social benefit'.

These quotations serve to direct our attention to at least the following three sets of propositions which begin to set the framework for any humane discussion of criminological problems in their social (and philosophical) context.

(i) There is no satisfactory evidence to support the belief that there is a 'right sort' of penal sanction, which if we could find out what it was and apply it would result in a reduction of the crime rate and it is difficult to see what would contribute satisfactory evidence for such a belief.

(ii) The type of behaviour we call crime has some deep roots in the economic and social structure of society.

(iii) Punishment of offenders as we at present practise it and especially in the form of imprisonment, is unlikely to reap any lasting social benefit if we think of that benefit as reduction of the crime rate.

The probable truth of or in these propositions gives us cause to think furiously and critically about our present penal practices and about the implied or expressed theories which are alleged to justify them and our putting hope in them as useful social and human activities. When we proceed with this urgent critical thinking further wide-ranging questions arise. For example, the concepts of 'crime and punishment' and 'law and order' are not just slogans (although in popular agitation they often are). In criticising their popular use we have also to consider all the important moral and practical human and social questions which surround the defining of anything as a crime and the complexity of psychological and evaluative human responses which are bound up in the language and practices of punishment. We have also to face up to the urgent pressures we are under to work out the actual and desirable roles of law in our society and the inescapable dilemmas which any society has about the necessity to preserve ordering structures and the threats which actual attempts to preserve such order also entail. Further, any talk of the 'causes' of crime clearly raises wide issues. It is true that one does not have to be a Marxist to believe that there is a great deal of evidence leading one reasonably to locate factors causing crime 'deep in the economic and social structures of society'. But it is not an observation it is a judgement to go on and hold that 'the causes of crime' lie there *in toto*. This involves a theory about human beings and society which (i) goes beyond the evidence (like all theories) and (ii) many people do not believe it is desirable to hold. So discussing what it is (allegedly) obvious about crime and penal policy is no simple matter.

I put forward these considerations because they help me at any rate to clarify for myself the nature and cause of a curious unease which I felt throughout the consultation and on reconsidering the papers given and the notes I made during the subsequent discussions. The unease eventually focused in the question 'But what are we talking about?' I describe this as 'curious' because in one sense it is obvious enough what we are talking about. As Professor Preston puts it, pretty concretely, we are talking about 'the apprehension, trial and treatment of criminals'. I would suggest, rather less concretely, that we are talking about the response of society to these offenders whom it dubs criminals. But while this sufficiently points to the practical focus of the discussion it only names 'the tip of the iceberg'. The subject seems inevitably to be something much more like how we understand and view human beings and society, with our entry point into these wide questions being the problem of offenders/criminals in society and our desired aim being effective contributions to both the theory and practice of the response in society to that problem.

All this raises the question of the status of the discipline or separate subject of 'criminology' and where it fits into the wider discussion of these social questions. To an outsider it looks as if a concentration of interest and attention on a recognisable area of social concern and social institutions (to do with definition of and response to offenders) at one stage attempted to become specialised into a quasi-science. This may well explain one very important factor which makes the present confusion of criminology worse confounded. This is the lingering effects of the assumption that criminology (or the most valid and careful methods and procedures within criminology) *is* a science and, secondly, that science provides objective methods which can sufficiently settle questions to do with 'treating crime'.

There seem to be parallels here with the current difficulties and confusions in our society about the National Health Service and the best or most feasible means for treating disease and promoting health. Public, professional and social expectation is all focused on scientific and technological medicine. (And this is where vast public funds are invested.) But 'scientific' medicine has no internal resources to deal with the social, political and structural questions which are raised by seeking for a more healthy society. ('Health' is, in any case, not a *medical* concept) and treatment of disease has a very small contribution to make to these improvements in the conditions and quality of living which are most contributory to healthy personal and social functioning. But when it becomes clear that medical expertise cannot be relied upon to give 'scientific' judgements about how society should handle its pursuit and promotion of health, people (whether 'expert' or 'lay') do not know where to turn either for a vision (of human healthiness or worthwhileness) which might sustain them and give general guidance in wrestling with social unease and disease or for a set of values which would enable discriminating judgements to be made about what needs to be done or aimed at in the immediate, the medium or the long-term.

I would suggest that, like many other disciplines in the broad field of so-called social sciences, criminology continues to show the effects of an atmosphere of opinion which has inherited a mistaken view that scientific investigation in itself produces the necessary material for discriminating value judgements and the determination of human and social aims. This adds to criminological confusion by saddling this '-ology' with expectations which it cannot fulfil (and which, indeed, most of its practitioners no longer hold for themselves). Responses to the problems of crime in society cannot be worked out without recourse to value judgements and philosophical theories which go beyond the scope of criminology (whether or not it is a science) and of scientific procedures in general. I would further suggest that a great deal (although certainly not all) of the use of the notion of 'model' in current discussions is tinged with, or still liable to encourage, this false 'scientific' expectation. The rehabilitative model (for treatment) has been proved not to work. The justice model might therefore be a possible substitute. But the models often seem to be assumed to be capable of playing roles which are much more like those of scientific models within a scientific theory than of symbols or foci of philosophical theories addressed to problems of human life in society.

It is now, however, pretty clear that a criminologist is not any sort of a scientist but a person who — under some more or less formal auspices — spends more time than most on thinking about and investigating problems, practices and ideas in the area which society in practice defines as crime and response to crime. Both 'thinking' and 'investigating' cover a wide spectrum of activities from the most generally philosophical to the most particularly empirical but there is at present no methodology or theory which clearly differentiates the various types of thinking and investigating or clearly relates them together so that the necessary distinctions between reasonably established facts and persuasively supported value judgements or recommendations can be made. Thus, on purely internal and logical grounds, criminology cannot have any criteria which are purely its own for recommending how society should respond to what society defines as crime. Whatever clarifications or insights can be properly obtained by its own discipline, tradition and methodology, decisions concerning policy, practice and reform or revolution must require value judgements and philosophical perspectives which fall outside the scope of criminological analysis or expertise and into the scope of broader human responsibility and sensitivity, an area in which, nowadays, very few people feel at home. (See below on our pluralistic society.)

The fact that criminological confusion cannot be sorted out or lived with by criminological argument alone is not only made clear by examination of the internal methodology and intrinsic status of criminology. It is equally made clear by an examination of the content and context of the debates and problems covered in this consultation. The issues that arise when we consider what is being done about, and what should be done about, those offenders whom society defines as criminals are clearly symptomatic of wider current problems about society and about human self-understanding and human aims.

Thus the 'crisis in British penology' seems to impinge at a number of levels. First there is the basic one of resources for the system as it now is. The pressures here are now immense and force issues of both internal priorities within the system and of the social priorities in society at large. But there is much uncertainty in 'society at large' about how to respond to fears raised by increasing crime and violence. This is matched by uncertainty among those directly concerned with penal policy and practice both about what practices, if any, 'work' and about what theories or understandings could or should contribute to better ways of 'working' (or even surviving). All this is in the context of a more general 'crisis' or at least disagreement and uncertainty about authority and about the State which is reflected in a number of tensions, if not contradictions. For example, people demand decisive and authoritative action. But, at the same time, other people (or even the same people) are very suspicious of 'the authorities'. Anyone cast in an authoritarian role is in a highly ambivalent position. Further, there is very widespread and often deeply authentic questioning about the ways in which social and political institutions function. Nothing can be taken for granted in their working presuppositions. Indeed, there are influential groups who take it for granted that what has hitherto been taken for granted in running various institutions is, *ipso facto*, false. For example, the 'justice of the courts' is so plainly class 'justice' that it is equally plainly injustice. A consideration of 'the crimes of the powerful' or of the statistics about the high proportion of committed prisoners who come from Social Classes IV and V clearly give grounds for this type of questioning.

Thus everything is called into question at all levels, whether we are concerned with the various levels of institutional practice or of the various levels of theoretical understanding. (A further theological comment will be made below about living positively with an interim state of affairs that is radically called in question.) Criminological confusion is a produce and symptom of a much wider human and social confusion. What needs to be clarified is how criminology can and should play its proper part in the general human quest for a better society and a greater fulfilment.

This clarification of what criminology is as a discipline and what is its focus of concern within the broader human and social issues is necessary if we are to see how theology *might* come into criminological discussion and why theology (or its equivalent) *must* come into criminological discussion. But to develop this point it is first necessary to indicate the working definition of theology that I am assuming for the purpose of this discussion.

I write as a Christian so whatever is meant by 'theology' it is Christian theology which is being referred to. (Reference will be made below to the pluralistic context of religious, philosophical and value commitments in our society.) By theology, then, I mean a disciplined and responsible reflection on the traditions built up in and through the various Christian communities, about what is believed to be discovered about God, man and the world, through the corporate exercise of a faith focused on God through Jesus and assisted by the Spirit. That is to say that theology is a discipline exercised on traditions about man, the world and God built up from the discoveries of Faith developed through the Christian communities. A theological response to a discussion of some area of human and social concern is a considered Christian response drawing on these Christian traditions under the pressures of and in the light of the considerations raised and the problems encountered in the best contemporary engagements with this particular field of concern. (Professor Preston's paper refers to some of the difficulties inherent in this enterprise.) The interest of such a theological response is to contribute to a systematic attempt to relate the doings, reflections and aspirations of men and women in society to the knowledge and resources believed to be offered by God.

If therefore, one is to make a theological response to criminological confusion one must be as clear as possible about what sort of human activity criminology is and about what particular aspects of human and social living and its problems is the focus of criminology. In other words, in what distinctive ways does criminology as a discipline or activity attempt to come to grips with what is going on in society and what particular goings on in society is it focused on? For theology cannot make a direct response to problems, confusions and aspirations arising out of what is going on in society just by a mere inspection of these goings on, for theology has no expertise about such 'goings on'. Theologians are dependent in any particular sphere on the proper secular expertise in that sphere.

Theology therefore can only engage in a social disturbance area which has become the focus of a discipline or expertise by entering into dialogue about the way in which the current exercise of this expertise expresses or implies values and more general presuppositions about 'what it is or might be to be human in the world'. That is why it is part of a theological investigation to consider the possibility that some of the current aspects of criminology still show the influence of a false view of criminology as a science and/or a false view of what science on its own, and as such, can contribute to problems which involve decisions and perspectives about human values and human aims. Secondly, theology has to enter into the discussion by sharing in the efforts made by the experts, as human beings and concerned citizens, to bring their expertise to bear on judgements of value involved in such questions as:

What is wrong or undesirable in what is going on?
What ought to be aimed at?
What are legitimate methods for living with what we've got
and for moving towards what ought to be aimed at and
which we are right to think of as possible objectives?

From the point of view of a believer who already accepts theology as in some way authentic it is necessary to be clear that theological responses can be made only through those aspects of expert and specialised dealing with what is going on in society which reveal or can be made to reveal evaluations, hopes and decisions about what it is or ought to be to be human in society. It is equally important to notice, however, that whether one is a Christian believer or not (or whatever sort of believer or non-believer one is) it is not possible to avoid occupying a theological stance *or its equivalent*. For it is quite impossible to operate in a socially focused field such as that which is the concern of criminology without explicitly acknowledging or implicitly expressing a perspective and commitment about what it is to be human in society.

Consequent Collaboration in Promoting the Human

The argument of this chapter so far has been designed to establish the thesis that there is no way of dealing constructively or realistically with the present criminological confusion which does not include, as a necessary element, a search for a theological response or its equivalent. It is also meant to indicate methodological considerations which are relevant to introducing such a theological or equivalent response into the criminological discussion; and to the human search for a better society of which the improving of attitudes and responses to 'offenders' is a part.

When it comes to looking for clearly valuable and clearly practicable proposals for dealing with problems and practices in this area it turns out that there is scarcely any strictly *scientific* guidance available and that *expert* guidance is not as straightforwardly applicable or decisive as might have once been thought or is, perhaps, still looked for in some quarters. In any case for the evaluation and application of whatever guidance there is or might be obtained we have to draw criteria from whatever we decide are the views which we can or should entertain about society and about human beings.

But one of the most striking and often commented-on features about our society at present is the widespread pluralism of views current in it about 'the views which we can or should entertain about society and about human beings'. Indeed, apart from some Christians, more Marxists, some few adherents of other world religions which are now establishing themselves in the West and a handful of old fashioned Humanists, it seems that people scarcely entertain at all the notion that there could be a 'view about society and about human beings' which is clearly enough articulatable or sufficiently establish-able to be an effective source for criteria of action, of purposes and of hope. Further, scarcely anybody but some of the Marxists seem capable of envisaging a practical relationship between any view about human beings and society which they do hold and the making of discriminating and practical judgements within the actual running of society. If, then, we see serious difficulties both about the overall Marxist view(s) of man in society and about the Marxist proposals for applying these views in society we are in a difficulty.

For when the pressures of the social problems and of the confusions about them force us to the point where we want guidance or direction we cannot fall back on science or on pragmatism. Science cannot provide guidance without the addition of values and views on the human drawn from outside it and pragmatism is by no means as 'matter of fact' as its name implies. For it is the assumptions about what count as 'pragmata' (i.e. the 'things' which you must 'of course' take into account and which are 'obviously' decisive), and the assumptions about the working rules of thumb which are to be 'pragmatically' applied, which are precisely what are called into question by the new presentation of facts and the new ways of looking at things which contribute to and arise out of the confusion which we are seeking to analyse and respond to. How then to proceed?

It seems necessary to recognise that the overall context of all discussions is that of a human quest for better conditions in and of society and, within that context, to recognise the strict limits on the contribution which criminology as such can make, the necessity and ubiquity of questions of value and of perspectives on the human, and the obligation to proceed with full awareness of the plurality of approaches to these questions and perspectives. This involves an awareness by criminologists and others who make a speciality of advising and practising in the field of response to crime that they are far more often advocates than experts, that their expertise has to be subordinated to the pursuit or reopening of important human questions and that the bringing into clear awareness of the value and human perspectives questions, together with the development of whatever collaboration is available for, and appropriate to this task, is an essential part of criminological contributions to the theory and practice of society in matters of criminality. What are the criteria for responsible advocacy?

In working out how to proceed in the light of the considerations adduced above, it is to be noted that the 'necessity' to take account of questions of value and human perspectives arises in two distinct but interacting ways. Firstly there is a logical (and, perhaps, pragmatic) necessity. When we probe into the current discussions and confusions in criminology and in the social context of these we soon find that we are either implying values in our arguing or else need value criteria to proceed with the argument. For example, in arguing for the abandonment or taking up of a particular 'model' for guiding penal theory and practice one is, among other things, declaring or implying one's beliefs about what it is or should be to be human in society. But there is a second and more existential 'necessity' involved or likely to be involved. This is the impulsion exercised upon us by a perception of human suffering or frustration or injustice or exploitation. This is the demand made upon us by a perception of things going humanly wrong and it is related to demands or desires for things going humanly right. It is here that some form of 'faith' and 'commitment' is inescapable, however disturbing it may be to recognise this or however difficult it may be to know how to respond to this. It is this existential demand and commitment which adds passion to the advocacy which often rapidly supersedes or overcomes the expertise and which turns arguments about practices and policies into conflicts. Criminology cannot avoid being a field in which passionate questions arise about how to care for and promote justice for human beings and a field which is fraught with conflicts arising from human commitment, human mistakes and human defensiveness.

Since Christian theology arises from and is essentially related to a particular set of traditions of human faith and commitment it clearly must seek to collaborate in this field of criminology, as in all other fields of serious commitment to human and social struggles, problems and possibilities. Because it is an articulated example of response to a particular tradition of human faith and commitment with its own understanding of what is and ought to be involved in human life in the world, it also clearly has a strong claim to be considered as an appropriate collaborator for those aspects of the criminological task which must take into account human values, perspectives and commitments. In the circumstances of pluralism this claim must go along with, face the conflicts of, and be prepared to come to terms with other such claims. But this pluralism should not be either uncongenial or unhelpful to Christian theology. When Christianity was the official philosophy of those who enjoyed a temporary and geographically limited cultural monopoly in the days of 'Christendom' it was possible for Christian theology to slip into and enjoy what we can now see to be a sinful dogmatism and an overwhelming imperialism. The authorities of the Church could claim to be the unquestionable authorities of last resort on all matters of human (and eternal) significance. Now however history has mercifully (and Christians must surely say providentially) cut these claims down to size. Theology is not the absolutely authoritative interpretation, as required, of the meaning and application of a revelation given once for all and inscribed, as it were, on tablets of stone for all time. Theology is rather a servant discipline for a pilgrim people. (For a more extended discussion see the sections on 'Wilderness and Progress' and 'Men and Women' below). Both Christian theology and Christian faith have to make use of the traditions and the resources they have inherited to sustain and develop themselves in a current and rigorous encounter with contemporary human living, thinking and acting. Dogmas do not determine answers. As focusing symbols of the corporate experience of faith they provide material for searching for creative responses, critical judgements and promising hopes in the midst of current confusion, controversies and conflicts. Christian discipleship, assisted by theological reflection, is an exploration of human possibilities under God. The effect of pluralism is to induce in Christian faith and theology a readiness for collaboration and questioning which combines an agnosticism about answers with an assurance about God. Faith has to be lived into as well as out of.

Thus the developing of a set of theological responses to and in current criminological confusions could be a substantial contribution to the building up of appropriate collaboration in that part of the human quest for advance in society, and in human living which is focused on society's definition and treatment of offenders. The very provocative, awkward and now frequently rejected aspects of theology, and the faith which lies behind it and seeks guidance through it, may at least serve to keep alive some of the provocative, awkward and frequently rejected aspects of what is involved in, and what is sought by, the struggles to be human which are reflected in the problems of criminology. The keeping alive of this provoking and frequently rejected awkwardness is essential if penal theories and practices are not to sink men and women into the cruel apathy of an unimaginative and grimly defensive pragmatism or to force them into the mould of an unrealistically utopian and arrogantly self-righteous totalitarianism.

The constructive facing of any specialised set of questions about how things are going humanly wrong and how things might go humanly more right can only be collaborative. Specialities on their own cut off acquaintance with and consideration of the greater part of what human life is about or should be open to. Claimed monopolies on the definitition of what we must put our faith in, or of what is to be thought about man, society and the world shut human beings up in the as-yet inadequate fantasies and sometimes dreadfully distorting dreams of the would-be monopolists. But faith, commitment and vision in some form or forms there must be and they must be relatable to the details of the practices and problems of social living as detailed and disciplined analysis and reflection show them to be. Theological responses drawn from a living tradition by those who find their human faith and commitment in and through that tradition are therefore a humanly legitimate contribution to criminological discussion. In the eyes of those who hold the faith from which they are drawn the responses are a necessary human contribution; and a general case may be stated for claiming that they are or should be a helpful human contribution. They must however be sought after, set out and received as contributions to that general human quest of which criminological discussion and research is a part. In this human quest theology has as much to learn as to contribute.

It is in the light of the above arguments and considerations that I put forward the more obviously recognisable theological comments and suggestions in the rest of this chapter. But I would close this first part of my chapter by adding that the above inquiry and argument is, in fact, part of a *theological* comment, This is so because Christian theology requires:

(i) A constant attempt to increase clarity and understanding about contemporary reality. This is so because God is understood as making Himself known through engagement with the realities of contemporary life and history.

(ii) A radical exposure of presuppositions and taken-for-granted beliefs and assumptions. This is so because it is an obligation to receive awareness of and judgement upon what is going on and what is the nature of current commitment so that they may be corrected ('converted') into more humane directions. (The Christian concern for the Kingdom of God.)

(iii) A steady refusal to be content with the shutting-up of human beings in any theory or set of ideas and practices stemming from any source, scientific, political, philosophical or religious. This is so because men and women being in the image of God, they are known to have infinite possibilities and an infinite context.

Hence the probing of any set of social activities and disciplines is itself a theological activity and does not have to be given a specifically theological content or expressed in distinctively theological language. A concern for God is primarily a concern for Himself and for men and women in His world not for His religion and its cultic ways of talking and thinking.

I wish now, therefore, to indicate some aspects of and items from Christian ways of thinking about God, men and women and the world which could serve as bases for developing theological responses to and theological contributions in criminological discussion, both regarding theory and practice. They are put forward because my reflections on the papers and discussions of this consultation have put me in mind of these aspects of Christian tradition. They are meant to set out the beginnings of a process not the end of one. There is, as yet, little evidence of many products from collaborative and conflictual dialogue between criminologists and theologians at the level which I have tried to outline in the first part of the chapter. My listing and discussion can therefore constitute only a first item in what should be, if the arguments of this chapter have any validity, a continuing discussion and exploration.

Part II: The Contents of a Theological Response —
Contributions to Dialogue and Practice

We observe that in our society the response to and the treatment of offenders is going very wrong and we want to know how to put things

right or, at least, how to contribute to substantial human improvement. I have argued or assumed, that the materials used or pointed to
in the papers and discussion of this consultation support the following
picture of our concerns and our difficulties in this particular social
problem area.

It is an observable feature of human behaviour in any society
known to us that human beings have the capacity to offend. That is to
say they are liable to do things which 'come up against' other members
of society either directly or as 'offences' against those things which
society, for the time being, regards as necessary or desirable to keep
society going and in being as a society. A certain set of these offences
are held to be so offensive, or offensive in such a way, that they are not
to be tolerated by society and are therefore regarded or designated as
wrongs which are crimes, against which it is necessary to have socially
and formally recognised and socially and formally organised means of
response.

At any given time society, or a society, finds itself with an
elaborate set of responses to this set of problems. These at present
include a system of criminal justice, prisons and those who run them,
and other services (such as the probation service) dealing with
convicted offenders and measures for crime prevention and detection.
The responses also extend into various manifestations of public
opinion and public pressure, some of them very general and some of
them much more specialised and organised by particular pressure or
interest groups. This is the field studied by criminology. Once
criminology becomes recognised as a separate and continuing
discipline and expertise then, of course, criminologists themselves
become one of the manifestations of organised and formalised
response in society to this area of social disturbance and concern.

Criminology, it seems, has developed at one stage in the hope of
being at least a quasi-science working on the further hope that it would
be possible to find a way through all these confusions and dissatisfactions by the use of methods, both of investigation and of argument,
which partook of the neutrality and objectivity of science. Through
the exercise of these methods on the appropriate subject-matter the
criminologist and his or her associates would partake of the nature of
man the problem-solver arriving at enlightened ways of responding
to man the problem (in this case 'man the offender') and to society,
in its present structures and dynamics, as the problem-producer.
(Compare, for example, Blom-Cooper's remark that 'you do not
have to be a Marxist to observe that the causes of crime lie deep in the
economic and social structures of society'.)

It turns out, however, that criminologists, together with a broader
range of socially concerned persons and groups who are, surely

rightly, deeply dissatisfied with present social responses to the problem of offenders and offences, do not have available to them any such clearly agreed or established neutral or objective way of proceeding. There is great and growing concern and dissatisfaction in society at large but no signs of any general or informed consensus about how to respond to this state of affairs. Criminology shows no signs of enabling the production of a new consensus, nor, as I have argued, is it capable of doing so on its own. There is widespread disagreement about the basis, the methods and the aims of programmes and procedures which should shape our understanding of the policies and practices which will improve responses in society to the problems presented or represented by offenders. Yet the urgency of working out improved responses is clear for a variety of practical and humanitarian reasons.

If we accept that this is a sufficiently accurate or at least not too inaccurate picture of the state of affairs to be responded to and if we see this as a particular area of problems within the general context of our struggles to put things more right for human beings in society, then what are some possible theological responses both to the situation in general and to particular problems within it? I propose now to set out two ways in which theology offers illuminating perspectives on the general human situation which are relevant to our responses to and handling of the present state of the case in society with regard to crime and punishment. I then propose to put forward aspects of three theological doctrines which have something to say about some of the questions at issue in the criminological field. Finally, I shall describe two ways in which appreciations arising from theology contribute to the practical stances required to maintain constructive ways of living with the current difficulties in penological theory and practice.

Theological perspectives

(i) Wilderness and Progress — the Values in Confusion

In the West at any rate the hopes and practices of society have tended to be dominated by dogmas. For centuries a version of Christianity, shaped through a 'Christendom' culture, supplied religious dogmas. The enlightenment and rise of science provided scientific dogmas, out of which there, thirdly, emerged the political dogmas of Marxism. The perspective on human life and society remains, however, in one vital respect the same. Accept and apply the true dogmas given by revelation or established by science, or by Marx (who according to Engels' 1888 introduction to the 'Manifesto' transferred science from nature to history: see Marx and Engels 1848, p. 63), and you will be part of salvation, progress or liberation, that is, of that which in the current or accepted dogmatic picture, is the true end of man. We, however, find ourselves required to incorporate frequent references to 'pluralism' into any argument we develop about policies and social and human aims because the hold and extent of any dogmatism has greatly weakened. There are widespread intellectual doubts about the authority usually claimed for dogmatisms, and increasing practical doubts about what the systems activated by the various dogmas actually 'deliver'. (For example, science delivers pollution and Marxism delivers Stalinism. The deliveries of a dogmatic Christendom were discredited before the contemporary argument started.)

When dogmatisms break down and practical results cause distress there is, of course, confusion. Taken-for-granted frameworks and an implicit consensus for decision-taking and problem-solving (and for facing situations where decisions cannot be taken and answers to problems are not available) fade away or are found to be no longer viable or available. When the absence of these supports becomes widely obvious or generally suspected it looks as if society is 'breaking-down' and there is much talk of and wrestling with 'crises' of various sorts. (A crisis of confidence, of politics, of law and order; a crisis in the health service, in the prison service; etc.) Such persons and groups as attempt to respond actively and consciously to the crisis or crises tend either to try to reassert some aspect of a dogmatic system which has been found wanting or to develop some new causal diagnosis or explanatory theory which can be made dogmatically central to the description of and response to 'the crisis'. (A mild form of this is to concentrate on replacing a discredited central model by an arguably 'better' one which will still remain central and decisive.) One theological perspective to be drawn from the Bible and from Christian tradition could suggest that these 'dogmatic' responses are inadequate and unlikely to promote creative human and social living.

The theological perspective in question is suggested by stories about and symbols of passing through the Wilderness, being on a journey, maintaining a pilgrimage, going out 'not knowing whither he went' (cf. Abraham, a central symbolic figure, as referred to in Hebrews ch. 11 vv. 8 ff.) having 'no permanent city, . . . (but) looking for the city which is to come' (Hebrews ch. 13, v. 14) and so on. It must be said at once that this is a perspective which has frequently been ignored or rejected by the Christian church with its own various dogmatisms and establishments. But there are two theological comments to be made on the evident fact that Christian communities very often live in contradiction to, or at least askew from, central insights of their own faith and tradition. The first is that a central Biblical theme is that of the divine activity which will not abandon a faithless and disobedient community but is always recalling them to their central insights and tasks and so renewing them and making them once again effective. The second is that this recalling and renewing task is frequently seen to be advanced through secular and contemporary pressures. Thus it would be theologically consistent for Christians to be recalled to an insight and perspective which is important both to them and to their fellow human beings by a general and secular questioning of the false expectations and undesirable effects of dogmatisms in general, including Christian dogmatisms in particular.

A contemporary renewal of this perspective would suggest that a valid and practical way of construing our human situation is to see it in the light of a divine offer of a pilgrimage which is neither progress according to a recognisable blueprint nor a random and ineffective wander, dominated by mere reactions to unavoidable determinisms and by an ultimate hopelessness. Rather the pilgrimage is in search of a shared purpose, shared between God and Man in such a way that both the emergence and the achievement of the purpose depends upon a collaboration between Man and God. The pilgrimage is also sustained by a promise of eventual achievement and enjoyment which goes beyond time and space because the promise is underwritten by the investment of God in time and space. Thus any particular segment of human history, and in particular the one which we are experiencing, is not to be seen as a determined section in a fixed and coherent plan (conceived with the aid of God, or Science or of Marx), nor as a set of random happenings in a galaxy of randomness, but as a set of possibilities for collaborative exploration and invention which can be looked for and developed in the midst of uncertainty, frustration, suffering and wickedness. Thus purpose, promise and hope are maintainable whether or not any particular set of models, theories and policies are at the moment 'working' with regard to the particular field of social and human disturbance on which our concern is focused.

In fact, positive values are to be detected in a period of confusion about social aims and social institutions. Signs of 'not working' can be seen as threatening breakdowns and these threats may come to be realised in local or wider ways (e.g. the Hull prison riot and its aftermath, or the possibility of crippling deficiencies in prison security and order because of overwhelming pressures arising from over-crowding, increasing obsolescence of buildings and irresistible pressures towards industrial unrest among prison staffs). Nonetheless there is a possibility of using these threats of breakdown as pressures for and indications of ways of breaking out of a received wisdom and practice which has ceased to be, or ought to cease to be, humanly acceptable. A primary task of criminological investigation and reflection is to direct dissatisfactions and fears into channels and directions which could lead to a breakthrough into improved ways of handling or understanding the threatening problems in society's response to crime and to offenders.

The main human point of the criminological confusion is to be seen, in terms of the pilgrimage perspective, to be in the pressures to move on. Thus it is to be understood and received as basically a good thing from the point of view of human development and welfare that the present functioning of the criminal justice system and of penal theory and practice should be called in question at both the practical and moral levels. It is a mistake in the understanding of what it is to be human to act upon the notion that any functioning social system is good enough for human beings and their potentialities. Uncritical acceptance of what has become established can thus rapidly allow tyrannous and cruel developments to settle in or to be taken for granted. (This is the more likely in view of that apparently persistent element in human affairs which theology refers to as 'sin' but this will be referred to below.)

It is also humanely good that models and theories should be cut down in size and be shown not to be capable of explaining everything on their own or of covering everything that needs to be covered or taken into account. Rather, it becomes clear that models and theories are not revelations nor determining total descriptions of what must be the case or of what must be aimed at. They are, properly understood and used, heuristic devices developed with as much rigour, discipline and responsibility as possible for getting to grips with what is going on, for understanding this as sensitively as possible and thus for assisting us to improve our responses to human social problems and to what is happening to human beings in them and through them. With such an understanding of the provisionality of the methods and of the limitations of the tools available to us it should be possible to develop a healthy clarity with regard to penal proposals or to criminological theories as to what part of them can properly be claimed to reflect analysis, what part represents an infusion of values into the argument and thus what emerges as clear advocacy advanced on grounds of human commitment in order, so it is believed, to preserve something of human importance or develop something of greater human worthwhileness. A renewing of the search, or a discovery of new ways to search, for the more truly human is an essential part of human pilgrimage.

I will close this part of my discussion by some comments on the effect which seeing things in the above perspective might have on two issues which arise in criminological discussion: these are the issues of the State, and of polarisation.

In this consultation it was pointed out that some of the developments of the justice model imply a minimalist understanding of the role and significance of the State. Other approaches suggest or even demand a much more active role for the State and a much higher evaluation of the State as a necessarily prime factor in the shaping of society. It might seem therefore that one of the prerequisites for clarifying criminological confusion is to clarify our theory or evaluation of the State. It would then further follow that our theological response to this confusion ought to be some theological contribution to a theory of the State.

The pilgrimage perspective, however, suggests caution here. It is clear that when discussing criminological issues we must remain sensitive to the fact that we are investigating issues which either demand or imply a view of the State and the ways it does or should work. The views need to be given explicit articulation so that we can see whether we wish to maintain them or whether it is possible to maintain them. It is also clear that Christian theological traditions contain a great deal of material about the State. However, if we are 'strangers and pilgrims' we are engaged (or invited to be engaged) in discovering and adapting patterns of State existence and State activity quite as much as (or even more than) in conforming to or maintaining the existence of a pattern of the State or a theory of the State which is already given.

The State is not to be deified. It is not even to be sanctified. That is to say that it is never to be absolutised and it is not even to be treated with special respect whenever it becomes clear that State institutions and arrangements are failing to promote purposes which we now see to be humanly desirable or are actually maintaining or producing effects which we now see to be humanly undesirable. For 'here we have no permanent city' and we 'look for a city which is to come', that is we know we must always be ready to move on. On the other hand, we are not encouraged by theological perspectives to be unrealistic pilgrims. We are not therefore invited to write off the State or to adopt a dogmatically minimising view of it. The State has to be taken seriously for a number of reasons. An immense amount of human investment has gone into the development of State activities for the promotion of human welfare. The running of human and humane societies at the scale and level of complexity which is now inevitable, clearly involves both the necessity and the persistence of elaborate social structures. Further, within a theological perspective, human living clearly has vital communal, corporate and collective features although this has been somewhat obscured by the way in which one influential strand in modern (post-Reformation and post-Renaissance) Christian thinking has over-concentrated on individualism.

Within this perspective, therefore, criminological reflection and the pursuit of more humane and more workable penal policies are seen to be one important element in exploring what, at this juncture in our affairs, we ought to mean by 'the State' and what we want of the State. We do not have to wait for the emergence of a new consensus about the State on the one hand, or to insist on suspension of critical judgement about our own theory of the State on the other, before we can legitimately and effectively put forward criminological suggestions and consequent penal proposals. On a pilgrimage there is no practical contradiction between being provisional and being purposeful.

Considerations such as these lead to reflection on a second issue in current criminological controversies, that of polarisation. There seem to be two sets of questions which crystallise out in current discussion. The first set are about man, society, criminal justice, punishment, law and order, all as a whole and in relation to fundamental views of, and hopes for, men and women and society. I have argued in the first part of this chapter that it is because this set is inevitable and always impinges on the second that a theological contribution or its equivalent is both possible and required for furthering criminological discussion. The second set of questions are about immediate and short-term action, about legislating for and administering the system as it obtains now, about keeping things going and about sustaining where we must and ameliorating where we can, while discovering the rules for, and enabling the conditions of, such new ways of doing things as seem to be demanded by practical necessity and moral insight. Whilst these two sets of questions are clearly logically interwoven, in practice they seem to get set against one another (hence the problem of polarisation).

The first (the 'fundamental') set of questions tends to be pressed by people and groups who have a strong sense of moral outrage about much that goes on in the system as it is and who ally this protest with utopian theories and idealistic visions of what ought to be and what could be. They are convinced that the questions raised cut to the very roots of society, that the protests justify a fundamental calling in question of what now goes on and that the new state of affairs which is longed for makes absolute demands upon us. These convictions lead to the judgement that nothing worthwhile can be done about the second set of questions as long as there is no revolutionary change in the structures and attitudes prevailing in society. It is further argued, with a great deal of force, that to become engaged in attempts at dealing with the second set of problems is to be diverted from the basic fight for the revolutionary changes which can alone make possible real amelioration and to risk almost certain co-option into support of the *status quo.*

The second (the 'practical') set of questions is likewise made the exclusive focus of debate and action by many of those who have the direct responsibility for running or taking part in present institutions, by those who can see that there are troubling moral and human questions raised by what happens at present but who do not see that a sense of moral outrage or a utopian vision can offer any useful or practical ways of responding to such unease, and by those who are persuaded or persuade themselves that the running of persisting structures and making the best job one can of keeping things going is the most important contribution that can be made to the maintenance and improvement of society. Such preoccupations tend to result in all questions being telescoped into their most severely and immediately 'practical' end. A strongly negative value is attributed to the raising of wider questions or to the insistence that questions to which there are no immediate answer or no clear prospect of a practical answer are none the less real questions which must be faced by practitioners and for the sake of practice. Thus the polarisation between the 'revolutionary' questions and campaigners and those who struggle to maintain and hope to improve the *status quo* seems often to be more complete in practice than would seem necessary in logic or in theory. Further, any person or group who seeks to avoid or deny this polarisation is liable to be made to feel guilty by the 'revolutionaries' for not being sufficiently urgent and utopian in their moral commitment and to feel useless and irrelevant by the 'practitioners' because they are not offering an immediate contribution to what needs to be done in the next few days or months.

Yet within a theological 'pilgrimage perspective' this polarisation must be both clearly recognised and firmly rejected as definitive of possible attitudes and activities. What is to be rejected is the limited and limiting absoluteness of both sides. As I shall shortly argue when I put forward relevant theological suggestions arising from the doctrinal areas of sin and of eschatology, the severity of revolutionary judgements and the demands of revolutionary hopes point to essential elements in and pressures on the human pilgrimage. But the demands and pressures of present problems, present structures and present persons (including presently defined 'offenders') in their present forms cannot be ignored in the light of, or sacrificed for the sake of, 'the future'. For the future is neither a fixed pattern nor an agreed goal (still less an established guarantee) but a set of possibilities yet to be realised and always to be corrected. The material for and the context of our human pilgrimage is constituted by that contemporary whole which

includes both the revolutionary thrusts and the maintenance necessities. 'Revolutionary righteousness' is neither infallible nor impregn-
able and prescriptions for change cannot escape the necessities of social
continuity and survival. On the other hand those who perform and are
committed to the task of maintenance, management and containment
can equally readily absolutise the continuing necessity of some such
tasks and the current routines and assumptions for performing them
into pragmatic idols which represent nothing so much as entrenched
self-interest and vested habit.

In practice, these arguments and perspectives suggest that
criminological research and penological concern should currently
focus on such tasks as finding better ways of running prisons while
accepting the force of arguments for the abolition of imprisonment
and for the decriminalisation of much of the law and treatment to do
with offenders. A second focusing task would be to search for ways of
concentrating on the statistics and descriptive diagnoses of rising
crime rates and of demands for 'law and order' in such a way that the
pressures for developing more effective ways of responding to
offences and offenders were turned back on to society at large rather
than directed solely to the agencies on whom society has devolved this
task.

If we are to follow up this approach within this perspective then we
shall apparently be inviting those who bear the brunt of penal practice
and criminological confusion to face more tensions and more
uncertainties rather than offering them elements of solutions to clearly
seen and sharply felt practical problems. But this is precisely the point
of the theological response which is to claim that the pilgrim
perspective points us to more realistic and more hopeful ways of living
with our problems than do either the pragmatic or the dogmatic.
Further, other features of a theological response are directed to
providing support for living with the inevitable tensions in such a way
that they can remain hopeful and creative rather than paralysing and
destructive. These include the theological support for 'courage
concerning values' which is the subject of my next section, the
maintenance of radical demands under all circumstances which stems
from the doctrinal insights about men and women, sin and eschatology, to which I shall be referring, and the understanding of the
pilgrim perspective itself as issuing in a style of life which combines
commitment to the demands of the present context with a readiness
for detachment in the interest of moving on in the direction of that
which promises less inhumanity and more worthwhileness. It is not
possible to offer theological responses without making suggestions
about a way of life, just as it is not possible to analyse the context and
implications of criminological confusion without falling into ques-

tions about ways of life presupposed, promoted or hindered by the society whose responses to crime we are considering.

In this section I have therefore argued that a first theological response is to suggest a perspective within which human life and its problems and thus criminological problems, are to be viewed. This perspective, which I have labelled the 'pilgrim perspective', has effects on our understanding of problems and of our approach to problem-solving. I have made some initial suggestions as to how it would affect our handling of the issue of the State when it comes up in criminological investigation and I have suggested how it might affect our response to any apparent polarisation in criminological argument and advocacy. This raises problems about maintaining necessary tensions and conflicts if one rejects polarisation while also rejecting any 'toning down' of the importance and the sharpness of the issue raised by the taking up of the polarised positions. This leads naturally into some further theological comments which are also relevant to other aspects of the discussions in the consultation.

(ii) Theology and Courage Concerning Values

Much attention has been given in this consultation and in this chapter to the current lack of consensus or assurance about how to analyse and evaluate problems of crime and punishment in our society. It is also generally accepted that our society is 'pluralistic' in that different value systems and life-philosophies compete and co-exist within it. A possible effect of all this is to emasculate the motivation and commitment which visions and values have inspired in men and women. All values are to some extent valuable but none are very valuable. Thus there is nothing to long for, to fight for or to reach out for. Moral outrage and utopian hopes are exaggerated and useless responses to the regrettably undesirable and the wistfully unobtainable. The institutions which society has evolved must be run with as little trouble as possible and where trouble gets too disturbing there are two possible reactions. One is to fall back on a response from a localised and fragmentary interest-group (a trade union, a profes-sional association, a pressure group) which will fight the troubles in terms of the symptoms which particularly affect the members of the group. This is a sort of defensive sub-tribalism. The other is to become enthusiastic and potentially violent supporters of some simplistic solution which may or may not be bolstered by an allegedly explanatory theory. (It's all to do with class, or lack of discipline in schools and families, or immigration, or State interference with freedom or. . . .) This is a sort of irresponsible messianism. These two reactions are often reflected in the polarisation between the 'practi-tioners' and the 'revolutionaries' referred to earlier.

If we hold that the only possible basis of consensus in a pluralistic society is some form of utilitarianism, which is, I think, the thread of the argument in at least a part of Dr. Plant's chapter, then we are up against the problem that the generally accepted notion of utility seems to have sunk to a very bureaucratic, routine and self-centred one. Such a notion cannot generate either the motives or the insights which could rise above or force a way through the present confusions. Nor can it begin to do justice to the 'something more' which there is or ought to be about being human which is glimpsed by those who feel moral outrage, long for utopian hopes or are simply moved to compassion by what is happening to some of their fellows. It will also need more than a consensus and minimum utilitarianism to combat the problem which Professor Bottoms cites from Malraux as 'a key problem of our time', that is, whether it is 'possible to pursue an active but pessimist philosophy that is not, in fact, a form of Fascism' (above, p. 20).

Here theology would seem to have a particularly important response to make. Christianity, through history and in practice, has displayed as much variation and as much failure in the pursuit of professed values as any other organised philosophy of life. There are and always have been many differences of opinion among Christians as to what values mean and what they properly demand. But there is absolutely no doubt at all about the existence of supreme and glorious Value, of the necessity to seek responses to it and of the possibility of being blessed by it. Thus a theological response offers in the first place not so much detailed guidance about the application of values nor a claim for universal submission to its interpretation of value and values but an unambiguous and whole-hearted reinforcement to those who feel and seek to sustain courage about values. Theologically it is clear that men and women do well to feel moral outrage (even if the particular content given or the particular conclusions drawn are mistaken, inept or inapplicable). Likewise we do well to entertain utopian hopes, impossible longings and risky compassion. For all these are appropriate responses to the Mystery and the possibility which is bound up in being human. Theology thus offers a perspective which endorses and motivates human propensities to protest, to long, to explore and to suffer and which refuses to accept any policy or programme which subordinates these propensities decisively and wholly to the world of hard facts and inevitable institutions.

Ways in which this perspective comes more precisely to bear on particular aspects of penal theory and practice can be more easily indicated by reference to particular theological doctrines to which I now turn.

Theological Doctrines

(i) *Men and Women 'in the Image of God'*

I am assuming that when I use the term 'a doctrine' I am referring in a shorthand way to a traditional locus of discussion about some particular aspect of the life of men and women in the world in relation to God or of some particular aspect of the relationship between God and the world. I do not myself hold that doctrinal talk is literally descriptive talk but rather that its principal terms are icons or symbols which serve to build up informative and dynamic pictures or story-ways of talking about God, men and women and the world in such a way that they point towards realistic understandings and possibilities. These understandings and possibilities are developed through the ways in which one is invited or provoked into viewing what is going on, the resources one is invited to look for and the responses one is invited to make. (For a fuller discussion on the ways 'doctrines' work, see Jenkins 1976, chs. 6, 10.)

It is on this basis therefore that I draw on doctrines to indicate theological responses which have something to say about questions at issue in the criminological field. To refer to men and women as 'in the image of God' is to begin to make a theological contribution from a Christian point of view to a question to which anyone must have some sort of answer when dealing with criminological matters. This is the question 'What positive view and evaluation do you take of men and women, including yourself?'. 'In the image of God' symbolises a very positive view about and evaluation of men and women as to their status and potentialities. It is a claim that whatever may be the most accurately supported current accounts of the physical origins and the physical, psychological and social operating of men and women their total context and range of potentiality extends as far as the transcendence and infinity of God and that this transcendence and infinity of God has traces and possibilities which are or can be operative within them both in their discreteness and in their relationships. 'Image of God' is a symbol of the presence of transcendent and infinite personal possibilities.

This is very relevant to arguments and allegations about the cause or causes of crime. A symbolic doctrine claiming that human life is to be seen and lived in a wider, indeed in a transcendent context, stands, at the very least, as an important reminder of the limits of a disciplined analysis carried out in terms of a particular theory and a particular methodology (e.g. an analysis of recidivism in matched samples of prisoners, correlated with the treatment which they received; or an analysis of the social background of a scientifically selected spectrum of types of offenders). For the claim of the symbol to be pointing to a valid evaluation of human reality serves to indicate that it is a critical value judgement and the expression of a commitment to a particular perspective on being human to argue and act as if any analytic causal account of human behaviour is, as such, comprehensive and a sufficient exposure of what needs to be taken into account when deciding how to respond to the problems analysed or the results revealed. No psychological, sociological or political approach with its consequent methodology is the generator on its own of a policy, a programme or a decision which can claim sufficient authority by virtue of its conformity to an 'objective' or 'scientific' method. This becomes even clearer when one comes to the stage of overt advocacy of a line of action. It is always appropriate and necessary to pose the additional question about whether it is right to treat human beings like that or to regard them like that in view of their 'being in the image of God'. Reductionism is not a necessity, it is a decision.

It must also be stressed, however, that because 'Image of God' symbolism is part of a wider symbolism and a wider story of Creation, it cannot legitimately be used to interfere with or to push on one side the procedures and findings of properly autonomous scientific-type inquiries. The Creation story invites a theological perspective on what goes on in the world. It does not provide theological directives about either how we find out what is going on or about the details of these 'goings on'. As I have already argued a theological response is possible (and it or its equivalent is inevitable) at the level of evaluation, decision and advocacy. Thus in any theological response the interposition of the 'Image of God' question or perspective has to be accompanied by the most sensitive assessment possible of the best available evidence and theories about the influential shaping factors which are at work in the human and social area concerned. What a theological response must be concerned to maintain is that while the details of analysis are essential to a responsible approach to any problem these details are neither totally decisive nor wholly definitive.

Thus, speaking from a theological and faith perspective which takes 'Image of God' symbolism seriously when it comes to decision and practice it is more important to risk treating people as free than to risk treating them as determined. It would be irresponsible to ignore well-established evidence which clearly casts doubt on areas of freedom or choice but it would be inhuman either to take the question as closed or to fail to search for an area in which freedom can be assured, provoked or risked. A clear grasp of the divine evaluation of men and women ought to provide an effective tool for facing up to the uncertainty and confusion about theories of punishment, about penal practice, and about the wider issues of authority and of the State that have been widely referred to in this consultation and in this chapter.

For example, rehabilitation may not 'work' in the sense that when experts monitor the follow-up to policies and treatments held to aim at rehabilitation there is no evidence that anyone has been changed (say in respect of their contribution to the crime rate). It is also clear that there are some practical and moral problems about coercive attempts to change people under duress. But if anyone can help anyone else to 'rehabilitate' himself or herself surely this attempt must continue to be made out of sheer respect for human beings and it is very necessary to both reflect and organise to keep that element alive in both criminological reflection and penal practice.

Similarly to assume that sentences pronounced in the course of criminal justice give people their 'just deserts' may invite a proper cynicism. But society will go on coming up against 'offenders', we have to reckon with both wickedness (see below re 'Sin') and responsibility and we have to respect people as people. Therefore *some* attempt at working out 'what is deserved' must continue as a sheer necessity for recognising and attempting to do justice to these features of human life and society. We have to learn to be always trying here and always recognising our failures.

Further, whatever the confusions about the State and about authority, simple awareness of the value of persons constitutes a demand that we continue to struggle to structure a community which protects and enables human living together and to build up or uphold an authority which can protect members of the community against the aggressive or reckless and which can help to balance out conflicting claims. We ought not to invest too much in our expectations of what our models and theories will enable us to understand and provide. They are tools to guide us in our deciding and our hoping. But because we believe that men and women are 'in the image of God' or because we agree that it is worth treating them as if they have or can be open to a transcendent dimension we have to be prepared to take the practical risk of refusing to be too utilitarian about rehabilitation or to be too merely regulative about 'justice'.

(If this were a more extended discussion, rather than a series of notes indicating lines along which theological responses could and should be developed, it would be necessary to show how the 'image' perspective ought not to be used to justify any approach to crime and to the offender which is over-individualised. But it is not possible here to follow up the relational and social aspects of 'the Image' arising from its context in biblical and traditional Christian thought.)

(ii) *Sin*

'Image of God' symbolism, the faith which it provokes and the understanding which it encourages, enable and direct a positive evaluation of men and women. This is part of the Christian contribution to answering the question everyone must have some working answer to, *viz.*: 'How do I view what it is to be human?'. There is another side to this question which is equally inescapable. This is 'How do we understand and face up to the negativities in human beings and in society?'. This is clearly of peculiar importance for any discipline or any social institution which is aligned on the identification of and response to 'offenders'.

The doctrine which is central to a Christian understanding and evaluation of what is wrong with, and what goes wrong in, the human situation is that of 'sin'. As with all terms or symbols which are central to Christian doctrines the term 'sin' is a strictly theological one. That is to say one cannot appreciate the proper use of the term without some understanding of the dynamic picture of men in relation to God which it is designed to convey or suggest. This picture cannot be outlined here (i.e. I do not have space to attempt a sketch of 'the doctrine of sin'). I can only refer to certain aspects or implications of this picture and indicate their relevance to some features of current criminological discussion.

The doctrine of sin then is an attempt to locate 'what is wrong' within a certain perspective and to suggest how this wrongness is to be faced with realism, creativity and hope. The general picture of men and women and their situation which is portrayed is built up out of notions like man before God, man against God, man falling short of the glory which God offers, man choosing less than the best or deliberately choosing that which is bad, man directing his energies, understanding and interests in on himself and thus turning himself against other men. There are three implications of this portrayal (among doubtless many others) which occur to me as relevant to a theological response to criminological problems. These are implications about responsibility, about wickedness and about optimism.

The picture of Man as sinner is not a demeaning picture of Man, however it has been misinterpreted and abused to enable the self-styled 'righteous' to justify power exercised in their own interests over 'sinners'. (This frequent abuse, of course, is a type-specimen example of what the doctrine of sin is about!) For as a 'sinner', Man is understood as a being with responsibility before God and his fellows, with the potentiality of choice and with a nature and a destiny which is not defined by the abuse of these possibilities nor by the situations of chaos, misery and helplessness in which he is (we are) often trapped.

With reference to criminological problems, the implications about responsibility to be obtained from this picture reinforce the considerations about risk already discussed under 'Image of God'. This may be of particular importance in evaluating any attempt to advocate and work out the details of a 'regulative' approach to the administration of justice. It may very well be that 'the question of just deserts' can function only as a question which is a disturbance and a puzzle rather than as a question whose pursuit could lead to a clear guide in the providing of sentencing 'tariffs'. But, whatever the difficulties and limitations of discriminatory sentencing, it would seem to be potentially dehumanising not to leave a space in which a representative or representatives of the community have to face up to the recognition (however difficult to do so 'justly') of a person's responsibility and deserts. Again, it is important not to lose sight of the element in rehabilitation which seeks to enable people to be responsible just as it is important to remain critical about indeterminate sentences, aimed at providing 'time for rehabilitation' but which leave too much responsibility in the hands of people who have, effectively, arbitrary power over an offender. This perspective on responsibility also suggests that the concepts of prisoners' rights and of prisoners' participation in the management of their affairs must be pressed. A human concern for all human beings requires this, whatever may be the immense practical difficulties at present because of inadequate buildings, inadequate staffing and an understandable reluctance on the part of a majority of staff and among the public to acknowledge that prisoners have rights.

The implications about 'wickedness' are perhaps more difficult to assimilate by persons of a liberal or utopian cast of mind but they are of particular importance if we are to build up a realistic and hopeful resistance to the latent fascism and aggression which sometimes seems so near the surface in public reactions to problems of crime and of law and order. The doctrine of sin does not explain wickedness, it recognises it. That is to say it faces the fact, and holds it to be a fact, that one of the elements in human living in the world is an inexplicable or, perhaps better, a non-explicable tendency, to which human beings may lend themselves, to do, cherish or create wrongness or evil for its own sake, or out of a desire to deny or defy goodness. It is part of the greatness and tragedy of human beings to be able to exercise freedom to the extent of choosing and promoting evil.

Such a theological perspective has its own internal difficulties (e.g. the relation of God to free-will and to evil), it presents many difficulties of acceptance and interpretation and the doctrine has been made use of in many difficult and destructive ways. But as a claim about an element or feature of human living which must perforce be taken into account it at least serves as a warning against underestimating what we are up against in human and social wrongness, and also against tendencies to adopt oversimple mono-causal (or even single theory) explanations of 'what is wrong'. Whatever is done and whatever is responsibly judged to be the case there is still the necessity to be on one's guard for evil, sin, wickedness. On the other hand this apparently pessimistic realism is located within a very positive overall approach to human life (Sin is a feature of 'fallen' human 'nature'. That is to say that its presence, power and potential ubiquity does not define either what human beings are meant to be or what they are able to become.) It is related to a doctrine of redemption which asserts, in various ways, that powers and possibilities are available which can confront, suffer, absorb and overcome sin and it is thus part of an approach to man which combines a readiness to face the worst with a reason for moving towards and hoping for the best.

This approach can throw light on some pretty intractable problems both about some offenders and about those who have power over offenders. Thus, it suggests that we have consciously and clearly to face, as one such problem, the continuing existence of people who are so violent, dangerous or malignant that society is obliged to exercise coercive restraint against them. This is not to say that we can ever be satisfied with how we define, detect and treat such people for insofar as society contributes to their wickedness, it is our wickedness, just as it is our society. But this does not alter the fact that it is also their wickedness and that it is wickedness and has to be restrained as such. On the other hand it also means that men and women who add to or express wickedness are still men and women and must be treated as such. This points to another area where practical tensions have to be maintained as, for example, in high security prisons. The problems and tensions have to be lived with and cannot be defined and administered away either in the direction that humans are never wicked or in the direction that the wicked have no rights as humans.

Further, however, this existence of tendencies to wickedness has implications also concerning all those who have power over offenders or are involved in administering criminal justice and what follows from it. No one and no one group is to be trusted without question or without accountability, whether they are placed in positions of power, regarded as experts or charged with the carrying out of orders. Hence the need to be always pressing for an increasingly public system of inspection, checks and balances at all levels of criminal justice and penal practice. This is not because we are particularly suspicious of 'the authorities' but because we know that no one is to be trusted absolutely (save in the glorious risk of certain mutual relationships of love), including ourselves, and that power over fellow human beings gives particular opportunities for self-centredness that can turn into tyranny and wickedness. Sin is not something of which one primarily accuses others but something which one recognises in and confesses of oneself and then takes into account in contributing to the structuring of institutions and of society.

As Professor Preston has already pointed out, this whole perspective should make one particularly sensitive to false pretensions and to the necessity for provisionality and frequent reassessment. One area in which this sensitivity needs to be applied is concerning the very notion of the 'offender' who becomes the proper concern of criminal justice. In view of the possibilities of sin it is always necessary to be questioning the persons and processes who define offences and offenders. The connection between the 'administration of justice' and justice in any ideal or fulfilling sense is bound to be fragile and in need of constant questioning and improvement. To absolutise 'the law' in any way as the expression either of morality or of the proper will and need of the State is to blaspheme against humanity and to ignore the evident sinfulness of human beings from which neither moralisers nor State officials are in any way exempt. This is not to question the inevitability of some criminal justice system, only to insist upon its necessary provisionality.

A further theological response which makes use of the notion of sin could be developed from a rather different feature of the biblical tradition than has been drawn on so far. This is to do with the perception of sin in the structures of society. While the Old Testament prophetic tradition in no way idealises the poor there are not infrequent references to the way in which God's wrath is directed against society because of the way the poor are treated within it or of the way in which they are left to their fate. A society is judged in the light of those who are found to be marginals within it or cast out on the fringes of it. This is a perspective on sin in society or even the sins of society. Such a perspective lends a great deal of support to those who argue, for example, from the high proportion of the lowest social classes that characteristically are to be found in the prison population, that criminal justice is largely an instrument of class bias and that our prisons are the dumping grounds in which the more prosperous and successful part of society attempts to shut away those of its problems which it cannot or will not face. The suggestion is that we must face the serious possibility that there are features of our sentencing system and of our prison systems which ought to be read as far more a condemnation of our society than of the convicted. Any theological response to our present criminological confusion would seem to involve the raising and pressing of this severe question, whatever compromises might be judged to be inevitable in practice out of the sheer necessity of sustaining society and under the pressure of what society will at present allow. In particular it would seem necessary to reinforce readiness to stand up against public opinion which is notoriously given to self-righteousness against scapegoats, outcasts and problems. It is also necessary to reinforce those who are struggling, however unpopularly and seemingly unpractically, to enable a prisoner's voice to be heard in the debates and reassessments which have to go on to find a more viable and more humane penal policy and practice. The doctrine of sin helps to make it clear that there is no clear cut division between men and women who are problem-solvers and men and women who are problems ('offenders'). Rather 'we' as human beings, and as constituting with 'them' our society, are all part of the problem. Distinctions, of course, have to be made, and to be maintained in practice, but in the search for more creative ways forward all voices (of 'them', as well as of 'us') need to be heard.

(iii) *Eschatology and Expectation*

In discussing the doctrines of 'Image of God' and of 'Sin' I have been discussing how criminological questions may have theological responses contributed to them from, respectively, a doctrinal area which points to positive evaluations about being human and one which faces up to what goes wrong in being human. In moving to the doctrinal area of 'Eschatology' I am moving to one which addresses the question of what expectations it is realistic to hold about human achievements and human failures in the process of living in the actual world *between* the ideal and hopes indicated by our positive evaluation of what it is to be human and our experience of what goes wrong in and with human living in society. This is a further problem area to which it is necessary to have either a theological response or its equivalent because in choosing and pursuing policies, programmes and patterns of action everyone has to have some view of what they *expect* from these actions and how they handle what results from the failure to achieve the expectations or from the frustrations of them or from the unexpected effects of their partial achievement.

'Eschatology' in traditional and systematic discussions of Christian doctrine is, formally, 'the doctrine of the four last things' ('Eschatos' refers in Greek to the last, the final, the end). These 'four last things' are Death, Judgement, Heaven and Hell. The significant thing about them, from the point of view of this discussion, is that they represent 'things' (whether their status is mystical, symbolic or 'flatly' realistic) about which men and women can, in the last analysis, do nothing and which depend for their resolution, if there is or will be any, on the action or presence or power of God as God. That is to say that if death is to be overcome then it must be God who 'raises up the dead'; if the tension between the terrible wrongness of things and the glorious rightness of things is ever to be finally resolved, then it is God who must 'execute the judgement'; if there is a state of affairs, a condition of being or a realm of enjoyment which is seriously and essentially consistent with the seriousness of moral commitment and the infinity of personal possibilities then it must be God's 'place and province'. ('Kingdom of God' language in the mythology and symbolism of the Bible is, for example, addressed to the same problems and possibilities.)

This type of language is very clearly at the best symbolic and at the worst fantastic. It is indeed a matter of faith whether one finds oneself allied with those who hold that the language stems from and points to realistic possibilities. It is also a matter of the lifetime of each believer and, as the believers would say, of eternity, to find out fully to what this realism leads. But even if the symbolism ('the doctrine') is not held to point to any credibly meaningful answer to worthwhile human questions, it does serve as one way, with a great deal of tradition behind it and a great investment put into it, of persistently pointing to the existence of limits, of limits to human achievement and of the dubious basis for many human and social hopes.

A theological response to this aspect of human and social struggles could be particularly relevant in our society at the moment. For our society has become trapped in a false set of expectations about our inevitable progress, guaranteed improvement and expanding pos-sibilities. These expectations have been built up by an amalgam of beliefs about liberal humanism, scientific progress and the political reorganisation of society. While the beliefs started from and were sustained by immense advances of the human spirit and intense moral insights, they have developed into an idolatry of the (very real and immensely valuable) human capacities for reason, science and political management. But reason, science and a proper understanding of political realities were supposed to have driven God out of the universe (or revealed his non-existence). Thus when they prove unable to deliver what was expected of them there is nowhere to turn. People then plunge into a depressive pessimism, localised apathy or privatised pursuit of self-fulfilment which is quite as unrealistic and potentially dehumanising as the previous euphoric and romantic optimism.

'Eschatological' language however points to insights of faith which are not about automatic progress but are about continuing possibilities of movement in a worthwhile direction which will have its promise ultimately fulfilled. (They tie up, of course, with what earlier I have described as 'the pilgrim perspective'.) It is God who 'brings in the Kingdom' in His own time and place and He does it both through human collaboration and in spite of human obstacles. This belief in commitment to the Kingdom of God is particularly apt for keeping alive and striving towards the highest ideals and hopes for human beings in the midst of repeated failures, obstacles and short- or medium-term bafflements and confusions. It is not what we immediately experience or expect which becomes decisive but what faith enables us to hope and work for. This 'practical eschatology' links the rejection of utopian expectations with an assertion of the constant relevance of the pressure of utopian hopes. The limitations on human powers of achievement are fully recognised but without the corresponding diminution in the power and importance attributed to human beings and human hopes. The practical effect of this should be to relativise the significance and effect of institutional 'last words' on what can be done about offenders, their treatment, and penal and criminal theory and practice, because of current managerial, administrative or political constraints.

What is to be aimed at, under the pressure of an eschatological understanding, is to devise ways and means of taking utopian hopes as seriously as practical necessities. For example, the demands and arguments of those who introduce the notion of 'Abolition' into criminological debate and the fights for penal practice are to be seen as presenting a perfectly proper human demand which must be entertained as pointing to something which could become an increasingly possible practice. There are plenty of reasonable grounds, some of them referred to in the preceding section, for holding that the practice of imprisonment is as much an example of what is wrong with society as an institution which protects society against wrong. This 'judgement' has an important part to play in maintaining humane pressures on our struggles to develop a better penal policy and indicates a direction in which we should always be striving to move however much we must again face the fact that, in any foreseeable practice, there will always be people who have to be detained and people who have to be treated as offenders. This understanding also reinforces the practical necessity of developing information and openness, and such a system of checks and balances about what actually goes on, that there are constant pressures to rethinking what we at present accept and to reforming current practices and attitudes.

Eschatology therefore requires that we continually press radical questions and look for ways of moving towards radical solutions (like the abolition of imprisonment and the decriminalisation of offences, wrongs and conflicts). At the same time however, it is also made clear that we cannot expect society and its institutions to be simply and directly moral. It is as much a mistake to be simply moralistic about the way structures and institutions work as it is to deny moral and human pressures on the grounds of pragmatic necessity. The morally and humanly worthwhile is something we have always to be seeking and constructing. We cannot be content with our structures and institutions nor can we do without them. We are bound therefore to be working and struggling for both changes which develop structures which will function in more humane ways and for working into any structures that which is more humanising or at least, less dehumanising. Hence the polarity between the 'revolutionary' and the 'practical men' referred to earlier is to be rejected and an attempt has to be made to combine radical criticisms and radical aims with a much more routine perseverance with what we actually have in order to bring about improvement.

Within prisons, the prison service and its surrounding official and voluntary bodies this suggests the persistent development of sensitive and corporate policies which strengthens people to bear the tension of how 'in the wrong' they are without developing more than normal guilt for or resistance to this knowledge. One may well have to do the undesirable and live routinely with the intolerable. But there is no way of keeping humane possibilities open or of searching for better alternatives if the undesirable becomes accepted as desirable and the intolerable becomes the norm of what is to be tolerated. To deny that the inhumane is inhuman must be dehumanising. The challenge and the hope is to find ways of supporting one another in acknowledging what is wrong while having to live with it, contribute to it and yet fight against it.

With reference to people committed to action within and about prisons this approach might suggest that they have at least three worthwhile areas of task open to them. First, they are doing a piece of work which society, as yet, finds inevitable and necessary. There are good grounds for thinking of it as a piece of society's 'dirty work' and there are many grounds for severe criticism of the way it is carried out. But insofar as society requires it and there is no worked out substitute for it, it is an authentic and honourable task which because it has to be done is worth doing. This essentially societal value of the task is not undermined by all the uncertainties about it and pressures upon it. Secondly, within the context and constraints of the task as required by society there is the unremitting task of doing all that can be done to make the actual transactions and procedures as humanly creative as possible (or as little dehumanising as possible). This holds regardless of what theories do or do not stand up in penal policy and in criminological investigation. It is a betrayal of one's own humanity and of everyone else's to act upon the assumption that 'nothing I can do will make any difference'. Thirdly, there is the task of being prepared to be part of considered and organised pressures for improvement, reform or even revolution in, and in relation to, the system which at present operates. A view about the absolute necessity of task (3) or the virtual impossibility of task (2) does not yet remove the present necessity and authenticity of task (1).

On the other hand, it does not remove the possibility either that particular conditions or tasks in the system as it is reach a point of inhumanity where all creative energies ought to be directed into putting a stop to these conditions or preventing the very existence of such tasks.

Such a way of seeing the possibilities and the requirements in human living and in the handling of social problems clearly makes considerable demands on our capacity to sustain tensions and maintain the pursuit of aims, ideals and visions. I wish therefore finally to turn to theological responses to the problem of living with tensions and 'in the interim' i.e. between the pressures of practical necessities and the pressures of ideals and hopes.

Theology and practical stances for living with tensions

(i) A Question of Identity

An eschatological perspective on our expectations means that both those who see their main task as keeping things going (as well as possible) and those who believe the humanly necessary investment must be chiefly in radical change with varying degrees of rapidity are required to accept tensions which they may interpret solely as threat — either to the possibility of maintaining their practice or to the possibility of pursuing their visions. An eschatological understanding insists that the tensions are necessary, the threats are real but that is what we all have to live with. If this is accepted as a valid and helpful approach then a further requirement of fruitful criminological exploration and penal experiment is that ways should be found of assisting all those who have vested interests in the criminal justice system to face what may well be experienced as a continuing 'identity crisis'. This requirement extends not only through the authorities, experts, operatives and offenders in the system but also to the public at large insofar as they are understood as those threatened by offenders and those demanding protection from offenders.

The pressures of penal problems and criminological confusions produce at least some symptoms of such an identity crisis because what is called in question is the way in which people and groups have come to regard themselves, how they understand their roles in the system and what they, and society at large, expect of the system. For example, to develop a stress on and a practice of 'giving prisoners rights' is to ask that prison officers and officials shall understand themselves differently and behave differently. This means that they require new structures of support and to be the subjects of different public expectations. They cannot be left to bear the additional burdens (e.g. of procedures designed to pay more attention to prisoners' rights and of their effects) while all the old pressures and problems go on as before. If public or pressure group demands increase or bear on different points than hitherto then public or pressure group support must also increase or change their form. But this requires the emergence, evolution or conscious construction of new forms of communal and group relationships, structures and understandings. While these are being fought for, waited for or painstakingly searched for individuals and groups are under immense strain.

The search for a new identity and a new community which is in one sense demanded and in another sense offered is a central theme in theological thought and in the practice of a life of faith. It is assumed that men and women (as 'sinners') do not yet express themselves in ways which are adequate to a satisfactory fulfilment of themselves or which can bring about an adequate community of mutual fulfilment. We are required therefore to see ourselves as 'under the judgement of God' (our identities, our relationships and our roles called in question), to be ready to exercise 'repentance' (the consequent reassessment and reappraisal which is called for by the judgement on current shortcomings), to accept 'forgiveness' (an understanding that we are dependent for creative moving forward on the acceptance by God and our fellows of the wrongness we are involved in without a corresponding rejection of or hostility to ourselves) and to be ready for constantly renewed attempts at 'building the Kingdom' (attempts to construct out of the material which is available to us and in the light of judgement, repentance and forgiveness, a state of affairs which corresponds a little more closely to the best insights we so far have and which will serve as a base for the next struggle of judgement, repentance, forgiveness and achievement or failure).

Such a 'theological response' to the problems and strains inherent in any attempt to advance criminological policy and penal practice is, clearly, more a statement of a task for theology and faith than a worked-out response. But it may serve as an initial indication of a practical or practising stance which is addressed precisely to living in and with identity-crises and institutional confusion. For it sees the disturbance of having one's identity called into question as part of a process which is potentially a necessary and healthy (a 'saving') part of constructive growth and activity. One's essential identity as a human being, and the meaning and hope which goes with it, does not lie finally and definitively, in the group to which one is accustomed to belong, the role which one has become accustomed to perform or the status which one has become accustomed to enjoy or deplore. Thus there are resources available to cope with just that identity-disturbance and those confusions of a search for new communal understandings and structures which are inevitably demanded if any social institution under heavy pressure is to develop creatively.

(ii) *Living in the Interim*

The enjoyment and development of the possibilities indicated by the theological responses described above require the existence of groups of people committed to working out the responses and to one another. Similarly, the persistent pursuit of penal betterment in the midst of the criminological and more general confusions of our society requires the existence of groups of people whose commitments, aims, attitudes and actions make them something deeper and more lasting than mere pressure groups. Or if, as seems very possible, the direct contributions to change in society are to be made through pressure groups, then the members of those pressure groups need to be sustained and directed by something more than the aims and the membership of the pressure groups themselves. Temporary enthusiasms and limited aims directed by necessarily limited social diagnoses are not enough for keeping alive a search for humanness which faces up to both the complexity of social problems and the range of human possibilities and hopes. Nor are they sufficient for enabling people to bear, and even enjoy, the types of tensions to which we have been drawing attention.

Thus the final theological response which I wish to make in this initial exploration is to point to the question or possibility of 'the Church' or 'a Church'. There is, I believe, a convergence of theological and secular practical reasons for working for a revival, renewal, rediscovery or adaptation of 'a Church' or its equivalent in relation to the sustained pursuit of social and human aims in the midst of inevitable and currently irresolvable confusions and tensions. We need to develop communal resources which will both support those who are concerned to face the tensions of identity and judgement and also help to maintain a common sense of value and direction.

From a theological perspective this would be seen as working for a 'renewal of the Church' locally, contextually, and intimately.

I put 'renewal of the Church' in inverted commas because the mutual living together we need to sustain hopeful living in our pluralist society must include men and women of differing explicit (or not so explicit) ultimate convictions but who share a common concern (in this case the concern to relate prisons and prisoners to wider human possibilities and the reforming of our common social life). I believe it is a particular calling of the committed, explicit and organised church to support those who will work at the evolving and maintaining of such committed groups of people who can be sustained in pursuing their common concerns in all the pressures and frustrations of running an actual institution within our existing system. The groups have to be 'local', i.e. within a sufficiently small geographical area for people to be able to come together regularly and seriously. They have to be 'contextual', for the object is to sustain and enable people who share this common problem and a common working area. And they have to be 'intimate', for a sufficient trust has to be developed to enable the free sharing both of 'impossible ideals' and actual failures and frustrations. From a theological point of view such groups may be 'substitute churches', agents of God's work in the world but freed to work without explicit acknowledgement of Him, and if Christians are to play their part in these 'bases for renewal' within our institutions, then they have to seek particular sustenance and renewal from their explicit Christian fellowship and worship. But the convergent practical need is for organised and sustained minorities who see the point of pursuing the values glimpsed and the changes desired whatever the practical difficulties and pressures. Since we are in the pluralistic situation so often described and since we are in the social uncertainty already discussed it is clear that any persons or groups committed to the long-term and persistent pursuit of ideals related to social particularities are bound to be in the position of what Peter Berger (1971) calls a 'cognitive minority' i.e. a group who look at, and seek to respond to, the world in terms that are not widely shared or generally taken for granted.

This is a very 'church-like' situation and one familiar to theological tradition with its talk of 'the Elect', 'the Faithful', 'the salt of the earth' and so on. There is therefore, a clear theological contribution to be made to working out ways of developing the necessary communities and groups, with appropriate disciplines and means for encouragement and renewal of aims and hopes (e.g. prayer, worship and fellowship), which will sustain consistent campaigns and searches for human values and humanising changes under the limitations of the pressures and necessities discussed elsewhere in this consultation and this chapter.

At one practical level it may well be that it is in this area that the efforts of those Church Chaplaincy services which still exist should be largely concentrated. Welfare services and ordinary 'pastoral' care should be part of any prison, probation or offenders' service. The distinctive contribution of a group of persons who continue both to be 'official' and to owe their distinctive role to their church authorisation should probably be to have concern for the creation or recreation of those groups who can live and work at the frontiers of current institutions and their problems and take a positive attitude to the tensions and difficulties which this involves. Positive developments here would offer much that would be useful not only to reforming our secular institutions but also to renewing the Church as a base for various more effective ministries to contemporary society. The main point, however, of raising these suggestions here is to indicate how following up a theological understanding of the Church as a sustaining and worshipping community, living necessarily in an interim world which always includes many tensions and problems, could contribute to the contemporary secular problem of sustaining those minorities who see and are prepared to work for deep and valuable human changes in our institutions, including those concerned with criminal justice and the penal treatment of offenders. It is not possible to rely on a general and enlightened public opinion or a well-established corporate consensus or widespread agreement about values which will clearly be the basis for advance or improvement in this area. Some form of mutual support and of mutual strengthening and correcting of aims, methods and objectives are clearly required among those who have more than a theoretical interest in criminological theory and penal practice. What this requirement makes of a theological understanding of the Church and how a theological understanding of the Church can contribute to resources for meeting this requirement are clearly matters for urgent investigation.

Conclusion

If my argument about the possibility and the nature of theological responses is at all valid then it is inevitable that an exploration of possible theological responses to apparent criminological confusion should conclude by leaving a lot of loose ends and a series of pointers to possible practical implications which can become more concrete only as and if they are taken up and worked out. What has had to be discussed has been the interaction between the fundamental human possibilities of developing what is involved in being human and the development of a disciplined and specialised approach to a particular social problem area. The combination of a concern for human values and the specialised study has to feed in to present practices in existing institutions and be concerned with changing those institutions.

Thus we are concerned with some particular strands in the processes of social living and human search. What I have tried to show is ways in which theology can be a contributory part of this process and this search. From a theological point of view, two things at least are clear. Firstly, the questions which have to be faced and the problems which have to be worked out are quite as disturbing and difficult for theologians and for Christians as for anyone else. No one has the answers. It is a matter of rallying resources for living with the questions and finding creativity and hope in the problems. Secondly, how theology is to be an effective part in this whole process can be found out only by further participation in the process itself. Therefore if there is any substance in what I have written it must serve as the sketch of a programme quite as much as, if not more than, the outline of an answer.

11

Retrospect and prospect

by A. E. BOTTOMS and MICHAEL H. TAYLOR

The chapters of this book (apart from that by David Jenkins) were originally prepared for presentation on the specific occasion of the Consultation at Manchester in April 1978 (see Preface). In drawing the volume to a close, it is fitting that we should refer rather more specifically than has previously been appropriate to the content of the discussions at the Manchester weekend. Yet we are very conscious of the limited interest of most published reports of conference debates, so we shall make no attempt to provide a detailed account of the deliberations, rather using the opportunity for some more general concluding reflections.

The purpose of convening the Consultation was two-fold — to examine present and future penal policy options in the light of the 'collapse of the rehabilitative ideal', and to consider whether the social theologian has any contribution to make to this debate (above, p. vii). In reflecting retrospectively upon the discussions, we accordingly return to three central issues: the collapse of the rehabilitative ideal, present and future penal policy options, and the future of criminological-theological collaboration.

The Collapse of the Rehabilitative Ideal

In the written contributions to the Consultation, the 'collapse of the rehabilitative ideal' was generally treated as substantially established, both on empirical and theoretical grounds. This was because most of the written contributions came from academic criminologists, amongst whom there is a considerable (though not absolute) consensus about the 'collapse'; and the chapters by non-criminologists (Raymond Plant and Ronald Preston) took as their starting-point this criminological consensus.

At the Consultation, however, there was strong representation not only from academic criminology, but from the world of penal policy, administration, and practice; and those from these fields (whom we shall call, for want of a better term, 'practitioners') were far from happy with some of the assumptions about the collapse of the rehabilitative ideal made by criminologists.

Four points made by practitioners are perhaps of special importance:

First, it was suggested that many academics had a rather simplistic picture (perhaps derived from their extensive reading of American materials) as to how far penal policy and practice in Britain was, or recently had been, dominated by the rehabilitative ideal, and consequently of the extent to which there had been a change of practice. In particular, it was pointed out that Britain (unlike the U.S.) had not adopted the indeterminate sentence in any extensive way, and that most sentencing in British courts had always been based primarily on retributive and deterrent criteria, not on the principle of rehabilitation.

Second, there was a concern that talk of the collapse of the rehabilitative ideal could have a seriously damaging effect within the penal services. As one participant put it in a subsequent informal note: 'Those of us with a concern with penal practice delivered some fairly blunt warnings about the possible effect on morale and behaviour in the services of too much heady academic talk about the irrelevance of what ordinary practitioners did'. Some particularly feared the impact on the prison service; for if rehabilitation were abandoned except for optional voluntary programmes (perhaps provided mainly by 'outsiders'), then the pessimism implicit in the prison officer's remaining job of 'secure and humane containment' could lead to cynicism, brutality, or worse.

Third, there was opposition to the view that one of the reasons why rehabilitation fails to work is because it takes place within the coercive framework of a penal system. It was argued, by contrast, that many institutions in society such as schools and factories are in part coercive; to attempt constructive personal growth within a penal system is not qualitatively different from attempting it within one of these other institutions. Indeed, some felt that all relationships are in part coercive, and that society should not be oversensitive about the use of coercion as such.

Fourth, there were some specific comments from members of the probation service. They felt that the service's original aim of 'advise, assist and befriend' still held good, and that the goals of changing people, and of reducing crime, had to some extent been foisted upon them. Moreover, some felt that the use of 'treatment' did not deny the responsibility of the offender (cf. the chapter by Plant), but that the kind of people with whom the service was dealing were largely unpowerful people who often need a lot of help and guidance, and who cannot make 'free voluntary choices' about treatment very meaningfully.

Once doubts of this kind began to be expressed by practitioners, it became clear also that most of the theologians present had a strong tendency to resist talk about the collapse of the rehabilitative ideal. Christians are generally committed to a doctrine of man which stresses the possibilities of each individual's human fulfilment in response to the grace of God, and to abandon the rehabilitative ideal might seem to involve abandoning such insights.

These various objections must be taken seriously, for they were each the expression of serious concern. It would be easy, in response, to make the obvious debating point that the first and second of the practitioners' objections cannot both be wholly true, since if there had been little change of practice with the advent of rehabilitation there could scarcely be a seriously damaging effect if it were to collapse. But such a response would be unworthy, not least because these two points do both contain true statements, but in different contexts. The *sentencing structure* in Britain has been relatively immune from structural change created by the rehabilitative ideal; the *prison and probation services* have been much more influenced by the ideal, and there is no doubt that its possible collapse does create genuine anxiety amongst members of both services, which anxiety could have damaging effects on offenders in their charge.

Equally, the theologians' concern with human fulfilment is a legitimate and important one. No penal system should lightly abandon possibilities of developing, or allowing to develop, the human potential of offenders in its care; and every civilised penal system should clearly demonstrate its respect for the persons it deals with. It is precisely because totalitarian penal systems deny respect and stifle hope that we justly condemn them.

But, whilst conceding these important points to the critics, it is crucial to point out that none of this goes to the heart of the original critique of the rehabilitative ideal. That critique, it will be remembered, was two-fold — empirical and theoretical. The impirical critique doubted the effectiveness of reformative treatment in preventing recidivism; the theoretical critique saw the rehabilitative ideal as (at least in its 'scientific' version) 'theoretically faulty, systematically discriminatory . . . and inconsistent with justice' (American Friends Service Committee 1971, p. 12). *None of the points raised by practitioners or theologians at the Consultation effectively refuted these criticisms.* Rather the concern was with human fulfilment, with damage to morale in the penal services, with affirming the possibilities of personal growth even within a necessarily coercive penal system. It was not denied that the results of treatment had been usually poor, nor that an espousal of the treatment ethic could lead to the taking of excessive power over others' lives in the name of 'welfare', nor that arbitrary and discriminatory decisions could flow from treatment concepts.

The dual considerations in the previous paragraphs lead to some interesting possibilities. The criticisms levelled against the rehabilitative ideal by justice model theorists and others have been especially concerned with some of the *penal structures* the ideal produced. Might it be possible to eliminate treatment thinking from structural features of penal systems, but within those structures to keep alive the possibilities of hope and of respect for persons?

The abandonment of treatment justifications for structural aspects of the penal system would have major consequences. For example:

(i) It would call into serious question the existence of parole systems, whereby offenders given the same sentence length by courts are then (in effect) given different sentence lengths by an executive body, often on the very doubtful grounds of 'response to treatment'.

(ii) It would mean an endorsement of Norval Morris and Colin Howard's (1964, p. 175) dictum that 'power over a criminal's life should not be taken in excess of that which would be taken were his reform not considered as one of our purposes'. And, as these authors note, the endorsement of such a principle would have major practical consequences for most existing Western penal systems: 'had it guided reform hitherto, the unjust excesses of the reformative treatment of children and adult sexual offenders, and the improper use of the indefinite or indeterminate sentence, would not have occurred'.

(iii) It would mean the abandonment of assumptions that treatment methods are crime-reducing, and can be justified to courts on those grounds. This potentially has especial relevance for the justification of probation orders, which are frequently recommended on treatment grounds at the present time.

The abandonment of those structural features of the penal system which reflect rehabilitative concepts would at a stroke remove many of the original critics' objections to the rehabilitative ideal. The absence of empirical evidence of treatment effectiveness is of much less significance if crucial features of the system and decisions made within it no longer assume such effectiveness. The possibilities of systematic discrimination and of injustice, as charged by the American Friends Service Committee, become much reduced if the structures of rehabilitation are removed from the penal system, though we should not forget the Friends' other message that a just penal system is ultimately only possible within a just society.

Within such a penal system, might it then become possible to build in procedures and practices which reflect respect for persons and hope for the future of unique individuals? We believe so. Exactly how this would be achieved is exceedingly difficult and complex to work out in practice, but that is not to say it is impossible. Indeed, in the months following the Manchester Consultation, two of its participants (in partial collaboration with a third) spent many hours working out a paradigm for probation practice which built explicitly upon what were regarded as the central Manchester insights of (*i*) *acceptance of the empirical and theoretical critique of treatment*, and (*ii*) *insistence that hope for the future and respect for persons must not be abandoned.* This paradigm has been published elsewhere (Bottoms and McWilliams 1979) and must of course be judged upon its own technical merits or demerits. But it does illustrate at least one practical possibility arising from the kind of theoretical considerations which began to be aired at the Consultation.[1]

What, finally, of the American Friends' charge that the treatment model is 'theoretically faulty'? As one might expect in a predominantly Christian gathering, the deterministic assumptions of the treatment model found little support at Manchester. But it is important to remember that there was a pre-scientific version of the rehabilitative ideal, largely based on liberal Christian beliefs, which was very influential in Britain before the Second World War. In what has been said above about insisting on hope and on respect for persons, are we simply advocating a return to such a model?

A clear answer to this question is required, and that answer is in the negative. A leading penal thinker in the liberal Christian mould was Alexander Paterson (see Ruck 1951), and it is noteworthy that the Vinerian Professor of Law at Oxford has in recent years gone on public record as saying that one of Paterson's penal aphorisms[2] makes him 'feel sick', because it is 'one of the most pernicious manifestations of the disease of "PLU" (people like us)' (Cross 1971, pp. 131–2). By this Cross means that Paterson was essentially engaged in attempting to inculcate middle-class and public-school values in the minds of working-class Borstal boys; to make them 'people like us'.

Manifestations of 'PLU' have not been confined to Paterson. Indeed, the Director of Corrections of a powerful American state once announced specifically to his executive staff, at a planning meeting, that 'the objective of the Department of Corrections was to change criminals into people like us' (Conrad 1974, p. 196).

There is a positive and a negative lesson to learn from these episodes. Positively, any State has to be prepared to espouse some values, and to uphold at least a quantity of those values in its criminal law. To that extent the criminal law of any State is inescapably about 'changing people into people like us' — *if* 'we' also live out the values, which often is not the case. Negatively, there is a dreadful arrogance in the American director's remark, and to an extent in Paterson's; and in the history of penology it is clear that this arrogance has been used to justify all kinds of interventions in the lives of the convicted (often by Christians). These interventions have typically gone well beyond those strictly required by the legal infraction — the purpose has been coercively to mould the *offender* in all his aspects, and not just to deal with his offence-behaviour. This coercive reformation has been justified always as 'in his own interests', but historical judgement suggests that this has often been a rationalisation for the interests of the treater, his organisation, or his class. To bid farewell to this kind of arrogance will be a gain. The justifiable attempt to retain respect for persons and hope for the future within the penal apparatus is not to be seen as an attempt again to assert this kind of unjustified paternalism.[3]

Present and Future Penal Policy Options

Ronald Preston (1975, p. 1), in his introduction to the first Manchester Consultation, indicated his Department's concern that 'after discussing carefully prepared background papers we should see if any consensus arose and, if so, "come off the fence" and state it, as a contribution to the formation of public opinion. If it did not arise, we should hope at least to identify and clarify the differences and the reasons for them.'

We have indicated above that one central insight did emerge as a consensus from the present Consultation; namely the acceptance of the structural changes in the penal system that the critique of treatment requires, coupled with the insistence that hope for the future and respect for persons must not be abandoned in penal systems. It would be idle to pretend that anything much else developed as an agreed conclusion: indeed one veteran conference-goer described the Manchester weekend as 'unusually inconclusive'. Nevertheless we would lay some stress on the one conclusion which did emerge, for sensitively worked upon it can yield rather more detailed guidance to penal policy-makers than may be apparent at first sight.

A wide variety of penal policy options were of course canvassed or discussed at the Consultation. These included the justice model, regarded by Keith Bottomley as 'the most valid framework for a critical penology of the future' (above, p. 25), but generally criticised by most participants as lacking a sound philosophical base or clear practical application to the details of a penal system — so that, as one participant put it, by the end many felt that 'the parsimony of the justice model is its only attractive feature'. Frederick McClintock's paper forced the Consultation to consider the abolition of the present criminal justice system, along lines first argued by the Dutchman Louk Hulsman; but this solution attracted little support amongst most participants, who regarded it as an unrealistic dream for a modern industrial society. There was much talk about the possible increase in the use of reparation as an alternative to existing punishments, and much support for the idea of courts considering reparation first, and then deciding whether there was any need to impose an additional penalty on the offender;[4] support was also engendered for an increase in regulatory penalties such as the fine. But within existing or foreseeable penal systems, most participants saw quite definite limits on each of these ideas: in particular, neither seemed applicable to the 'serious' offender, thus rendering a 'bifurcation' model inevitable if this line of policy were pursued, despite the known dangers and difficulties of a bifurcation model (see the introductory paper by Bottoms).

Theologians and others warned of the danger of getting trapped into seeing the penal world in terms of absolutist, exclusive 'models', and the limitations especially of single models was expressed. The need for interrelation, order of priority and levels of application of different possible models to the existing penal system was recognised, but not explored in detail.

The Consultation recognised that whilst these competing 'models' were being put forward by academics, many ordinary people in Britain have an increasing concern about the rising recorded crime rate, and a feeling that not enough is being done about 'law and order'. Meanwhile, the 'operatives' of the penal system (in the police, prison and probation services) uneasily feel themselves to be in a state of transition, but without any agreed goal, so that, as one Chief Probation Officer has succinctly put it, 'the certainties of our traditional knowledge base have gone' (Thomas 1978, p. 30).

The quotation from Karl Marx at the head of Frederick McClintock's paper usefully reminds us that no penal or social policy debate takes place in a vacuum, but only in a concrete historical situation. In what context did the Manchester debate occur, exposing as it did such substantial uncertainty about penal direction?

The brief answer to this is that the debate took place in a country which in the 1940s had united substantially behind the creation of a 'Welfare State society' (Addison 1975) but where for a variety of reasons that welfare consensus has largely evaporated, both in terms of the economic (Keynesian) solutions proposed at that time, and in terms of a widespread loss of faith in the ability of social institutions to deliver social benefits. Neither economically nor socially is there any clear confidence that solutions to these now chronic problems can be provided. To add to the complications, it is a country whose world standing has been reduced from first class to second or third class in 40 years; where expectations of the benefits and solutions to be provided by science and technology have diminished; and where traditional religion no longer carries the conviction that it once did. It is, in short, an anxious society, and one with a rising crime rate, no doubt causally linked to some of these wider developments. It will be no great surprise if, in such a society, simple solutions at least to the crime problem are sought through 'law and order' measures. The Manchester participants were united in rejecting such solutions as unlikely to lead to social benefit, but recognised in the very difficulties of penal debate that they encountered that to produce an alternative blueprint to the simplistic 'law and order' platform is no easy task.

A lengthy and important Marxist analysis published at about the same time as the Manchester Consultation argued that in the 1970s, because of structural contradictions in welfare capitalism, Britain entered the era of authoritarianism:

> The state has won the right, and indeed inherited the duty,
> to move swiftly, to stamp fast and hard, to listen in,
> discreetly survey, saturate and swamp, charge or hold
> without charge, act on suspicion, hustle and shoulder, to
> keep society on the straight and narrow. Liberalism, that
> last back-stop against arbitrary power, is in retreat. It is
> suspended. The times are exceptional. The crisis is real. We
> are inside the 'law-and-order' state. (Hall *et al.* 1978, p. 323)

Many would argue that, as an *overall* analysis, this is incorrect or at least premature. In the strictly penal sphere, for example (though admittedly this is not what primarily concerned the authors of the book), it hardly squares with the continuing official search for ways of reducing the prison population, and the constant rise of the fine and of compensation as modes of punishment in the Britain of the 1970s. But there is enough truth behind the assertion — for example in the renewed talk about capital punishment, in suggestions for longer sentences for 'dangerous' offenders, and in certain trends towards authoritarianism within the prison service (Fyffe 1977) — to cause any concerned citizen to think furiously about the present condition of penal policy, and hence too of the nature of the British State as it moves into the 1980s. For as David Jenkins correctly discerned as he listened to the debates of the Consultation (above, p. 176), to think about penal policy *is* ultimately to be concerned with how we view other human beings, society, and the State — it simply cannot be considered in splendid isolation from these wider issues.

In conclusion, then, to borrow from Jenkins again, overall the Manchester Consultation demonstrated only too clearly that:

> there is widespread disagreement about the basis, the
> methods and the aims of programmes and procedures
> which should shape our understanding of the policies and

practices which will improve responses in society to the
problems presented or represented by offenders.

To duck these disagreements and conflicts would be cowardly. To
pretend that one weekend's consultation solved them would be
foolhardy. But we do hope that collectively the chapters of this
volume will have helped to clarify some of the issues, and have helped
readers to reflect upon them.

The Future of Criminological-Theological Collaboration

The papers by Ronald Preston and David Jenkins have in different
ways set out the case for regarding theology as relevant to penal policy
debates. Attempts to state this case are long overdue: the present
volume is almost unique as a serious recent endeavour in this
connection.[5] But Preston and Jenkins would be the first to recognise
that their papers are inevitably only preliminary soundings, and in no
sense final. It is therefore right to consider what form the future of
criminological-theological collaboration might take.

We understand Christian theology to involve a continuing process
of reflecting on experience in the light of faith. During this process
faith may itself be re-formed as well as our understanding of
experience revised. The purpose of such reflection is to discover and
rediscover how to think and act in ways which are compatible with a
commitment to Jesus of Nazareth as the vision of the good, not to say
the vision of God. Such a view of theology already presupposes some
of the results of reflection which we must leave on one side, such as the
importance of struggling at all with this-worldly affairs; and it is not
the only view of theology, a fact to which we must return.

This understanding of theology suggests a number of answers to
the question about how it might be of assistance in debates about penal
policy, though we acknowledge the theologian's reluctance to make
too many claims at this point. He does not imagine that his
interventions will necessarily assist discussion and action. He can be as
obtuse as the rest. He would not claim that there is no wisdom,
especially moral wisdom, apart from what he has to say. Indeed the
desire of theologians to engage in inter-disciplinary work like the
Manchester Consultation suggests a recognition of their own lack of
wisdom without assistance from, in this case, the criminologists. If
theologians are nevertheless convinced that their ongoing reflections
do yield insights which are not 'theological' in a pejorative sense, but
are too important for the practical man to ignore, the criminologist is
not obliged to take any notice unless he can be persuaded to agree.

From time to time reflection will crystallise into judgements and
opinions — some of them fleeting, others more enduring. What were

often referred to in the Consultation as formal 'theories' (theories of punishment, theories of the State, and theories of man) are good examples and suggest one of the more obvious contributions that theology has to make. Their importance was sharply illustrated in the papers and during the discussion. For example, Frederick McClintock's paper advocates developments which presuppose a minimalist view of State activities and apparatuses; this was opposed by Ronald Preston who (for reasons hinted at in his chapter — above p. 117) regards a stronger vision of the State as *theologically* necessary, a view from which McClintock (himself a Roman Catholic layman) dissents. It is fairly clear from this exchange that some kind of clarity about the views of the State with which one is working is necessary in criminological-theological discussion; it is also clear that the Christian tradition has developed much material about theories of the State which could and should be fed into such a discussion, though this was not done in any systematic way during the Manchester Consultation.

Another 'formal' theological subject of great importance is the theory of Man. In the Consultation this was not much alluded to as such, though it clearly underpins notions such as 'sin' which are used in both Preston's and Jenkins' papers. Once again there is a wealth of Christian writing in this area,[6] and this is specially important in a social science context because the central Christian traditions about Man reject many of the assumptions about human nature with which social scientists in different traditions habitually work — such as behaviourist determinism, Cartesian dualism, or the Marxist view that man has no 'essential' nature at all, but is the product of his 'social being' at a given moment in history. Reinhold Niebuhr's (1941–3) Gifford Lectures represent one of the most powerfully stated articulations of a Christian theory of man in our era: very briefly summarised, Niebuhr fully affirms two aspects of man's nature — that he is a biological creature (with all that that entails), and that he is made 'in the image of God', with a unique spirit and creativity and the power of self-transcendence. Yet these two aspects are held together in a unified, and not a dualistic, nature. Moreover, he holds, 'the Christian view of human nature is involved in the paradox of claiming a higher stature for man, and a more serious view of his evil', than any other philosophical position. It is clear that such a position differs somewhat (or more than somewhat) from the ontological assumptions made by for example positivism, phenomenology, or Marxism; therefore it is vital that in any future criminological-theological debates the exact differences between these positions are worked out and clearly articulated, so that it is clear on what ontological assumptions a Christian view is being put forward.

When we ask more carefully what we mean by a theological

'theory' it is clear that we mean something more than a compact way of organising empirical knowledge. Theories are not merely commentaries on what is the case (analysis) or what is possible or practical; nor are they technical commentaries on how such things as punishment work. As David Jenkins points out: 'they go beyond the evidence'. A theological theory is developed in part in the light of our observation and experience of empirical realities (even where in the past this has been tacitly denied by dogmatic theologians, and theological theories have been regarded as simply 'revealed'), but it incorporates judgements and values made about reality on the basis of fundamental convictions which are of universal application.

These convictions might be called 'faith-commitments' because whilst they are held partly in the light of experience, and are used to make sense of experience and handle it and are therefore constantly tested by it, they are not wholly justified by experience to the extent that given the reasons for holding them any reasonable man would be bound to accept them for himself. For example, to value human life and to regard every human life as of equal value is not unreasonable, and it does much to shape and make sense of our experience. But experience also in some ways makes nonsense of it, and it cannot be wholly accounted for without reference to what we can only confess to believing (faith) and the commitments we have which 'go beyond the evidence'.

These faith-commitments include convictions about personal responsibility (see for example Ronald Preston's comments, p. 118) as well as the equality of persons and a concern for personal fulfilment which makes 'rehabilitation' so much more than the reintegration of the offender into an existing social order. Faith-commitments not only speak about God (theology in the strictest sense) but about man and the purpose of his existence under God in this world and the next. A crucial faith-commitment for Christians is of course the supreme value they place on the vision of good and of God as seen in Christ.

These commitments suggest that a second contribution that theology can make has to do with its concern about the values and assumptions that are implicit in all human debates, including debates about penal policy. It could be said that these concerns, evaluative rather than technical or descriptive, are its special subject-matter. Theology will insist that such commitments are a constituent part of most if not all opinions and judgements, so that its special area of interest intrudes into all others. It will ensure that along with empirical, practical and technical issues about which it has no special expertise, these commitments are exposed and discussed, especially where their existence tends to be denied or overlooked; and it will want to argue that its own commitments are worthy of attention and respect. This is not to say that the values and faith-commitments of Christians (for example, that the shared life of man in this world, including the penal system, is sufficiently worthwhile to be improved) are necessarily different from those of others. On the contrary they will often be shared, and in a plural society where common ground is at a premium, Christians should be glad when that is the case.

The relation between faith-commitments and formal theories suggests the first of several methodological points that can be made about the ways in which theology might be of assistance. It is critical and constructive. It will ask about the implications of its values and fundamental perspectives on man and his life in this world and endeavour to construct opinions (including theories) which take them into account, so that a theory of punishment, for example, or a sentencing procedure may commend itself for respecting man's personal responsibility (see Ronald Preston, p. 114 and D. E. Jenkins, p. 199). But no theory is likely to take all faith-commitments fully into account, not least because those who construct them are inevitably limited and unable to see things whole, and being perverse or sinful are unwilling to see things whole. Consequently faith-commitments transcend any conclusions arrived at in the process of reflection, and are likely to criticise and call them into question as much as lend them support. Creativity lies as much in the one as in the other. Values in their turn may be equally discomforted if kept in touch with the supreme critical principle for Christian faith of the vision of God in Jesus. Here for example we may find much to support a fundamental commitment to the value of human life, and yet something that disturbs it in a man who suggested more than once and in several ways that there may be occasions when even human life, and not only our own, must take second place.[7]

This critical constructiveness or constructive criticism is reflected in Ronald Preston's discussion of the way in which the radical Gospel ethic of forgiveness cannot be directly related to, yet must not be allowed to become irrelevant to, theories of punishment; and in Terence Morris' concern for a supervening moral order which is respected by the State whilst limiting its powers.

If the resulting picture is one of constant interaction between particular opinions and more generalised convictions, between the theoretical and the empirical, between principle and practice, between the interpretative and the descriptive, the theologian will not complain. To mention a second methodological point (which might not have been made by another generation of theologians more self-reliant and dogmatic in their approach) theologians will contribute to discussions by encouraging such a co-operative and corporate approach. They will be unhappy when decisions about human beings are made in watertight compartments. This is not only because of their own need for inter-disciplinary occasions, like the Manchester Consultation, in order to obtain the data for their own reflection. They will argue for it on the basis of their values, perspectives and faith-commitments as well. Man made in the image of God (see D. E. Jenkins, pp. 185, 197ff.) can never be adequately understood within a narrow frame of reference. Or again a commitment to the world as created by God and as being the arena of his ongoing creative activity will lead theology not only to interpret the present in the light of a truth it knows but to expect to discover truth in the present which it did not know before. Joining in the corporate inter-disciplinary enterprise and paying attention to the historical particulars however critically, along with everybody else, will be theology's way of taking seriously a world it believes to be God's.

We have spoken of theology's contribution by way of faith-commitments, substantive insights such as formal theories, and a methodology which includes critical-constructiveness, serious attention to empirical realities and an inter-disciplinary approach to problems.

What should now be made clear is that there is no universal agreement amongst Christians on any of these matters. Theology for some, for example, would be seen as more declaratory than reflective, passing on revealed truths rather than attempting to learn from experience or interpret it. But even if we restrict ourselves to our own understanding of theology and its task we are confronted by a daunting variety of opinion. We have referred to two theories of the State (the 'thick' and the 'thin'), but any Christian text book on the subject will indicate that there are many more than that. Protestants and Catholics have held different views of man and have often disagreed quite sharply about his capacity to discern what is good and true. We might expect to find differences of opinion when Christians come to work out the detailed implications of their faith, but in fact we are confronted with variety even when it comes to quite basic faith-commitments. Thus, understanding of Christian hope has ranged from a utopian belief in a perfect society realisable on this earth, through apocalyptic expectations of an abrupt end to this world, to the quieter assurance that whatever the immediate outcome it is well worth making a steady attempt to transform our common life into something more like what we imagine to be the Christlike Kingdom of God. Christians have also disagreed profoundly over whether to take life in this world seriously or withdraw or detach themselves from it and prepare for the next, and this in turn has produced very different attitudes in practice to the value placed on human life. And when we reassure ourselves that despite the differences, all Christians share a common reference point since all are committed to Jesus as the vision of good and of God, it cannot be forgotten that although the Gospels and the rest of Scripture remain as common source materials to which all Christians pay their respects, they are interpreted in different ways; and Christian history, not to mention the contemporary Christian community, has produced a bewildering assortment of pictures of the 'real Jesus'.

This variety is not hard to explain even if it is not easy to come to terms with. The forming of Christian opinions whether they are about Jesus, or hope, or the nature of man, or the State, or the penal system, or the importance of life in this world is as much affected by historical contingencies as the forming of all other opinions. People think what they do and about what they do partly because of the sort of people they happen to be, partly because of the social, economic and political circumstances in which they find themselves and the historical pressures under which they live and work, and partly because of the climate of opinion whether they accept it or react against it. These things change so that however real the continuities in life, which allow us for example to compare one society or period of history with another, there are equally real discontinuities. Times change and values change.

Variety is therefore inescapable unless we are going to narrow the range of opinion by means other than the kind of critical discussion which tries to choose between one opinion and another. In the past and still in the present many Christians have thought this possible by an appeal to an authority such as an infallible Bible or an infallible church. But the more we understand that these too are limited, conditioned and relative, subject to the same contingent factors as the options between which they are asked to arbitrate, the more unsatisfactory this seems to be. This is not to say of course that all opinions are equally as good but that the grounds on which we decide to respect the Bible, or within the Bible one book or author over against another, are not dogmatic but open to critical scrutiny like the grounds for all our other decisions.

Some will find this diversity difficult and even disappointing, since it only adds to the confusion and seems to deny us the fixed points that theology might be expected to supply. Some will welcome it and find it interesting and enriching, different views complementing as well as competing with each other. Some will regard the way diversity reflects changing contexts as the mark of authentic theological reflection. We see no alternative to accepting it and to working creatively with it. It suggests to us a number of concluding reflections on future collaboration and the contribution which theology might make.

First, the diversity of Christian opinion reinforces the need for corporate reflection and decision-making and adds to it a further dimension. Just as any sensible theologian is careful not to lean too heavily on scientific experts and recognises that they disagree among themselves, so the criminologist who is interested in the contribution of theology will ensure that he is aware of a wide range of Christian opinion; and the theologian who knows his job will try to open it up rather than present any one approach as typical of the whole.

Second, the diversity of Christian insights warns theologians especially against seeing the contribution of theology too much in terms of loyalty to the past. We have suggested that theology might contribute its faith-commitments and its formal theories to the debate. But they must not be given too much respect. Even if all the participants are within the Christian tradition, theologians and criminologists are in no sense tied to some Christian view of the State or of man or of punishment however insistently it comes to them from the past. They will take note of whether or not it has persisted and won support (as Ronald Preston takes note of the impressive amount of support given by Christian history to the retributive theory of punishment, see above, p. 114) and will ask why that is so. They will subject it to criticism and they will allow it to criticize and inform their own discussion. They will compare it with other views and debate it. But it remains a product of human reflection with all its inevitable limitations and they are not obliged to defer to it; indeed to regard it too highly and forget that it is human and to some extent perverse can be as misleading as refusing to take cognizance of it at all.

Third, this negative point about not being overawed or restrained by the past suggests a more positive one which finds support in experience and the Christian doctrine of man made in the image of God. The past should not and does not wholly determine the present and the future, any more than do all the other considerations which a debate about penal policy must take into account. The necessary business of engaging with other points of view, including the insights of the past and the fruits of past experience; of taking account of empirical data and of practical and technical advice — all this will not of itself determine the decisions we finally or provisionally take. They will influence the way in which people are informed and so take the decisions, and they provide the indispensable raw material out of which opinions and judgements are made; but at the end of the day man in his freedom, limited but real, must make or create these judgements for himself and take responsibility for them. This element of creativity is in line with the 'pilgrimage' perspective discussed by David Jenkins which invites us to be engaged for example 'in discovering and adapting patterns of State existence and State activity quite as much as (or even more than) in conforming to or maintaining the existence of a pattern of the State or a theory of the State which is already given' (see above p. 191).

Fourth, the implications of Christian diversity outlined above suggest that it may not be altogether a bad thing that a Consultation involving theologians turned out to be 'unusually inconclusive'. The outcome would be questionable if it reflected indecision and a refusal to live in the everyday world, or an unwillingness to act on an emerging consensus which carried some conviction. The outcome would be disappointing if the remark about it being inconclusive hinted at a lack of fresh insights. But an inconclusive result is acceptable insofar as it acknowledges that there can be no final conclusions free from human limitations and able to embrace all our human concerns, and that what we are engaged in is a creative enterprise the possibilities of which are not easily if ever exhausted. Theologians should not need to apologise for widening a debate.

Fifth and finally, pilgrimage and creative enterprises and open-ended discussions run risks not least of growing weary or disillusioned in well-doing. Here we can remind ourselves of a further contribution the theologian can make by way of the supportive rather than the substantive insights which result from his reflection on experience in the light of faith. To mention two of them, his convictions about the sinfulness of man may persuade him not to expect too much and to expect to run into trouble, and so guard him against disappointment; whilst his convictions about a hope for man may persuade him not to expect too little, and that even a troublesome enterprise is well worthwhile, so guarding him against discouragement.

NOTES

1. Nothing has been said specifically here about the fourth practitioners' objection listed above (concerning the probation service), but this issue is dealt with in the paper by Bottoms and McWilliams (1979).
2. Namely, that 'there is an individual good in each, and among nearly all an innate corporate spirit which will respond to the appeal made to the British of every sort, to play the game, to follow the flag, to stand by the old ship'. The phrase was used of Borstal boys in the 1930s.
3. Cf. the comment by Isaiah Berlin (1969, p. 157): 'Paternalism is despotic, not because it is more oppressive than naked, brutal, unenlightened tyranny, nor merely because it ignores the transcendental reason embodied in me, but because it is an insult to my conception of myself as a human being, determined to make my own life in accordance with my own (not necessarily rational or benevolent) purposes, and, above all, entitled to be recognised as such by others'.

4. Ken Pease's paper takes the view that this is impractical, given the length of time suggested by Christie (1976) for this procedure; but it would be possible to reverse compensation and punishment without moving all the way to Christie's 'neighbourhood court' model. To do so would, however, require major reconceptualisation of the present rigid boundary between civil and criminal law.
5. For some precursors see the Clarke Hall Lecture by Archbishop William Temple (1934), and the Anglican booklets on *Punishment* and *Prisons* (Church of England 1963, 1978).
6. Some of it by David Jenkins himself: see Jenkins (1967), (1970).
7. Cf. Matthew ch. 10, vv. 37–9 and Luke ch. 14, vv. 25–7 where it is suggested that the demands of Christian discipleship will from time to time require us to behave with an apparent disregard for human life. In the case of Jesus at least, these 'hard sayings' turn out to be far from exaggerations.

Consolidated list of references

Abrams, P. (1978) 'Community care: some research problems and priorities', in: K. Barnes and N. Connelly (Eds.), *Social Care Research*, London, Bedford Square Press.

Abrams, P. and McCulloch, A. (1976) *Communes, Sociology and Society*, London, Cambridge University Press.

Addison, P. (1975) *The Road to 1945*, London, Jonathan Cape.

Advisory Council on the Penal System (1970a) *Non-custodial and Semi-custodial Penalties* (Chairman of Sub-Committee: Baroness Wootton), London, H.M.S.O.

Advisory Council on the Penal System (1970b) *Reparation by the Offender* (Chairman of Sub-Committee: Lord Justice Widgery), London, H.M.S.O.

Advisory Council on the Penal System (1974) *Young Adult Offenders* (Chairman: Sir Kenneth Younger), London, H.M.S.O.

Advisory Council on the Penal System (1977) *The Length of Prison Sentences: Interim Report* (Chairman: Baroness Serota), London, H.M.S.O.

Advisory Council on the Penal System (1978) *Sentences of Imprisonment — a Review of Maximum Penalties* (Chairman: Baroness Serota), London, H.M.S.O.

Allen, F. A. (1959) 'Criminal justice, legal values and the rehabilitative ideal', *Journal of Criminal Law, Criminology and Police Science*, 50, 226–32.

Allen, F. A. (1964) *The Borderland of Criminal Justice: Essays in Law and Criminology*, Chicago, University of Chicago Press.

American Friends Service Committee (1971) *Struggle for Justice*, New York, Hill and Wang.

Andenaes, J. (1974) *Punishment and Deterrence*, Ann Arbor, University of Michigan Press.

Anon. (1978) 'Compensation orders', *Justice of the Peace*, 8 April, 203–4.

Auden, W. H. and MacNeice, L. (1937) *Letters from Iceland*, London, Faber and Faber.

Bailey, W. C. (1966) 'Correctional outcome: an evaluation of 100 reports', *Journal of Criminal Law, Criminology and Police Science*, 57, 153–60.

Barker, E. (1948) *Traditions of Civility*, Cambridge, Cambridge University Press.

Barnard, E. E. (1976) 'Parole decision-making in Britain', *International Journal of Criminology and Penology*, 4, 145–59.

Barry, B. (1973) *The Liberal Theory of Justice*, Oxford, Clarendon Press.

Baxter, R. and Nuttall, C. (1975) 'Severe sentences: no deterrent to crime?', *New Society*, 31, 11–13.

Bean, P. (1976) *Rehabilitation and Deviance*, London, Routledge and Kegan Paul.

Beccaria, C. (1764) *On Crimes and Punishments* (Eng. trans. H. Paolucci (Ed.) (1963), Indianapolis, Bobbs-Merrill).

Berger, P. (1971) *A Rumour of Angels*, Harmondsworth, Penguin.

Berlin, I. (1969) *Four Essays on Liberty*, London, Oxford University Press.

Berntsen, K. and Christiansen, K. O. (1965) 'A resocialisation experiment with short-term offenders', in: K. O. Christiansen (Ed.), *Scandinavian Studies in Criminology, volume 1*, London, Tavistock.

Beveridge Report (1942) *Report of the Inter-departmental Committee on Social Insurance and Allied Services*, Cmd. 6406.

231

Beyleveld, D. (1978) 'The effectiveness of general deterrents as against crime: an annotated bibliography of evaluative research', Cambridge, University of Cambridge Institute of Criminology (microfiche publication).

Biestek, F. (1961) *The Casework Relationship*, London, Allen and Unwin.

Bishop, N. (1974) 'Aspects of European penal systems', in: L. Blom-Cooper (Ed.), *Progress in Penal Reform*, Oxford, Clarendon Press.

Black, D. (1976) *The Behaviour of Law*, New York, Academic Press.

Boss, P. (1967) *Social Policy and the Young Delinquent*, London, Routledge and Kegan Paul.

Bottomley, A. K. (1973) *Decisions in the Penal Process*, London, Martin Robertson.

Bottomley, A. K. (1979) *Criminology in Focus: Past Trends and Future Prospects*, London, Martin Robertson.

Bottoms, A. E. (1973) 'The efficacy of the fine: the case for agnosticism', *Criminal Law Review*, 543–51.

Bottoms, A. E. (1974) 'On the decriminalisation of English juvenile courts', in: R. G. Hood (Ed.), *Crime, Criminology and Public Policy*, London, Heinemann.

Bottoms, A. E. (1977) 'Reflections on the renaissance of dangerousness', *Howard Journal of Penology and Crime Prevention, 16*, 70–96.

Bottoms, A. E. (1979) *The Suspended Sentence After Ten Years* (Frank Dawtry Memorial Lecture), Leeds, University of Leeds Centre for Social Work and Applied Social Studies, Occasional Papers No. 2.

Bottoms, A. E. and McWilliams, W. (1979) 'A non-treatment paradigm for probation practice', *British Journal of Social Work, 9*, 159–202.

Boyle, J. (1977) *A Sense of Freedom*, London, Pan Books.

Brody, S. (1976) *The Effectiveness of Sentencing* (Home Office Research Study No. 35), London, H.M.S.O.

Brunner, E. (1945) *Justice and the Social Order*, London, Lutterworth.

Butler Report (1975) *Report of the Committee on Mentally Abnormal Offenders*, Home Office and D.H.S.S., Cmnd. 6244.

Carson, W. G. (1970) 'White-collar crime and the enforcement of factory legislation', *British Journal of Criminology, 10*, 383–98.

Carson, W. G. (1974) 'The sociology of crime and the emergence of criminal laws', in: P. Rock and M. McIntosh (Eds.), *Deviance and Social Control*, London, Tavistock.

Christie, N. (1974) 'Utility and social values in court decisions on punishments', in: R. G. Hood (Ed.), *Crime, Criminology and Public Policy*, London, Heinemann.

Christie, N. (1976) *Conflicts as Property*, Sheffield, University of Sheffield; reprinted (1977) *British Journal of Criminology, 17*, 1–15.

Christie, N. (1977) 'The view of the sociologist', in: World Health Organisation, *Forensic Psychiatry; Report on a Working Group*, Copenhagen, Regional Office for Europe.

Church of England (1963) *Punishment* (A report of the Board for Social Responsibility), London, Church Information Office.

Church of England (1978) *Prisons and Prisoners in England Today* (A report of the Board for Social Responsibility), London, Church Information Office.

Clarke, D. H. (1978) 'Marxism, justice and the justice model', *Contemporary Crises, 2*, 27–62.

Clarke, R. V. G. and Sinclair, I. (1974) 'Towards more effective treatment evaluation', in: European Committee on Crime Problems, *Collected Studies in Criminological Research (Council of Europe), 12*, 53–87.

Cohen, D. (1972) 'Out of jail', *New Society, 20*, 234–5.

Cohen, S. (1974) 'Criminology and the sociology of deviance in Britain', in: P. Rock and M. McIntosh (Eds.), *Deviance and Social Control*, London, Tavistock.

Cohen, S. (1975) 'It's all right for you to talk', in: R. Bailey and M. Brake (Eds.), *Radical Social Work*, London, Edward Arnold.

Cohen, S. (1977) 'Prisons and the future of control systems', in: M. Fitzgerald, *et al.* (1977), *Welfare in Action*, London, Routledge and Kegan Paul.

Cohen, S. and Taylor, L. (1972) *Psychological Survival*, Harmondsworth, Penguin.

Cohen, S. and Taylor, L. (1978) *Prison Secrets*, London, Radical Alternatives to Prison and National Council for Civil Liberties.

Conrad, J. P. (1974) 'Winners and losers: a perspective on penal change', in: L. Blom Cooper (Ed.), *Progress in Penal Reform*, Oxford, Clarendon Press.

Croft, J. (1978) *Research in Criminal Justice* (Home Office Research Study No. 44), London, H.M.S.O.

Cross, R. (1971) *Punishment, Prison and the Public*, London, Stevens.

Cross, R. (1975) *The English Sentencing System*, 2nd ed., London, Butterworth.

Daniels, N. (Ed.) (1975), *Reading Rawls*, Oxford, Basil Blackwell.

Davis, K. C. (1969) *Discretionary Justice: A Preliminary Inquiry*, Urbana, University of Illinois.

Dawson, R. O. (1969) *Sentencing: the Decision as to Type, Length and Conditions of Sentence*, Boston, Little Brown.

Donnison, D. (1978) 'Special unit', *New Society*, *43*, 60–1.

Downes, D. and Rock, P. (Eds.) (1979) *Deviant Interpretations*, London, Martin Robertson.

Durkheim, E. (1893) *The Division of Labour in Society* (Eng. trans. 1933, Glencoe, Free Press).

Durkheim, E. (1901) 'Two laws of penal evolution' (Eng. trans. 1973, *Economy and Society*, *2*, 278–308).

Duster, T. (1970) *The Legislation of Morality*, New York, Free Press.

Ehrlich, I. (1973) 'Participation in illegitimate activities: a theoretical and empirical investigation', *Journal of Political Economy*, *81*, 521–65.

Eriksson, J. (1970) *Revolt i Huvet*, Stockholm, Bonniers.

European Committee on Crime Problems (1974) *Short Term Treatment of Adult Offenders*, Strasbourg, Council of Europe.

Fitzgerald, M. (1977) *Prisoners in Revolt*, Harmondsworth, Penguin.

Flegg, D. (1976) *Community Service Consumer Survey 1973–6*, Nottingham, Nottinghamshire Probation and After-Care Service.

Fogel, D. (1975) *'We are the Living Proof': the Justice Model for Corrections*, Cincinnati, Anderson.

Fogel, D. (1976) 'Prison: the fortress model vs. the justice model', in: R. J. Gerber (Ed.), *Contemporary Issues in Criminal Justice*, New York, Kennikat Press.

Foucault, M. (1975) *Discipline and Punish: the Birth of the Prison* (Eng. trans. 1977, London, Allen Lane).

Foucault, M. (1977) 'Prison talk: an interview with Michel Foucault', *Radical Philosophy*, *16*, 10–15.

Fowler, G. W. (1977) *Report of an Inquiry by the Chief Inspector of the Prison Service into the Cause and Circumstances of the Events at H.M. Prison, Hull, During the Period 31st August to 3rd September 1976*, London, H.M.S.O.

Fox, L. W. (1952) *The English Prison and Borstal Systems*, London, Routledge and Kegan Paul.

Fox, S. (1974) 'The reform of juvenile justice: the child's right to punishment', *Juvenile Justice*, *2*, 2–9.

Frankel, M. E. (1973) *Criminal Sentences: Law without Order*, New York, Hill and Wang.

Frankenberg, R. (1966) *Communities in Britain*, Harmondsworth, Penguin.

Fyffe, A. (1977) 'A most peculiar absence of monsters', *Prison Service Journal*, 27, 12–14.

Gibbs, J. P. (1975) *Crime, Punishment and Deterrence*, New York, Elsevier.

Gladstone Committee (1895) *Report of the Departmental Committee on Prisons*, C.7702, H.M.S.O.

Gouldner, A. (1973) *For Sociology*, London, Allen Lane.

Greenberg, D. F. (1977) 'The correctional effects of corrections', in: D. F. Greenberg (Ed.), *Corrections and Punishment* (Sage Criminal Justice Systems Annuals, vol. 8), Beverly Hills, Sage.

Griffith, J. A. G. (1977) *The Politics of the Judiciary*, London, Collins.

Gunn, J. (1977) *Epileptics in Prison*, London, Academic Press.

Gunn, J., Robertson, G., Dell, S., and Way, C. (1978) *Psychiatric Aspects of Imprisonment*, London, Academic Press.

Gusfield, J. R. (1963) *Symbolic Crusade*, Urbana, Illinois University Press.

Hall, S., *et al.* (1978) *Policing the Crisis*, London, Macmillan.

Hall Williams, J. E. (1975) 'Natural justice and parole', *Criminal Law Review*, 82–91, 215–23.

Hall Williams, J. E. (1978) 'The Advisory Council Report: Sentences of Imprisonment', *British Journal of Criminology*, 18, 396–400.

Hampshire, S. (1972) 'A new philosophy of the just society', *New York Review of Books*, 24 February, 38–9.

Hart, H. L. A. (1961) *The Concept of Law*, Oxford, Clarendon Press.

Hawkins, K. (1973) 'Parole procedure: an alternative approach', *British Journal of Criminology*, 13, 6–25.

Haxby, D. (1978) *Probation: A Changing Service*, London, Constable.

Hay, D. (1975) 'Property, authority and the criminal law', in: D. Hay, *et al.*, *Albion's Fatal Tree*, London, Allen Lane.

Hayek, F. A. (1976) *The Mirage of Social Justice*, London, Routledge and Kegan Paul.

Hegel, G. W. (1821) *The Philosophy of Right* (Eng. trans. T. M. Knox (1942), Oxford, Clarendon Press).

Heijder, A. (1975) 'The recent trend towards reducing the prison population in the Netherlands', *International Journal of Offender Therapy and Comparative Criminology*, 18, 233–40.

Hindelang, M. (1976) *Criminal Victimisation in Eight American Cities*, Boston, Ballinger.

Home Office (1959) *Penal Practice in a Changing Society*, Cmnd. 645.

Home Office (1969) *The Sentence of the Court*, London, H.M.S.O.

Home Office (1974) *National CDP Inter-Project Report*, London, H.M.S.O.

Home Office (1975) *Report of the Working Party on Adjudication Procedures in Prisons*, London, H.M.S.O.

Home Office (1977a) *A Review of Criminal Justice Policy 1976*, London, H.M.S.O.

Home Office (1977b) *Prisons and the Prisoner: the Work of the Prison Service in England and Wales*, London, H.M.S.O.

Home Office (1977c) *Report of the Parole Board 1976*, London, H.M.S.O.

Home Office (1977d) *Report on the Work of the Prison Department 1976*, Cmnd. 6877.

Home Office (1978) *Prison Statistics: England and Wales 1977*, Cmnd. 7286.

Home Office Statistical Department (1977) *Probation and After-Care Statistics 1975 and 1976*, London, Home Office (mimeo).

Hood, R. G. (1974a) 'Some fundamental dilemmas of the English parole system and a suggestion for an alternative structure', in: D. A. Thomas (Ed.), *Parole: Its Implications for the Criminal Justice and Penal Systems*, Cambridge, University of Cambridge Institute of Criminology.

Hood, R. G. (1974b) *Tolerance and the Tariff: Some Reflections on Fixing the Time Prisoners Serve in Custody* (N.A.C.R.O. Papers and Reprints No. 11), London, N.A.C.R.O.

Hood, R. G. (1974c) 'Young Adult Offenders: comments on the report of the Advisory Council on the Penal System: I The custodial sector', *British Journal of Criminology*, 14, 388–95.

House of Commons (1978) *Fifteenth Report from the Expenditure Committee: The Reduction of Pressure on the Prison System, vol. I — Report*, London, H.M.S.O.

Howard, J. (1777) *The State of the Prisons in England and Wales*, Warrington, William Eyres (Everyman Edition (1929), London, J. M. Dent).

Howard League for Penal Reform (1975) *Whose Discretion? Fairness and Flexibility in the Penal System: Annual Report 1974–5*, London, Howard League for Penal Reform.

Howard League for Penal Reform (1977a) *Making Amends: Criminals, Victims and Society*, Chichester, Barry Rose.

Howard League for Penal Reform (1977b) *Prisons in a State: Annual Report 1976–7*, London, Howard League for Penal Reform.

Hulsman, L. (1976) 'Strategies to reduce violence in society: 'civilizing' the criminal justice system', address to Annual General Meeting of the Howard League, October (unpublished).

Hulsman, L. H. C. (1978) 'Alternatives to criminal justice', address to Howard League for Scotland, Edinburgh, June (unpublished).

Hulsman, L. H. C., *et al.* (1978) 'The Dutch criminal justice system from a comparative legal perspective', in: D. C. Fokkema, *et al.* (Eds.), *Introduction to Dutch Law for Foreign Lawyers*, The Netherlands, Kluwer-Deventer.

Illich, I. (1977) *Limits to Medicine*, Harmondsworth, Penguin.

Jeffrey, C. R. (1977) *Crime Prevention Through Environmental Design*, Beverly Hills, Sage.

Jellicoe Committee (1975) *Boards of Visitors of Penal Institutions*, Chichester, Barry Rose.

Jenkins, D. E. (1967) *The Glory of Man*, London, S.C.M. Press.

Jenkins, D. E. (1970) *What is Man?*, London, S.C.M. Press.

Jenkins, D. E. (1976) *The Contradiction of Christianity*, London, S.C.M. Press.

Johnston, J. and MacLeod, C. (1975) 'Barlinnie's approach', *New Society*, 34, 482–3.

Karpman, B. (1956) 'Criminal psychodynamics', *Journal of Criminal Law and Criminology*, 47, 8–17.

Kittrie, N. N. (1971) *The Right to be Different: Deviance and Enforced Therapy*, Baltimore, Johns Hopkins.

Knowles, D. (1970) *Thomas Becket*, London, A. and C. Black.

Koestler, A. (1978) *Janus*, London, Hutchinson.

Kwartler, R. (1977) *Behind Bars: Prisons in America*, New York, Vintage Books.

Ladd, J. (Ed.) (1965) *Immanuel Kant: The Metaphysical Elements of Justice*, Indianapolis, Bobbs-Merrill.

LaFave, W. R. (1965) *Arrest: the Decision to Take a Suspect into Custody*, Boston, Little Brown.

Laing, R. D. (1967) *The Politics of Experience and the Bird of Paradise*, Harmondsworth, Penguin.

Lemert, E. M. (1970) *Social Action and Legal Change: Revolution Within the Juvenile Court*, Chicago, Aldine.

Lewis, C. S. (1953) 'The humanitarian theory of punishment', *Res Judicatae*, 6, 224–30; reprinted in: L. Radzinowicz and M. E. Wolfgang (Eds.), (1971) *Crime and Justice*, vol. II, New York, Basic Books; also in: C. S. Lewis, (1971) *Undeceptions: Essays in Theology and Ethics*, London, Bles.

Lewis, C. S. (1961) *Reflections on the Psalms*, London, Collins.

Lipton, D., Martinson, R., and Wilks, J. (1975) *The Effectiveness of Correctional Treatment*, New York, Praeger.

Logan, C. H. (1972) 'Evaluation research in crime and delinquency', *Journal of Criminal Law, Criminology and Police Science*, 63, 378–87.

Lopez-Rey, M. (1964) 'Analytical penology', in: M. Lopez-Rey and C. Germain (Eds.), *Studies in Penology to the Memory of Sir Lionel Fox*, The Hague, Martinus Nijhoff.

Lukes, S. (1974) *Power*, London, Macmillan.

Lukes, S. (1976) *Essays in Social Theory*, London, Macmillan.

McClintock, F. H. (1974) 'Phenomenological and contextual analysis of criminal violence', *Collected Studies in Criminological Research (Council of Europe)*, 11, 127–76.

McClintock, F. H. (1976) 'Studies of young offenders: problems of research into effectiveness of penal measures', in: W. T. Haesler (Ed.), *Neue Perspectiven in der Kriminologie*, Verlag der Fachvereine an den Schweizerischen Hochschule und Techniken (Proceedings of a seminar held at the Gottlieb Wuttweiler Institute, Switzerland, October 1974).

McClintock, F. H. (1977) 'The view of the criminologist', in: World Health Organisation, *Forensic Psychiatry: Report on a Working Group*, Copenhagen, Regional Office for Europe.

McClintock, F. H. (1978) 'The future of parole', in: J. C. Freeman (Ed.), *Prisons, Past and Future*, London, Heinemann.

McClintock, F. H. and Avison, N. H. (1968) *Crime in England and Wales*, London, Heinemann.

McConville, S. (1975) 'Future prospects of imprisonment in Britain', in: S. McConville (Ed.), *The Use of Imprisonment: Essays in the Changing State of English Penal Policy*, London, Routledge and Kegan Paul.

McIntosh, M. (1975) *The Organisation of Crime*, London, Macmillan.

Marris, P. and Rein, M. (1967) *Dilemmas of Social Reform*, London, Routledge and Kegan Paul.

Martinson, R. (1974) 'What works? — questions and answers about prison reform', *The Public Interest*, Spring Issue, 22–54.

Marx, K. (1852) 'The Eighteenth Brumaire of Louis Bonaparte'; reprinted (1968) in: *Karl Marx and Frederick Engels: Selected Works in One Volume*, London, Lawrence and Wishart.

Marx, K. (1853) 'On capital punishment', *New York Daily Tribune*, 18 February; extracts reprinted in: T. B. Bottomore and M. Rubel (1963) *Karl Marx: Selected Writings in Sociology and Social Philosophy*, Harmondsworth, Penguin, 233–5.

Marx, K. and Engels, F. (1848) *The Communist Manifesto*; Penguin edition (1967) with full prefaces, Harmondsworth, Penguin.

Mathiesen, T. (1974) *The Politics of Abolition*, London, Martin Robertson.

Mayhew, P., et al. (1976) *Crime as Opportunity* (Home Office Research Study No. 34), London, H.M.S.O.

Meacher, M. (1974) 'The politics of positive discrimination', in: M. Glennerster and S. Match (Eds.), *Positive Discrimination and Inequality* (Fabian Research Series 314), London, Fabian Society.

Menninger, K. (1959) 'Therapy not punishment', *Harpers Magazine*, August, 63–4.
Menninger, K. (1968) *The Crime of Punishment*, New York, Viking.
Michels, R. (1911) *Political Parties* (Eng. trans. 1949, Glencoe, Free Press).
Miller, C. A. (1977) 'The forest of due process of law; the American constitutional tradition', in: J. R. Pennock and J. W. Chapman (Eds.), *Due Process: Nomos XVIII*, New York, New York University.
Miller, F. W. (1969) *Prosecution: the Decision to Charge a Suspect with a Crime*, Boston, Little Brown.
Moore, G. (1978) 'Crisis in Scotland', *Howard Journal of Penology and Crime Prevention*, 17, 32–40.
Morgan, C. (1976) *Community Service in Gwent*, Cwmbran, Gwent Probation and After-Care Service.
Morris, A. M. (1974) 'Scottish juvenile justice: a critique', in: R. G. Hood (Ed.), *Crime, Criminology and Public Policy*, London, Heinemann.
Morris, A. M. (1976) 'Juvenile justice: where next?', *Howard Journal of Penology and Crime Prevention*, 15, 26–37.
Morris, H. (1968) 'Persons and punishment', *The Monist*, 52, 475–501.
Morris, N. (1974) *The Future of Imprisonment*, Chicago, University of Chicago Press.
Morris, N. and Hawkins, G. (1970) *The Honest Politician's Guide to Crime Control*, Chicago, University of Chicago Press.
Morris, N. and Howard, C. (1964) *Studies in Criminal Law*, Oxford, Clarendon Press.
Morris, T. (1978) 'The parlous state of prisons', in: J. C. Freeman (Ed.), *Prisons, Past and Future*, London, Heinemann.
Mountbatten, Earl (1966) *Report of the Inquiry into Prison Escapes and Security*, Cmnd. 3175.
Murphy, J. (1970) *Kant: The Philosophy of Right*, London, Macmillan.
Murphy, J. (1973) 'Marxism and retribution', *Philosophy and Public Affairs*, 2, 218–43.
N.A.C.R.O. (1977a) *Children and Young Persons in Custody*, Report of a N.A.C.R.O. Working Party (Chairman: Peter Jay), Chichester, Barry Rose.
N.A.C.R.O. (1977b) *Parole: a Case for Change*, Chichester, Barry Rose.
N.A.C.R.O. and S.C.P.R. (1976) *Vandalism: An Approach Through Consultation*, London, N.A.C.R.O. and S.C.P.R.
N.A.C.R.O. and S.C.P.R. (1978) *Vandalism: Cunningham Road Improvement Scheme — Impressions after Two Years*, London, N.A.C.R.O. and S.C.P.R.
Newman, D. J. (1966) *Conviction: the Determination of Guilt or Innocence Without Trial*, Boston, Little Brown.
Newman, O. (1973) *Defensible Space*, London, Architectural Press.
Niebuhr, R. (1941–3) *The Nature and Destiny of Man* (two vols.), London, James Nisbet; reprinted (1964) New York, Charles Scribners.
Niebuhr, R. (1965) *Man's Nature and His Communities*, London, Bles.
Nuttall, C. P., *et al.* (1977) *Parole in England and Wales* (Home Office Research Study No. 38), London, H.M.S.O.
Packer, H. L. (1969) *The Limits of the Criminal Sanction*, London, Oxford University Press.
Parsloe, P. (1976) 'Social work and the justice model', *British Journal of Social Work*, 6, 71–89.
Pearce, F. (1976) *Crimes of the Powerful*, London, Pluto Press.
Pease, K., Durkin, P., Earnshaw, I., Payne, D. and Thorpe, J. (1975) *Community Service Orders* (Home Office Research Study No. 29), London, H.M.S.O.
Pepinsky, H. E. (1976) *Crime and Conflict*, London, Martin Robertson.
Plant, R. (1973) *Hegel*, London, Allen and Unwin.
Plant, R. (1974) *Community and Ideology*, London, Routledge and Kegan Paul.

Platt, A. M. (1969) *The Child Savers: the Invention of Delinquency*, Chicago, University of Chicago Press.

Preston, R. H. (Ed.) (1975) *Perspectives on Strikes*, London, S.C.M. Press.

Radzinowicz, L. and Hood, R. (1978a) 'A dangerous direction for sentencing reform', *Criminal Law Review*, 713–24.

Radzinowicz, L. and Hood, R. (1978b) 'The doubts over stiffer sentences in a two-tier penal system', *The Times*, 19 July, 16.

Radzinowicz, L. and King, J. F. S. (1977) *The Growth of Crime*, London, Hamish Hamilton.

Rawls, J. (1972) *A Theory of Justice*, London, Oxford University Press.

Reppetto, T. A. (1974) *Residential Crime*, Boston, Ballinger.

Rheinstein, M. (Ed.) (1954) *Max Weber on Law in Economy and Society*, Cambridge, Mass., Harvard University Press.

Rhodes, R. P. (1977) *The Insoluble Problems of Crime*, New York, Wiley.

Robson, W. A. (1976) *Welfare State and Welfare Society*, London, Allen and Unwin.

Royal Commission on Capital Punishment (1953) *Report*, Cmd. 8932.

Ruck, S. K. (Ed.) (1951) *Paterson on Prisons*, London, Muller.

Rusche, G. and Kirchheimer, O. (1939) *Punishment and Social Structure*, New York, Columbia University Press; reissued (1968) New York, Russell and Russell.

Rutherford, A. (1977) *Youth Crime Policy in the United States*, Croydon, I.S.T.D.

Ryan, M. (1978) *The Acceptable Pressure Group*, Farnborough, Saxon House.

Sainsbury, E. E. (1977) 'The state of welfare', Inaugural Lecture, Sheffield, University of Sheffield; shortened version published (1979) *British Journal of Social Work*, 9, 1–14.

Schumacher, E. F. (1973) *Small is Beautiful*, London, Blond and Briggs.

Schur, E. M. (1965) *Crimes Without Victims*, Englewood Cliffs, Prentice-Hall.

Scottish Council on Crime (1975) *Crime and the Prevention of Crime*, Edinburgh, H.M.S.O.

Scull, A. (1977) *Decarceration: Community Treatment and the Deviant — A Radical View*, Englewood Cliffs, Prentice-Hall.

Seebohm Report (1968) *Report of the Committee on Local Authority and Allied Personal Social Services*, Cmnd. 3703.

Sinclair, I. (1971) *Hostels for Probationers* (Home Office Research Study No. 6), London, H.M.S.O.

Skinner, B. F. (1953) *Science and Human Behaviour*, New York, Macmillan.

Skogan, W. G. (Ed.) (1976) *Sample Surveys of the Victims of Crime*, Boston, Ballinger.

Softley, P. (1977) *Compensation Orders in Magistrates Courts* (Home Office Research Study No. 43), London, H.M.S.O.

Softley, P. and Tarling, R. (1977) 'Compensation orders in the Crown Court', *Criminal Law Review*, 720–2.

Sparks, R. (1971) *Local Prisons: The Crisis in the English Penal System*, London, Heinemann.

Sparks, R. F., *et al.* (1978) *Surveying Victims*, Chichester, Wiley.

Spence, J. and Hedges, A. (1976) *Community Planning Project: Cunningham Road Improvement Scheme Interim Report*, London, Social and Community Planning Research.

Strawson, P. F. (1974) *Freedom and Resentment*, London, Methuen.

Sutherland, E. H. (1949) *White Collar Crime*, New York, Holt, Rinehart and Winston.

Szasz, T. (1968) 'The mental health ethic', in: R. de George (Ed.), *Ethics and Society*, London, Macmillan.

Tarling, R. and Softley, P. (1976) 'Compensation orders in the Crown Court', Criminal Law Review, 422–8.

Taylor, C. (1977) 'Interpretation and the science of man', in: P. Connerton (Ed.), Critical Sociology, Harmondsworth, Penguin.

Taylor, I., Walton, P. and Young, J. (1973) The New Criminology: For a Social Theory of Deviance, London, Routledge and Kegan Paul.

Taylor, I., Walton, P. and Young, J. (Eds.) (1975) Critical Criminology, London, Routledge and Kegan Paul.

Temple, W. (1934) The Ethics of Penal Action, London, Clarke Hall Fellowship (First Clarke Hall Lecture).

Thomas, C. H. (1978) 'Supervision in the community', Howard Journal of Penology and Crime Prevention, 17, 23–31.

Thomas, D. A. (1974) 'Parole and sentencing', in: D. A. Thomas (Ed.), Parole: Its Implications for the Criminal Justice and Penal Systems, Cambridge, University of Cambridge Institute of Criminology.

Thomas, J. E. (1977) 'Hull '76: observations on the inquiries into the prison riot', Howard Journal of Penology and Crime Prevention, 16, 123–33.

Tiffany, L. P., et al. (1967) Detection of Crime: Stopping and Questioning, Search and Seizure, Encouragement and Entrapment, Boston, Little Brown.

United States (1967) President's Commission on Law Enforcement and Administration of Justice (Field Surveys I and II), Washington, G.P.O.

Vallance, E. (Ed.) (1975) The State, Society and Self-Destruction, London, Allen and Unwin.

Van den Haag, E. (1975) Punishing Criminals, New York, Basic Books.

Van Dine, S., Dinitz, S. and Conrad, J. (1977) 'The incapacitation of the dangerous offender: a statistical experiment', Journal of Research in Crime and Delinquency, January issue, 22–34.

Van Hofer, H. (1975) 'Dutch prison population', Kriminologi (Scandinavian Research Council for Criminology), No. 17, 104–50.

Von Hirsch, A. (1976) Doing Justice: The Choice of Punishments (Report of the Committee for the Study of Incarceration), New York, Hill and Wang.

Walker, N. (1975) 'Release by executive discretion: a defence', Criminal Law Review, 540–4.

Walker, N. (1976) Treatment and Justice in Penology and Psychiatry (The Sandoz Lecture 1976), Edinburgh, Edinburgh University Press.

Walker, N. (1978) 'Review of Doing Justice', British Journal of Criminology, 18, 79–84.

Weston, W. R. (1978) 'Probation in penal philosophy: evolutionary perspective, Howard Journal of Penology and Crime Prevention, 17, 7–22.

Whiting, J. R. S. (1975) Prison Reform in Gloucestershire 1776–1820, London, Phillimore.

Wiles, P. (Ed.) (1976) The Sociology of Crime and Delinquency in Britain, Volume 2: The New Criminologies, London, Martin Robertson.

Willetts, P. (1976) 'The love of offenders', Probation Journal, 23, 23–5.

Wilson, B. (1976) Contemporary Transformations of Religion, London, Oxford University Press.

Wilson, J. Q. (1975) Thinking About Crime, New York, Basic Books.

Winch, P. (1958) The Idea of a Social Science and its Relation to Philosophy, London, Routledge and Kegan Paul.

Winnicott, C. (1967) 'Casework and agency function', in: E. Younghusband (Ed.), Social Work and Social Values, London, Allen and Unwin.

Wolfenden Report (1957) Report of the Committee on Homosexual Offences and Prostitution, Cmnd. 247.

Wootton, B. (1978) *Crime and Penal Policy*, London, Allen and Unwin.
Wright, M. (1975) 'Tactics of reform', in: S. McConville (Ed.), *The Use of Imprisonment: Essays in the Changing State of English Penal Policy*, London, Routledge and Kegan Paul.
Young, M. and Willmott, P. (1957) *Family and Kinship in East London*, London, Routledge and Kegan Paul.
Young, P. (1976) 'The theory of the role of prisons in advanced penal systems', in: *Economic Crises and Crime* (Publication No. 15), Rome, U.N.S.D.R.I.
Zimring, F. E. and Hawkins, G. J. (1973) *Deterrence*, Chicago, University of Chicago Press.

Notes on Contributors

ELIZABETH BARNARD. Born 1945. Principal Organiser, National Association for the Care and Resettlement of Offenders since 1979. Previously Research Officer, Home Office Research Unit, and Lecturer in Criminology at the Universities of Keele and then Sheffield. Member of the English Parole Board 1974–7.

A. KEITH BOTTOMLEY. Born 1941. Senior Lecturer in Criminology, University of Hull since 1977; previously Lecturer in the same University. Author of *Prison before Trial* (Bell 1970), *Decisions in the Penal Process* (Martin Robertson 1973) and *Criminology in Focus* (Martin Robertson 1979); joint editor of *Criminal Justice: Selected Readings* (Martin Robertson 1978). Member of the Working Party on Prisons of the Church of England Board for Social Responsibility 1974–7. Co-editor of the *Howard Journal of Penology and Crime Prevention* since 1979.

ANTHONY E. BOTTOMS. Born 1939. Professor of Criminology and Director of the Centre for Criminological Studies, University of Sheffield, since 1976; previously Lecturer and Senior Lecturer in the same University. Co-author of *Criminals Coming of Age* (Heinemann 1973), *The Urban Criminal* (Tavistock 1976) and *Defendants in the Criminal Process* (Routledge 1976). Editor of the *Howard Journal of Penology and Crime Prevention* since 1975 (co-editor from 1979). Member of the English Parole Board 1974–6.

DAVID DOWNES. Born 1938. Senior Lecturer in Social Administration, London School of Economics, since 1973; previously Lecturer at the School, and Senior Research Fellow, Nuffield College, Oxford. Author of *The Delinquent Solution* (Routledge 1966), co-author of *Gambling, Work and Leisure* (Routledge 1976), and co-editor of *Deviant Interpretations* (Martin Robertson 1979).

DAVID E. JENKINS. Born 1925. Professor of Theology and Head of the Department of Theology and Religious Studies, University of Leeds, since 1979. Also Co-Director, The William Temple Foundation, Manchester, since 1979 (previously full-time Director 1973–8). Canon Theologian of Leicester Cathedral. Previously Fellow and Chaplain of The Queen's College, Oxford; later Director of Humanum Studies at the World Council of Churches, Geneva. Author of *Guide to the Debate about God* (Lutterworth 1966), *The Glory of Man* (SCM Press 1967), *Living with Questions* (SCM Press 1969), *What is Man?* (SCM Press 1970), and *The Contradiction of Christianity* (SCM Press 1976).

FREDERICK McCLINTOCK. Born 1926. Professor of Criminology, University of Edinburgh, since 1974; previously University Lecturer in Criminology and Fellow of Churchill College, Cambridge. Author of *Attendance Centres* (Macmillan 1961), *Robbery in London* (Macmillan 1961), *Crimes of Violence* (Macmillan 1963); co-author of *Crime in England and Wales* (Heinemann 1968), *Criminals Coming of Age* (Heinemann 1973). Justice of the Peace since 1968; co-opted member of the Treatment of Offenders Committee of the Magistrates' Association.

241

TERENCE MORRIS. Born 1931. Professor of Sociology with special reference to Criminology, London School of Economics, since 1969; previously Lecturer and Reader at the School. Author of *The Criminal Area* (Routledge 1957), *Deviance and Control: The Secular Heresy* (Hutchinson 1976); co-author of *Pentonville* (Routledge 1963), and *A Calendar of Murder* (Michael Joseph 1964). Justice of the Peace since 1967; former member of the Treatment of Offenders Committee of the Magistrates' Association. Former Editor of the *British Journal of Sociology*.

KEN PEASE. Born 1943. Senior Lecturer in Social Administration, University of Manchester, since 1978. Previously Principal Research Officer, Home Office Research Unit, and before that Lecturer in Psychology at Manchester University. Co-author of two monographs on Community Service Orders and one on parole, all published by H.M.S.O. in the Home Office Research Studies series; co-editor of *Community Service by Order* (Scottish Academic Press 1979).

RAYMOND PLANT. Born 1945. Professor of Politics, University of Southampton, since 1979; previously Lecturer and Senior Lecturer in Philosophy, University of Manchester. Author of *Social and Moral Theory in Casework* (Routledge 1970), *Hegel* (Allen and Unwin 1973), and *Community and Ideology* (Routledge 1974).

RONALD H. PRESTON. Born 1913. Samuel Ferguson Professor of Social and Pastoral Theology, University of Manchester, since 1970; previously Lecturer in the same University. Hon. Canon of Manchester Cathedral. Co-author of *Christians in Society* (SCM Press 1939), *The Revelation of St. John the Divine* (SCM Press 1949); editor of and contributor to *Technology and Social Justice* (SCM Press 1971), *Industrial Conflicts and their Place in Modern Society* (SCM Press 1974), *Perspectives on Strikes* (SCM Press 1975), *Theology and Change* (SCM Press 1975), and *Religion and the Persistence of Capitalism* (SCM Press 1979).

MICHAEL H. TAYLOR. Born 1936. Principal of Northern Baptist College, Manchester, and Part-Time Lecturer in Christian Ethics and Theology at the University of Manchester, since 1969. Previously held ministerial appointments in Tyneside and Birmingham.